AN INTRODUCTION TO HEALTH CARE ETHICS

# Theological Foundations, Contemporary Issues, and Controversial Cases

D1502549

*In gratitude, we dedicate this book to*

Dr. Ronald P. Hamel
Friend, Mentor, Colleague, Scholar

## Acknowledgments

Our thanks to the following individuals who advised the publishing team or reviewed this work in progress:

Dr. Debra Bennett-Woods, Regis University, Denver, Colorado

Dr. Janine Idziak, Loras College, Dubuque, Iowa

Dr. Karen Elliott, CPPS, Mercy College of Northwest Ohio, Toledo, Ohio

Dr. Ron Hamel, Catholic Health Association, St. Louis, Missouri

Rev. Steven O'Hala, Saint Vincent de Paul Regional Seminary, Boynton Beach, Florida

Dr. Tim McFarland, Saint Joseph's College, Rensselaer, Indiana

## AN INTRODUCTION TO HEALTH CARE ETHICS

# Theological Foundations, Contemporary Issues, and Controversial Cases

Michael R. Panicola, PhD

David M. Belde, PhD

John Paul Slosar, PhD

Mark F. Repenshek, PhD

Saint Mary's Press®

The publishing team included Leslie M. Ortiz, general editor; John B. McHugh, director of college publishing; prepress and manufacturing coordinated by the production departments of Saint Mary's Press.

Printed in the United States of America

7002

ISBN 978-0-88489-944-0

Library of Congress Cataloging-in-Publication Data

An introduction to health care ethics: theological foundations, contemporary issues, and controversial cases/Michael R. Panicola ... [et al.].
    p. cm.

Includes bibliographical references and index.

ISBN 978-0-88489-944-0 (pbk.)

    1.   Medical    ethics.    2.    Medical    ethics—Religious    aspects—Christianity.
I. Panicola, Michael R.

R724.I63 2007
174.2—dc22                                                                2007025889

# CONTENTS

# PREFACE

This book is intended as a faith-based introductory text in health care ethics geared toward college students. We believe this book offers something distinctive in that it does not assume extensive knowledge of theology, ethics, and medicine on the part of college students.

In many ways college students are only beginning to come to grips with their particular moral sensibilities. Therefore, this text provides ample opportunities for self-reflection and group discussion. It does this through interactive exercises and case studies that stimulate self-learning and class discussion. Our goal is to encourage moral reflection and moral discourse rather than resort to ready-made and proscriptive answers to concrete dilemmas. This book examines real-life concerns and issues that confront real people every day across this country. It is a realistic applied ethics textbook written by theological ethicists working in the field.

Four interdependent elements comprise the overall structure of the book: (1) a normative ethical basis; (2) examination of particular issues; (3) case studies; and (4) multimedia aides.

The normative ethical basis is presented in chapters 1–4. In our experience as college teachers and in our work within health care institutions we have learned that it is pointless to discuss controversial issues without some kind of normative framework. Without a normative framework, ethical discussion inevitably turns toward individual relativism. Our normative approach is not a moral method per se. That is, it does not provide a methodological process for ethical decision making. Instead, it presents a picture of who we ought to become as people living in community. The central concern of our normative approach is human and social flourishing. While principles and virtues are used to provide some objective basis for ethical decision making, our normative approach is rooted in a holistic view of the person and principally concerned with the role of discernment in attaining human and social flourishing.

The issues are presented in chapters 5–12. We focus on issues that arise in clinical medicine, examining them in the light of our normative approach. This normative approach is also concerned with the social conditions that contribute to making these issues ethically problematic. We ask that students and professors take these social conditions seriously: they are not simply "add-ons" meant to increase classroom dialogue.

Within the issues section we have included case studies to give real-life relevance to the book. Some of these cases we have confronted in our daily work. They are intended to show how particular circumstances have an impact on ethical decision making. The case studies can be incorporated easily into creative teaching and learning strategies. At the end of each chapter we recommend further readings and multimedia aides such as documentaries and movies that touch on the core themes of the chapter.

This textbook is the product of four authors. In it, you will encounter four different voices and writing styles. While our normative ethical basis is grounded in some values and concepts that are central to the Catholic moral tradition—such as human dignity, justice, and human flourishing—this book is not intended as a textbook on Catholic health care ethics.

As is often the case in ethics classes, you will no doubt encounter a range of opinions and perspective. We encourage such open discourse. We also ask that you share with us your opinions and perspectives regarding this text. In particular, we would like to know how we might modify the book so that future readers may benefit from your experience with it.

# CHAPTER 1

# Ethics and Its Role in Health Care

## Context for Understanding

Each of us encounters ethics every day, whether we are aware of it or not. We cannot avoid situations that force us to make ethical choices because ethics cuts across every facet of our lives. There really is no part of human life that is ethics-free—not politics, not sports, not journalism, not medicine, not education, not marriage, not friendships. Despite our daily experience with ethics, it remains one of the hardest concepts to define. Think about it for a minute. How would you define ethics? What descriptive words or phrases would you use?

# Understanding Ethics

## What Is Ethics?

Most people, when asked this question, say something about right and wrong actions and then highlight some of the sources of morality or ethics that shape how we act in concrete situations, like personal values, religious beliefs, rules, laws, customs, traditions, and feelings. How we act in concrete situations and what sources inform our decisions are definitely a part of ethics, but ethics is much more. So before we start talking about health care ethics and getting into the more complex issues of our day, we need to get a sense of what ethics is generally and what it requires. This will better prepare us for what lies ahead in this book and hopefully in life. To get us pointed in the right direction, consider the following cases.

**Case 1A:** Last night while out on the town with your friends you witnessed your best friend's boyfriend kissing another girl. He noticed that you saw him and he immediately came over to you to beg you not to tell. He tried to explain that he and your friend have been going through tough times and that the kiss meant nothing; it was simply a dumb mistake made while caught up in the moment. The next day you see your best friend, who asks you how last night was. Do you tell her what you saw?

**Case 1B:** You are a mid-level executive in a fairly large, fast-moving organization. You value your job and know that you would have a difficult time finding another like it in the same place with the same salary level—which is important, given your considerable school loans and other monthly bills. One unpleasant aspect of your job is that your supervisor seems less talented than his staff and is prone to violent outbursts with some of the lower-ranking employees in the department. Just recently he berated his administrative assistant in public for not having a report completed on time, even though he had given her the necessary data at the last minute. It was obvious to everyone in the department that he was attempting to blame someone else for his poor work habits. You would like to do something about his behavior, perhaps report him to one of his superiors. However, he has gained the favor of the president over the years, due largely to his ability to bring in the big accounts. Consequently, no one is willing to stand up to him and you will have to go it alone. You are unsure how your accusations will be handled. You fear that you will be seen as a "problem," and could even lose your job. What do you do?

Laying aside the question of what we should or should not do if we found ourselves in these situations, what do these cases tell us about what ethics *is*? Stated simply, these cases deal with ethics because any decisions made will have an impact on the well-being of people and communities. Whether we decide to tell our friend about the kissing incident or stand up to our boss will not only affect our character and quality as individuals but also that of other people and community life as a whole. This gets to the heart of what ethics is all about: the moral lives and actions of people and the impact of our actions on the well-being of others. Ethics always seeks to answer two interrelated questions: who ought we to become as people (*being*), and how ought we to act in relation to others (*doing*; see *Figure 1A*).

**Figure 1A:** What Is Ethics?

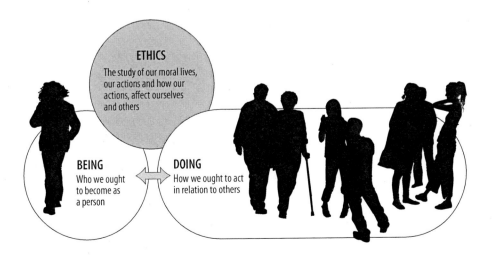

Consequently, ethics considers such things as:

- The ***goal(s) of human life*** and what our lives should ultimately be directed toward (e.g., love of God, right relationships, just social order)
- The ***virtues*** or character traits, attitudes, feelings, and dispositions that should define us as people and shape how we act in relation to others (e.g., love, compassion, honesty)
- The ***principles*** that should guide our decision making, conscience formation, and discernment in concrete situations (e.g., human dignity, justice, solidarity)
- The ***circumstances***, including the facts surrounding the situation and the consequences of our actions, that have an impact on our decisions

Understanding ethics in this way avoids the common misconception that ethics deals exclusively with how we act. Admittedly the focus of ethics is on our actions, which is why in ethics we tend to debate issues such as abortion, physician-assisted suicide, stem cell research, and genetic testing, all of which center on what we are doing in concrete situations. But this focus on actions tends to overshadow something that Socrates, Plato, Aristotle, Aquinas, and others took great pains to make clear, that is, our actions say something about who we are and determine to a great extent who we ultimately become as people. While we may not always act in ways consistent with who we are or ought to become, and while no one action may completely define us as a person, we cannot escape the fact that who we are affects how we act and how we act affects who we are becoming as people in relation to other people, to God, and to the creation.

Perhaps an example, using one of the cases above, will explain this a bit better. If you tell your friend about the kissing incident and consistently tell the truth in similar situations where it would be easier to lie, your actions would suggest that you value honesty and are or are on your way to becoming an honest person. The same is true in reverse. If you continuously lie when in tough spots, your actions would suggest that you are or are becoming a dishonest person—a liar. How could you claim to be anything else? The connection between the *being* and *doing* aspects of ethics is essential if ethics is to be understood properly. You cannot have one without the other because ethics is not just about what we do but also, and simultaneously, about who we are becoming as people (and communities) through our actions.

## What Does Ethics Require?

As a human endeavor concerned with who we ought to become and how we ought to act, ethics requires freedom and knowledge, reasoning and discernment, and a normative basis. Each of these elements constitutes a vital part of ethics; without any one of them it would be impossible to do ethics.

Freedom and Knowledge. In ethics, freedom is broken down into two aspects: freedom of self-determination and freedom of choice. Freedom of self-determination relates to *being;* it is that basic freedom to shape our lives and become the person we want and are called to be. Freedom of choice relates to *doing;* it is simply the ability we have to choose this or that. For example, it is the freedom we have to go out with friends versus study, or to buy Dove soap as opposed to Dial.

Some people argue that our freedom of self-determination is weakened, even crippled, by original sin, social forces, physical characteristics, or other factors. There is some truth to this; we are not *totally* free because of spiritual, social, biological, and other factors, which limit, at times, our choices and our ability to make good decisions. Yet despite these limitations, at the core of our being we are each free (barring extreme incapacity) to choose the type of person we want to become through our actions, even in the most challenging of circumstances. Viktor Frankl, a survivor of the Holocaust, provides proof of this:

> We who lived in concentration camps can remember the men who walked through the huts comforting others, giving away their last piece of bread. They may have been few in number, but they offer sufficient proof that everything can be taken away from a man but one thing: the last of the human freedoms—to choose one's attitude in any given set of circumstances, to choose one's own way.[1]

In addition to freedom, ethics requires that we have knowledge. Knowledge in ethics refers to the information we have at our disposal to make decisions in concrete situations. This knowledge can be personal, moral, or circumstantial. Personal knowledge has to do with ourselves in terms of who we are and are called to become as people in community. Moral knowledge deals with the sources of morality or ethics that guide us in making a decision. Circumstantial knowledge encompasses the circumstances surrounding the decisions with which we are faced. Obtaining the knowledge necessary to make an ethical decision may not always be easy: we may not know where to look, or may not have the energy to pursue the requisite knowledge. Nevertheless, if we have the capacity, we must seek to acquire the knowledge necessary to inform our conscience adequately.

With freedom and knowledge comes responsibility. Ethics presupposes that we have a choice in shaping our own lives through our actions in concrete situations and as such are responsible for the types of people we become and for the consequences of our actions on others. When we act with freedom and knowledge we are held morally or ethically accountable. Because our freedom or knowledge may be constrained at times, our moral responsibility can be diminished proportionately (i.e., in equal measure to our lack of freedom or knowledge).

In real-life situations, limiting factors may require us to assess our or another's accountability differently than we otherwise might. We see this all the time in law and it is no less true in ethics. When a child commits a crime with incomplete knowledge about the consequences of her actions, she is judged differently than an adult, who should know better. Or when a man is caught stealing food from a grocery store to provide nourishment for his starving family, his offense is considered less than what it might be if he were acting without this constraint.

One caution is in order: by describing how our moral responsibility can be diminished due to a lack of freedom or knowledge we do not wish to create a loophole in ethics. We simply wish to call attention to the brokenness of human life and the limitations we all experience as human people. Living morally or ethically is not easy; at times it is painfully difficult. Nevertheless, we can never use this as an excuse for making bad decisions that negatively affect ourselves or others. We have to take responsibility for who we are as people and strive, in any given situation, to make truly ethical decisions. This is what is required of us as moral beings living out our lives within communities.

**Reasoning and Discernment.** Ethics also requires the ability to reason through a situation and to discern which action, among various options, best reflects who we are called to become morally as people and promotes the well-being of others. Reasoning and discernment are not simply following the orders of an authority figure, blindly applying well-known rules or principles to a case, or succumbing to desires or feelings. Rather they involve: self-reflection in which we get a sense of ourselves, our hopes, motivations, intentions, and desires; contextual analysis and investigation whereby we consult the sources of ethics and try to understand the morally relevant circumstances of the situation; and critical evaluation whereby we consider the different courses of action against some well-established moral criteria. We will say more about this in chapter 4; for now it is sufficient to point out that we cannot do ethics without the ability to reason and discern, and we cannot do these things without a normative basis.

**Normative Basis.** This may not be a familiar term, but the concept is something you know quite well. We all have a normative basis, though most of us never give much thought to it. If we did not have one, we would never be able to say, "I really need to be a better listener," or, "You really are a good person," or, "I should not have yelled at him like that," or, "That was nice what you did for that woman." These statements indicate that you have an idea or an understanding, no matter how unformed, of who we should be as people and how we should act toward others. This is what a normative basis is—a framework, point of reference, or backdrop against which we judge people, actions, and the impact of actions on others. It gives us insight into the goals of human life, the virtues and characteristics that should define us as people, and the principles that should guide our actions in concrete situations.

Despite the differences we may have when it comes to specific issues or decisions (e.g., whether physician-assisted suicide is acceptable), most of us share many common thoughts about the elements that fill out a normative basis. There are many things we can say about human life and people from a normative perspective that transcend religious, cultural, ethnic, political, geographic, and other boundaries. For instance, most of us would agree with Aristotle and Aquinas that the goal of life is to flourish as people and communities. What "flourishing" means to particular people in particular times may differ, but how could one deny that this is a basic goal of life?

This is true also of the virtues or characteristics that people should strive to acquire and that constitute what is considered a good person. Who could deny that being a loving, compassionate, and courageous person is better than being a hateful, apathetic, and cowardly person? This is true also of moral principles. Although here we are getting closer to the concrete level of ethics where disagreements occur more frequently, it would be hard to argue against a principle that says "do not harm others" (the principle of nonmaleficence) or "promote the good of others" (the principle of beneficence). Likewise, it would be equally as hard to argue against a principle that says "people should be free to choose their own way in life" (autonomy) or "we should act fairly in our interactions with others" (justice). What "harm" and "good" and "freedom" and "justice" mean in different cultures or contexts might be debatable, but not the fact that we should not harm others, that we should promote the good of others, that we should be free to direct our own lives, and that we should act justly in relation to others.

These are just a few examples of commonly held, normative views. There are countless others. Yet in recent years some have questioned whether there really is an objective normative basis, themes or elements against which we can judge people and their actions. Some go so far as to claim that everything is relative and that the only value things (or people) have is what someone attributes to them. This is a very serious matter: without some form of an objective normative basis we would never be able to say that someone was a good or bad person or acted ethically or unethically, and as a result moral responsibility and accountability would be completely destroyed. Think about the implications of this for ethics, for life. How would we be able to judge and to hold someone accountable for stealing from another, being unfaithful to a spouse, cheating on an exam, or even killing someone? On what basis would we be able to speak out against the person's actions?

To put this into perspective let us consider the attacks of 9-11. If there were no objective normative basis of any kind, how could we say that the perpetrators were wrong? On what basis could we make such claims? Perhaps you could argue that the attacks were against innocent civilians, or that the people who were killed never agreed to it, or that the attacks disrupted the social order. However, isn't this saying something on a normative level? Why can't we kill innocent people, or take someone's life without their consent, or disrupt society? These things should not matter to us if, as some suggest, there is no objective normative basis and everything is relative. But they do matter! They matter precisely because we know through our shared human experience that people are of value, that we have a responsibility to treat others with respect, and that there should be peace and stability in society because holding to these ideals aids us in our attempt to flourish as human beings and communities.

We may not all agree on the specifics of a normative basis, but at a minimum we can agree that we need one, and we can begin to sketch some of the general elements of what this would look like—as we will in chapter 3. Here we simply observe that without a normative basis ethics would cease to exist because ethics is not simply about *describing* how we live as people and how we act toward others but *determining* how we ought to live and act as people in community.[2] This is the task of ethics, whether done personally in the context of everyday living or analytically in the context of a classroom.

## Ethics Defined

With this background we can now define ethics. Ethics is the study of the moral lives and actions of people *against a normative basis* that provides insight into who we ought to become (BEING) *and* how we ought to act (DOING) in relation to others (people, God, creation).

# Understanding Health Care Ethics

## A Field of Ethical Inquiry

Now that we have defined what ethics is generally, we can move on to health care ethics (HCE). Before we offer a definition of HCE and outline the various ethical issues that arise in health care, it is important to get a sense of why we study the ethics of health care in the first place. What is so special about health care that people dedicate their lives to studying its ethical dimensions? Why is HCE a fixture in course catalogs at colleges and universities? Why do we have codes for nurses, physicians, and other health care professionals with strict ethical requirements? In short, why is health care a field of ethical inquiry? There are three main reasons.

First, health care is a basic need we all have and supports perhaps the most basic of all human goods: physical health and mental well-being. Without these it would be difficult if not impossible to pursue life's other important goods, such as friendships, education, family, work, recreation, and religion. As the adage goes, "Without our health, we have nothing." This separates health care from other fields of ethical inquiry. While business, journalism, education, and other fields all have ethical dimensions, the goods they promote are not as basic as the good promoted by health care.

Second, patients tend to be vulnerable in relation to their caregivers. From a moral perspective, vulnerability means that one is at risk of not being seen as a person deserving of respect and loving concern. One could argue that we are always vulnerable, no matter what the situation, because theoretically someone could always treat us poorly and not value us as people. Nevertheless, in health care situations our vulnerability is much higher than in other settings because there is far more at stake and a real imbalance in the patient-caregiver relationship.

For one thing, patients are seeking services related to their physical health and mental well-being, which is certainly more important than mere material goods. Because they often know less about their condition than their caregivers, patients are also usually completely dependent on them to provide the necessary services, and must trust that they have the proper training and are motivated to promote their patients' best interests. Furthermore, patients often have to divulge sensitive information about themselves that could be embarrassing or even incriminating. Perhaps worst of all, patients may be sick, frightened, and uncertain about the future and may have to expose themselves physically and emotionally to people they do not know very well. Customers in a grocery store, readers of a newspaper, or students in a classroom do not experience this same degree of immediate vulnerability. Patients need ethical safeguards to ensure that their dignity and well-being will be protected.

Finally, health care is a profoundly social endeavor. The decisions we make in health care—whether on the policy-making, organizational, or clinical level—affect not only those directly involved but also society at large. Consider the following case.

Case 1C: John is in a very bad car accident and transported by helicopter to a trauma center. After extensive testing, John is diagnosed with a severe head injury and sent to the intensive care unit (ICU) for close observation and treatment. After several weeks in a coma receiving aggressive treatment and round-the-clock care, it is clear that John is not going to recover consciousness and will die sooner or later, depending on how long he is treated aggressively. The physicians suggest to John's wife that he be removed from the breathing machine because it is not improving his overall condition, and moved from the ICU to a nursing floor where he will receive comfort measures only. John's wife refuses and demands that everything be done. The physicians protest but, fearing a lawsuit, give in to her wishes.

Though this case focuses on decisions that unfold at the bedside of an individual patient, it highlights the social implications of health care. For one thing, continuing to provide aggressive treatment to John could negatively impact other patients. The resources (health care professionals, the ICU bed, the equipment, the money) being used to sustain John's life may not be available for other patients who may actually benefit from the treatment. This is not a theoretical problem. Hospitals do not have breathing machines for every patient, ICUs have only a certain amount of beds and trained staff, and emergency departments sometimes must close their doors to new patients because they cannot move their current patients to certain parts of the hospital due to lack of space.

In America we tend to think of health care resources as unlimited, a virtual bottomless pit. Yet in reality there is only so much to go around. Some people object to this because they assume that we could simply spend more money on health care. But experience shows that this would require much to be sacrificed in other areas and even then there is always a breaking point. The situation is a lot like our own finances. Every day we make decisions about the things we can and cannot afford because our checkbooks have only a limited amount of funds. We could obtain credit and go into debt for the things we desire, but this would limit us in other areas and eventually catch up to us. This is reality for most people, and it is the same reality we experience in health care.

Second, continuing to provide aggressive treatment to John could impact the lives of those caring for him. The physicians have already expressed their concerns about further aggressive treatment. Will their integrity be compromised because they went along with John's wife's demands against their better judgment? Will it change the way they think of medicine and the role of patients and families in decision making? What about the nurses and other health care professionals? They will have to continue to provide intensive treatment to John and manage the complications that will inevitably arise. What about their feelings? It may be difficult emotionally to stop treatment for a dying patient, but it can be equally hard to continue to provide aggressive treatment to a patient who may suffer longer because of it. Front-line caregivers such as nurses often feel this emotional entanglement most because of their closeness to patients and families.

The hospital and John's health insurance plan, assuming he is insured, could also be affected. Hospitals only receive a certain amount of money for the services they provide and sometimes the costs far exceed the reimbursement. Is it fair to hospitals to provide care that is not benefiting a patient when they have to absorb the costs? What if this limits their ability to care for other patients and to provide just wages and cost-of-living salary increases to their employees? Would it be right for other members of John's health insurance plan to have to pay higher premiums because of the costs associated with his care? An additional four dollars a month may not be a lot to some, but to others it can make the difference between being insured and going uninsured.

Third, continuing to provide aggressive treatment to John and other patients in similar situations could drive up overall health care costs and have an impact on society at large. In America we already spend over two trillion dollars on health care and this number is expected to rise to over four trillion by 2015, which will represent about twenty percent of our national spending.[3] This means that for every dollar we spend as a nation, twenty cents will go to health care. While this may seem justifiable because health is such a basic good, the fact is that this limits our ability to spend money in other areas that are also important for personal and community development, such as education, defense and homeland security, highway and road improvements, agriculture, and alternative energy sources. We should also keep in mind that health care insurance is getting more and more costly and the number of uninsured in the United States alone is well over forty million. These things will only get worse as health care costs continue to rise and the population ages as expected. Costs, limited resources, and the effect of our individual health care decisions on others are often overlooked in our individualistic society, but they constitute a vital reason why health care is a field of ethical inquiry.

## Definition and Description

We can now explain what HCE is. HCE, a specialty of ethics generally, is the study of how human people and communities are affected by medicine, medical technologies, and the decisions we make in health care on various levels. Like ethics generally, HCE is done against the backdrop of a normative basis.

Though ethical issues in health care seem rather common nowadays, HCE is a relatively new phenomenon. It only became a distinct discipline and a formal area of study in the 1960s. This somewhat misrepresents the fact that concerns about the ethics of health care (or medicine) surfaced thousands of years ago, as witnessed in the Hippocratic Oath (circa fourth century BCE), and that Christian theologians dating back to the early church have dealt with problems that we tend to group under HCE (e.g., abortion, contraception, sterilization, and euthanasia).

Several factors led to the recent rise of HCE as a formal discipline, none more than advances in science and medical technology. Ethical issues have always been present in health care, but as medicine became more advanced and developed the technologies capable of diagnosing complex conditions, doing elaborate surgeries, and, particularly, sustaining life, the number and complexity of ethical issues increased considerably. It is no mistake that one of the most prominent health care ethics cases to date, that of Karen Ann Quinlan, arose in the 1970s and had to do with the question of sustaining life. Once health care obtained its technological might, which continues to expand, the ethical issues and concerns were quick to follow.

There are other factors as well. Significant changes took place in the patient-physician relationship and in health care. Traditionally, physicians made decisions for patients; they not only had the technical expertise but also assumed responsibility for deciding what was in the patient's best interests.

This approach is called "paternalism" because it is similar to how parents assume almost complete decision-making responsibility for their minor children. Strange as it may seem to us, in the past physicians knew their patients quite well, often having cared for them from birth to death. In such a context paternalism tended to work well, as the physician could adopt a course of treatment that accurately represented the views of the patient and family. As health care itself changed—from family physicians who came into the home to complex delivery networks involving multiple structures (hospitals, clinics, insurance companies, government payers) and caregivers (not just physicians) who often know very little about their patients—the close relationship between patient and physician began to break down. People in developed countries started to crave individual liberty and wanted to make their own decisions. All of these factors led to a new model of the patient-physician relationship, one that is now driven by patient autonomy versus physician paternalism. This new model, while beneficial to a point, has led to greater conflict in health care decision making, such as we saw in *Case 1C*.

Other important events gave rise to HCE, perhaps the three most important of which were the Nuremburg Tribunal, the Tuskegee Syphilis Study, and dialysis committees. At the Nuremburg Tribunal several Nazi physicians were tried for performing unethical, harmful, and sometimes fatal experiments on concentration camp victims during World War II. What came out of Nuremburg was a commitment that all research subjects must be adequately informed about the benefits and risks of participating in medical research and must give their free and informed consent before anything is done to them.

The Tuskegee Syphilis Study was conducted by the United States Public Health Service and began during the great depression around 1930 and lasted until 1972. The study was conducted on poor, uneducated African-American men who lived in Tuskegee, Alabama, where a relatively high number of people were suffering from syphilis. The researchers at Tuskegee lied to the men about the nature of the study, were not honest with them about the extent of their disease, did not tell some men who acquired the disease while in the study that they were sick, and deceived the men into thinking they were receiving the best treatment for their condition. What is worse, when penicillin began being used effectively in 1946 to treat syphilis, the government blocked the men from receiving it. This was all exposed by a reporter for the Associated Press, whose story came out on July 26, 1972, and appeared on the front covers of most national newspapers. The story and the subsequent congressional hearings on Tuskegee opened the eyes of the American public about the danger of ethical abuses in medical research and practice.

Dialysis committees were fixtures in sophisticated acute care hospitals. They were charged with determining who, among patients with severe kidney disease, would receive a treatment known as dialysis, which essentially does the work of the kidneys outside the body by filtering the blood artificially and reintroducing the filtered blood back into the body. At the time, dialysis machines were not readily available and so hospitals could not meet the needs of all patients with kidney problems requiring dialysis. Dialysis committees "played God" by deciding who would receive dialysis and who would not—and would most likely die. This obviously raised questions of an ethical nature and people began to wonder how dialysis committees made their decisions and what criteria they used.

Advances in science and technology, changes to the patient-professional relationship and to health care generally, and landmark events such as Nuremburg, Tuskegee, and dialysis committees all contributed to the rise of HCE as a formal discipline of study. The ethical challenges posed by these developments could not be ignored and as a result people began in earnest studying the ethical dimensions of health care. At first, study was restricted primarily to the clinical level or issues related to patient care. However, it quickly became clear that HCE encompasses three interrelated levels: the macro level (health policy issues), the middle level (organizational issues), and the micro level (clinical issues). Decisions made at one level have an impact on other levels. We have already seen how decisions at the bedside might have an impact on the other levels (refer to *Case 1C*). This can also go the other way. For example, when the government started reimbursing for dialysis under Medicare, hospitals no longer had to make the difficult decision as to who would receive treatment

**Figure 1B:** Three Levels of Health Care Ethics

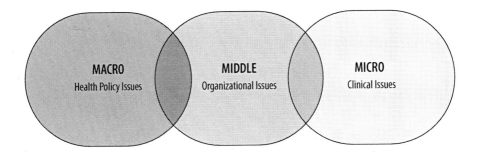

(middle—organizational level), and more patients were allowed access to the treatment and as a result lived longer than they otherwise might have (micro—clinical level; see *Figure 1B*).

Below we list the major ethical issues that arise in health care. As we move forward in this book, we will focus primarily on issues at the micro (clinical) level, but we will always keep an eye on how decisions at this level impact our relationship to others, our communities, and society at large. This is necessary because ethics is not just about who we are and how we act as individuals, but more profoundly who we are becoming in community and how our actions affect others.

## Macro Level (Health Policy Issues)

1. Health care organization and reform
   o Creating a just system, ensuring access to care, defining coverage and setting limits, allocating societal resources for health care, responding to the needs of the underinsured and uninsured, and establishing adequate structures for delivering care

2. Health care financing
   o Reimbursement, controlling costs, balancing societal values, and payment mechanisms (who pays and how best to structure payment: employer, government, insurers, out-of-pocket)

3. Public health concerns
   o Immunizations, infectious disease control, disparities in health care, safety programs, health infrastructure (lead paint, toxic substances, sanitation, water supply), and health promotion and disease prevention

4. Medical research
   o Protecting research subjects, allocation of public funds, Human Genome Project, and stem cell research

5. Health care regulation and legislation
   o Insurance, government-sponsored programs, patient privacy (HIPAA, the Health Insurance Portability and Accountability Act), patient-dumping (EMTALA, the Emergency Medical Treatment and Active Labor Act), physician-assisted suicide, embryonic and fetal research, and regulation of other research applications

## Middle Level (Organizational Issues)[4]

1. Health care organization as caregiver
   o Hospital staffing levels, provider shortages, clinicians and conflicts of interest, patient rights and responsibilities, admission (especially into specialty units like the ICU), providing futile or non-beneficial treatment upon request, medical mistakes, medical records, and billing procedures

2. Health care organization as employer
   o Employee strikes, union activity, justice and responsibility in hiring practices, just wages, downsizing, diversity and affirmative action, whistle blowing, sexual harassment, and executive compensation

3. Health care organization as insurer
   o Setting health benefits for a plan, reviewing appeals for denied coverage in a plan, coverage exceptions for contractually excluded benefits, prescription drug plans, covering disenfranchised populations, paying for investigational interventions for life-threatening conditions, and balancing commitment to individual enrollees with overall plan

4. Health care organization as citizen
   o Hospital closures, community needs assessment, fairness in selection of vendors, responsible advertising, environmental responsibility, mergers and acquisitions, investing (investment screens, proxy voting, and community investing), advocacy and lobbying activities, and charity care

## Micro Level (Clinical Issues)

1. Allocation of scarce resources
   o Life-sustaining treatments, organ transplants, intensive medical care, genetic technologies, and the goals and limits of medicine

2. Providing care to patients unable to pay
   o Addressing the needs of the underinsured and uninsured, charity care, and cost-shifting

3. Nature of the patient-professional relationship
   o Rights and responsibilities, conflict of ethical principles (e.g., autonomy, beneficence, nonmaleficence), advance directives, informed consent, patient competency, disparities in health care, and clinicians and conflicts of interest

4. Treatment of people living with HIV-AIDS
   o Vaccinations, treatments, pastoral care, partner involvement in treatment decisions, and aiding developing nations ravaged by the disease

5. Treatment of people living with mental illness
   o Access issues, stigmatization, and patient rights

6. Definition of death
   o Heart-lung versus brain death criteria

7. Withholding and withdrawing treatment at the end of life
   o Treatment criteria, who decides, case conflict, questions about futility, professional integrity, patient rights, and cost concerns

8. Euthanasia and physician-assisted suicide
   o Personal liberty versus societal restraints, and compassion or killing

9. Care of dying patients
   o Pain management, palliative care, hospices, and recognizing limits of life and medicine

10. Care of critically ill newborns
    o Pushing limits of viability, treatment criteria, parental authority in decision making, and cost concerns

11. Organ and tissue transplantation
    o Dead versus live donors, donation after cardiac death, artificial and animal organs, cloning for organs or tissues, transplants for questionable populations, and cost concerns

12. Reproduction and reproductive technologies
    o Personal rights, societal limits, abortion, maternal-fetal conflicts, fetal surgery, assisted reproduction, embryo adoption, and human cloning

13. Genetics, genetic testing, and gene therapy
    o Access, confidentiality, insurance and employment discrimination, the goals and limits of medicine, and safety and efficacy

14. Stem cell research
    o Allocation of federal dollars, access, the moral status of embryos, and the goals and limits of medicine

15. Research and experimentation on humans
    o Informed consent, progress versus limits, protecting vulnerable populations (children, prisoners, mentally ill), and research across borders

## Conclusion and Next Steps

By way of conclusion, we would like you to consider *Cases 1A* and *1B* again. This time, however, we *want* you to decide what you would do in each case. While

# Virtue Theories (VTs)

Virtue Theories find their roots in ancient philosophy. Both Plato and Aristotle, for example, constructed what we would call today virtue theories to describe how we ought to live and act in relation to others. In various works Aristotle outlined numerous virtues, including temperance, justice, courage, dignity, generosity, love, truthfulness, and others that he said had no name. No matter what virtues are emphasized, though, all VTs focus on who the person is and is becoming in light of some conception of the ideal human person and the moral (or good) life. Principles and consequences, which are linked with actions, maintain some relevance, but are secondary to virtues and a focus on the person.

It bears mentioning that VTs are not relativistic and should not be confused with ethical theories that determine right and wrong solely on the basis of an individual's feelings or intuitions. Rather, VTs are rooted in the virtues that we recognize (through shared human experience) as necessary in order to be a good person and live a good moral life in relation to others. While we may not all agree on an exact list of virtues, some are simply indispensable for living well morally. Take Aristotle's virtue of love, for instance. No one can deny that love is a virtue and something to which we should strive to acquire and live out in concrete circumstances. This is not relative; we ought to love others. What is subject to relative factors, however, is how the virtues are expressed by different people in different times and cultures. What love looks like in the context of real-life ethical situations may not be the same at all times and for all people. But we must love nonetheless.

The underlying premise of VTs is that who one is (*being*) largely determines how one acts morally (*doing*). In other words, we do what we are. If we are virtuous, then we will do good things. If we are vicious, then we will do bad things. Jesus had something like this in mind when he said, "In the same way, every good tree bears good fruit, but the bad tree bears bad fruit. A good tree cannot bear bad fruit, nor can a bad tree bear good fruit" (Matthew 7:17–18). If a child is taught and shown how to be kind, respectful, and compassionate, and this becomes ingrained in the child's character as she develops, then she will most likely act in these ways when faced with challenging ethical situations. Contrariwise, if mean-spiritedness, hate, and rage are impressed upon this child, then she will most likely act out these qualities.

Virtue can be described as what we do when no one is watching because it is who we are. For example, there are rules against cheating in school, which students generally follow, especially when a teacher is present and attentive and the consequences for cheating are severe. Most students even follow these rules when the teacher is not present and there is really no chance of getting caught. In some way this suggests virtue: doing good for its own sake because that is who we are. Some students, however, seize the opportunity to cheat when they can, especially when it is likely they will not be caught and punished. Such students do not exhibit the characteristics of a virtuous person. They tend to do the good not for its own sake but only because cheating would have bad consequences.

We have said a lot about virtues without yet saying what they are. Hopefully, from what we have outlined above you get the point that virtues are not just things "out there," imposed on us by others. In a real way, virtues become a part of us. They are the habits, character traits, feelings, and intuitions that make up who we are and that are necessary for being a good person and living a good moral life. When we acquire virtues and cultivate them into our overall moral character, they become second nature to us such that to act contrary to them feels awkward, like a right-handed person trying to write a letter or throw a ball with his left hand. Because virtues ultimately make up who we are, they are very personal, much more so than laws, principles, rules, or duties. Who we are (our identity) is bound up with virtues, and directly related to how closely we live them out in concrete ethical situations (our integrity).

Fortunately there has been a resurgence of interest in VTs; people are once again realizing that ethics is not just about what we do but also, perhaps even more so, about who we are becoming as individuals and communities. But VTs are not without their challenges. VTs must contend with three difficult questions: (1) What virtues are necessary to be a good person and live the moral (or good) life, and who decides what these are and on what basis? (2) How do we acquire these virtues and integrate them into our character? (3) How do we ultimately determine whether one is acting virtuously in concrete situations? These questions cannot be easily answered, which is probably one reason why we tend to focus on the doing dimension of ethics. Focusing on actions and consequences is much easier than trying to determine and defend some conception of the ideal person and the moral (or good) life.

Hopefully, you now have a good grasp of VTs. To further this understanding, let's go back to *Case 2A* for a moment. Of the three hospital representatives, which one argues primarily from a virtue perspective? Based on our brief overview of VTs you can see that the hospital president speaks mostly from a virtue perspective. His words are indicative of someone operating out of virtue. Someone who invokes integrity, as he does when he argues that this case "is a matter of personal and institutional integrity," is usually basing an ethical decision on virtue. Other words or phrases that point to a virtue perspective are moral character, values, personal qualities or characteristics, compromising or violating self, true to self, promoting the good of self/others, who I ought to become, living a good moral life, and of course, virtue. For the hospital president, the key question is, am I promoting in this situation the virtues necessary for living the good moral life? He does not refer to laws, principles, rules, duties, or even the potential bad consequences for the hospital. Instead, telling the truth to the patient, Noah, is directly related to who he is and wants to become as a person and what he believes the hospital should be or should become as an institution.

## Deontological Theories (DTs)

DTs can be traced back to the legal traditions of Judaic and later Roman thought. Philo of Alexandria and the Roman jurist Cicero are two of the oldest supporters. In modern times deontology has been linked mostly with the work of Immanuel Kant. DTs focus mainly on our actions, what we choose to do as the means to an end. What we do matters much more in DTs than who we are becoming, what we hope to achieve (ends), or what the results will be. As such, virtues, intentions, extenuating circumstances, and consequences have little to no relevance. The underlying premise of most DTs is that some actions are right *in themselves* and should be done always and everywhere, whereas others are always and everywhere wrong and should never be done. For DTs the ends can never justify the means.

In DTs the rightness or wrongness of our actions is reduced to our obedience or disobedience to some code of laws, principles, rules, or duties that are derived from an authority figure, such as God (divine law such as the Ten Commandments), nature (natural law), a ruler or government (civil law), or ourselves (autonomous law). Unlike VTs, which are more inductive in reasoning (meaning we derive a sense of virtues from our shared experience in a community with others), DTs use deductive reasoning. So, for example, if we were following divine law as articulated in the Ten Commandments, we would be forbidden from stealing in all instances no matter what the circumstances. Even if you had to steal bread to feed your starving family, you could not do so morally under DTs that hold to absolute prohibitions against stealing. Likewise, many governments have laws against torturing suspected criminals and prisoners of war. The famed character from the Fox television hit *24*, Jack Bauer, would be a frequent violator of such a law for his aggressive tactics in obtaining information from suspected terrorists, despite the fact that his intentions are always good and his actions often result in the saving of innocent human lives.

In DTs moral creativity comes from trying to figure out which laws, rules, principles, and duties apply to concrete situations. Difficulties arise for DTs when laws, rules, principles, or duties are in conflict with one another. Here deontologists must determine which of the conflicting deontological factors takes precedence over the other(s). Another example may help. In health care ethics there are three well-known principles: beneficence (do good for another), nonmaleficence (don't harm another), and autonomy (respect a person's wishes). As we saw in *Case 1C*, sometimes patients or their family members request treatment that physicians, nurses, and others believe will be harmful. What is a physician to do when a patient asks to receive a treatment that the physician knows or suspects will actually cause the patient more suffering? Respecting the patient's wishes (autonomy) in such cases may actually cause the physician to violate other principles to which she is bound. How does the physician determine which principle trumps or outweighs the others?

In addition, how do we know what set of laws, principles, rules, or duties to follow when they often compete one with the other? Do we follow those handed down by God, the government, a specific religion, or ourselves? What if we cannot trust the authority figure? Are we then free to break from the rules? Is there no room for our own conscience, or must we always follow the law? Are there no exceptions? What if following the principles results in greater harm to oneself or others? These obviously very serious questions highlight the limitations of DTs. Still, laws, principles, rules, and duties in ethics have their place, as we shall see later in the chapter.

With all that said, let's go back to *Case 2A* for a moment and apply what we have learned so far about DTs. Of the three hospital representatives, which one argues primarily from a deontological perspective? In this case the physician most exemplifies deontological theories. A telltale sign was her reference to duty when she spoke of "a duty to disclose the truth." Other words or phrases that identify the deontologist include obligations, beliefs, convictions, rights, responsibilities, principles, right and wrong, have to, always/never, bound by, requirement, and absolute. For this physician, the key question is, does my action in this situation conform to the relevant laws, principles, rules, or duties to which I am bound? What weighs most heavily upon her is not so much virtue and certainly not the consequences of her action ("no matter what the costs"). Rather it is the duty she has to her patient. For her, living morally is equated with fulfilling her duties.

## Consequentialist Theories (CTs)

CTs find their fullest expression in modern thought, especially in the British utilitarians Jeremy Bentham, John Stuart Mill, and Henry Sidgwick. Though there are various versions of CTs, they all focus on the consequences of our actions in light of the goods we are trying to promote through our actions. In

CTs the outcome of our actions matters much more than who we are becoming or what we are doing (*means*). As such, virtues and deontological factors such as laws and principles are seen as morally relevant only when they guide us to do that which results in the best outcomes, but failing that, there is no moral obligation to attend to them. The underlying premise of CTs is that some goods should be promoted regardless of the means used. In contrast to DTs, the ends justify the means for consequentialists.

The rightness or wrongness of our actions in CTs is determined by evaluating the consequences of our actions as these relate to the goods we are striving to promote. "Goods" in this sense is usually defined in broad terms, such as happiness (understood as pleasure and the absence of pain), preference satisfaction, or social utility; they are the ends to which we are striving and want to promote in each and every action. In essence, the morality of our actions within CTs is deduced through a cost-benefit analysis where we add up the positive and negative consequences and choose the action with the best overall results or consequences for the good or end we are seeking. According to one CT, known as utilitarianism, maximizing positive consequences consists in doing that which results in the greatest good for the greatest number of people (sometimes referred to as the "happiness principle"). So, for instance, while *24*'s Jack Bauer would often be condemned by deontologists, his actions would be considered morally acceptable under CTs because his aim is to promote the greatest good for the greatest number. His aggressive interrogation tactics and violation of government protocols often save lives in the end.

It should be noted that when we must choose between two or more negative outcomes, CTs say that we ought to do that which minimizes bad consequences, that is, we ought to choose the course of action that results in the lesser evil. This is a fairly common way of thinking through such situations. In fact we see it all the time on television and, to a lesser extent, in real life. To use another *24* example, in season three Jack Bauer was placed in an impossible situation. Terrorists demanded that Jack kill his superior, with whom he had worked for years, or else they would release a lethal virus in a populated area immediately.

Jack chose the former, which he perceived as the lesser evil—the killing of one person to save hundreds of thousands. In a similar way this consequentialist viewpoint about the lesser evil has implicitly provided the moral context for governmental decisions about military interventions and even the practice of medicine in some settings where values collide. A good example of the latter is the removal of a cancerous uterus from a pregnant woman as a way to treat and prevent the spread of cancer to other parts of her body, even though the surgery will result in the death of her pre-viable fetus. For consequentialists this is a classic case of lesser evil—rather than withhold treatment (resulting in the death of both mother and fetus), you do the surgery and at least save the woman.

For policy making as well as personal decision making, no one can deny the usefulness and popularity of CTs. Yet despite this, CTs have limitations just as the other ethical theories do. How do we identify the good for which we should be striving and against which we should be weighing consequences? If it is happiness, as some CTs hold, how should happiness be defined, and who gets to define it? More practically, what do we do when it is unclear which action will result in the best overall results or consequences? What if we cannot accurately predict what the consequences will be? And do the ends *always* justify the means? Are there any limits to this rule or can we do absolutely anything so long as we bring about the good? Like VTs and DTs, CTs raise difficult questions for which there are no easy answers. We hope to address some of these concerns later in the chapter and throughout the foundations sections of this book.

As a way of rounding out this section, let's apply what we have learned about CTs to *Case 2A*. Of the three hospital representatives, which one argues primarily from a consequentialist perspective? The rationale of the chief legal counsel is pretty clearly consequentialist or outcome-oriented. As he puts it, we don't have to inform the patient "because everything turned out fine for him" and if we do, "he will probably sue the hospital and there will be a lot of bad publicity." He may not use telling consequentialist words or phrases—such as outcomes, results, consequences, interests, goods, greater good, lesser evil, balance, weigh, exception because, ends justify the means—but his focus is on the negative consequences that will result from disclosing the truth. For him, the key question is, does my action bring about the best (or the least bad) results or consequences in light of the good I am trying to achieve? He understands the good as protecting the hospital's interests and, to a lesser extent, the well-being of the patient. He is not driven by virtue or deontological factors, but the potential negative effect on the hospital.

## Ethical Theories in Personal Decision Making

We have spent a good amount of time describing the classic ethical theories. Now we would like for you to consider which theory or theories you personally use most when reasoning through ethical situations. Listed below are a number of case scenarios that address issues in ethics.[1] Each scenario is followed by statements representing each of the classic ethical theories and supporting the position the scenario directs you to take. You may not agree with the position itself or the statements, but we would like you to choose the statement that best fits the way you would come down on the issue—if you had to—from the position given. This exercise is not meant to shape your viewpoints on the issues; it is only intended to provide some insight regarding what factors you most take into consideration when making ethical decisions. There are no right or wrong answers, so please respond truthfully.

1. The question of embryonic stem cell research (ESCR) has been a hot topic lately. While out with your friends one evening, the topic comes up. When asked of your opinion, you argue in favor of ESCR using embryos left over from in vitro fertilization because:

   a. The medical profession has an obligation to promote the best interests of sick patients by pursuing potential cures for deadly diseases.

   b. You can't imagine why anyone wouldn't support the research given that the embryos will be destroyed and discarded anyway, and the economy

| Scenario | Virtue | Deontology | Consequentialism |
|---|---|---|---|
| 1 | | | |
| 2 | | | |
| 3 | | | |
| 4 | | | |
| 5 | | | |
| 6 | | | |
| 7 | | | |
| 8 | | | |
| 9 | | | |
| 10 | | | |
| Total | | | |

It does not matter how you "scored" in this exercise. All three of these classic, common approaches to ethical decision making are acceptable; no one approach is necessarily better than any other because no single theory is normative. Therefore you do not have to worry whether you had more virtue responses or deontology responses or consequentialist responses. This exercise was intended to give you some indication of how you tend to approach ethical situations, and to do two other things as well.

First, reviewing your answers should help you to become more familiar with the classic ethical theories. This contributes to your own understanding, and also helps you as you engage in dialog on ethical issues. When talking about ethical issues with your friends or family there may have been times when you did not understand where they were coming from or the grounds on which they based their arguments. Perhaps you even became frustrated because you just could not fathom how they could think in such a way. By understanding the classic ethical theories better and recognizing some of the key words and phrases of each, you are now better positioned to understand the reasoning behind many ethical arguments and to engage more effectively in ethical dialog. Now when someone argues for embryonic stem cell research on the grounds that the frozen embryos they want to use for the research will be destroyed anyway, you will be able to see that this is a consequentialist argument instead of, for example, a deontological one ("it is never acceptable to destroy a human embryo"). Recognizing this will allow you to have more insight into ethical arguments and respond accordingly, perhaps even from the same perspective as the one(s) with whom you are debating.

Second, by forcing you to choose one statement representative of a single ethical theory for each case scenario, the exercise challenges you to accept one way of thinking through the ethical issue, to the exclusion of other approaches. For many people this is difficult because they do not like being confined to one theory or perspective. Rather, they feel more comfortable considering the issue from two, perhaps even all three, perspectives, and then arguing on the basis of whichever perspective provides the most compelling reasons either for or against. This is one reason why you probably did not answer all ten case scenarios from the same perspective. Intuitively you know that virtues, principles, and consequences are all important factors to be considered when analyzing ethical issues and making ethical decisions in concrete situations.

This highlights one of the major weaknesses of contemporary approaches to health care ethics, many of which are grounded in only one of the classic ethical theories: they tend to be too narrowly focused. By concentrating on one aspect predominantly, often to the exclusion of other morally relevant features, they are limited in their usefulness and applicability. We cannot do justice to the complex nature of ethical issues in health care by looking just at virtues or just at principles or just at consequences. It makes no sense, for instance, to consider just virtues to the exclusion of principles. Principles can support virtues by specifying what it generally means to be a just or honest or compassionate person. In fact, without principles or action guides, virtues remain a little abstract or unclear. Likewise, it makes no sense to consider just principles to the exclusion of consequences. Consequences need to be incorporated with principles because sometimes principles must yield to the concrete realities of the situation. Generally we should not steal or be overly aggressive with suspected terrorists, but there may be instances when the consequences dictate that we set aside the principle in a particular case. In the same vein, it makes no sense to consider just consequences to the exclusion of virtues. If we always do

Sketching a normative basis is a tall task, and there may be disagreements when we get down to particulars—after all, we are attempting to articulate the goals of human life, the virtues and characteristics that ought to define us as people, and the principles that should guide our actions in concrete situations. Yet we know that we need a normative basis and that we share many common normative beliefs.

## Describing a Normative Basis

A normative basis is something that gives us insight into who we should become as individuals and how we should act in relation to others (people, God, creation). A normative basis is a framework, point of reference, or backdrop against which we make ethical decisions and evaluate who we are as people, the morality of our actions, and the impact of our actions on others. Perhaps it will help if we think about a normative basis in terms of something with which you are more familiar, say, a sport like basketball. We all know that basketball referees call fouls on players. Although not every foul called may be warranted, fouls are called nonetheless based on some conception of how basketball players should conduct themselves while on the court. Over the years this conception of how the game should be played has evolved and has been codified in a rulebook that referees use to distinguish between appropriate and inappropriate behavior. In essence, this is a normative basis. It need not be as detailed as a basketball rulebook to serve as our blueprint for living morally. Human experience, revelation, community life, and other sources have afforded us some conception of who we should become as people and how we should act in relation to others. Ethics is nothing more than making ethical decisions and judgments in light of this conception, this normative basis.

## The Goal of Human Life

As we pointed out in chapter 1, we all make use of some normative basis, whether we know it or not. In fact, most everything we do socially or interpersonally is guided by a normative basis. Nevertheless, we do not all lead good moral lives or act ethically in each and every situation. How can this be if we all have and use a normative basis? There are many reasons for this. Experience and personal reflection tell us that we are imperfect people, beset by physical, intellectual, psychological, moral, and spiritual limitations, who live within a social context that is at once good but also sinful. Because of this, like St. Paul, we sometimes lack the moral strength and courage to do the good we desire and instead do the bad that we know we should not (Romans 7:19–20).

There are also practical reasons that account for our not acting ethically all the time. Sometimes we do not know what is the truly right or good thing to do, other times we may lack the capacity or energy to inform our conscience adequately so we can make the best ethical decision. Another reason, ever-present in our impatient world, is our tendency to be short-sighted about matters of ethics or morality, our failure to consider the big picture and to link our more immediate goals with the ultimate goals for which we are striving. Some people call this "moral myopia."

Every action we perform in life is directed toward particular goals. We brush our teeth to avoid cavities and to eliminate bad breath; we take classes in college to fulfill the requirements for graduation and to get a good job; we sleep to rejuvenate ourselves and to avoid getting sick; we work to have the means necessary to live a decent life and to develop our talents; we eat to be nourished and sustained physically; we see movies to be entertained and to escape from reality; we vote in democratic elections to help shape social structures and to ensure our rights are protected.

Our moral actions especially are directed toward goals. From an ethical perspective, however, it is important to recognize that beyond our more immediate goals is an even more basic or underlying goal that ought to provide the overall direction for our lives and guide our decisions. The first step in constructing a normative basis is to discern what this goal is, the goal for which we are ultimately striving as human beings. Individuals and communities have struggled with this question for thousands of years. People often say that the ultimate goal of human life is to have fun, to be successful, to be smart, to be compassionate, or to love others. These are indeed good goals for which we should be striving. Without these, life would not be nearly as meaningful. However, all these goals in various ways point to an even more fundamental goal, that of "human flourishing." Ethically speaking human flourishing supersedes all other goals, it is the goal to which all others should be directed. Think about it: we do not want to be successful just so we can feel good about ourselves and receive accolades; we do not want to be smart just to impress people or score high on an IQ test; we do not seek to be compassionate so people will say how kind we are. Rather, we pursue these goals because they offer us the possibility of living a good life, a life in which we flourish as individuals in relation to other people, God, and creation.

We encounter problems in our moral lives when we make ethical decisions without attending to the goal of human flourishing. When this happens our ultimate goal as human beings becomes subordinated to some other, more immediate goal, and our pursuit of human flourishing is often undermined as a result. Take, for example, *Case 1B* involving the abusive supervisor. If we focus on the more immediate goals, we might not report him to a higher-ranking executive although it is probably the right or good thing to do. Think about it: you value your job, make decent money, have bills to pay, enjoy the lifestyle to which you have grown accustomed, and would have difficulty finding another job. If your goals are limited to these issues and do not include human flourishing, your choice would be clear. However, when we compare these against the goal of promoting our own well-being and that of others, these immediate goals probably would take a back seat to doing the hard but ultimately right thing.

This is how a normative basis functions in ethics and acts as a corrective to moral myopia: it helps us "zoom out" so we see the bigger picture and make ethical decisions accordingly. It is like the Google map feature that many of us use when getting driving directions. While the map can zoom in to show us the street and particular area that we are attempting to find, it can also zoom out to give us a sense of where we are and where we are headed. In order to live a good moral life in relation to others it is critical that we "zoom out" by considering our more immediate goals against the backdrop of human flourishing and other morally relevant features.

## Understanding Human Flourishing

It is pretty hard to deny that human flourishing is the overarching goal of human life, as we pointed out in chapter 1. What is debatable is what it means to flourish as human beings. This is where we run into challenges because people can and do have different conceptions of human flourishing. Many of the ancient Greek philosophers who considered this question spoke of human flourishing in terms of *eudaimonia*—what we might call happiness. They believed that happiness is the only goal we seek for itself as the final end and never for the sake of something else.[1] Obviously the term "happiness" could easily be misconstrued to refer to having our desires fulfilled or achieving pleasure in every situation. This is not what the Greeks had in mind. Happiness for them was generally understood as having a well-formed character that allows one to live a life of virtue.

Think about what human flourishing means to you and what you think you need to flourish as a person. In the space provided below, list ten things that you feel are necessary for living a good life, a life of flourishing. These could be things such as money, a big house, health, sports, music, people or love, friendships, community, peace, religion—the choice is yours.

_____          _____

_____          _____

_____          _____

_____          _____

_____          _____

If you were forced to live without five of the ten items you selected above, which five would be most important for human flourishing? List them here.

_____          _____

_____          _____

_____

Now go one step further and consider which two of the five remaining items are most important for human flourishing. Write them below.

_____          _____

This can be quite a difficult exercise because it is hard enough limiting the items necessary for human flourishing to a list of ten, let alone two. Interestingly, as we do this exercise with students, health care professionals, and others, the two most common final items are health and relationships (which you may have listed as a specific person, your family, your friends, community, or something equivalent). Health is an obvious choice; without health it becomes difficult to pursue any goals or ends. Relationships, though, is another matter altogether. What makes relationships so essential for flourishing as human beings? This is where the Christian understanding of human flourishing is so instructive.

Although the Greeks equated human flourishing with *eudaimonia,* translated as best we can in today's terms as happiness, for Christians human flourishing is understood as love of God. What this means in practical terms is that we live truly rich and full lives when we love God in all that we do, when we direct our lives totally to loving God. Jesus made this clear when responding to the Pharisee who asked him what the first and greatest commandment was. Jesus' simple response was: "Love the Lord your God with all your heart and with all your soul and with all your mind" (Matthew 22:37). The Judeo-Christian story tells us that we have been created out of God's unconditional and unyielding love and that we are directed toward God as our ultimate end. Through human life we enter more fully into communion with God by loving God and giving glory to God in how we live our lives.

Admittedly, saying that human flourishing means love of God is quite vague, especially since ethics is a practical discipline. How do we love God when we do not necessarily encounter God immediately? Jesus' response to the Pharisee provides us with an answer to this question. After saying that we should love God with our whole heart, soul, and mind, Jesus went on to say that there is a second commandment, which is like the first: "Love your neighbor as yourself" (Matthew 22:39). The second part of Jesus' statement is as important as the first, for in it Jesus draws the link between relationships and human flourishing. Human flourishing, understood as love of God, is pursued most tangibly within the context of relationships. We encounter God primarily through relationships with others, though we can also encounter God in other ways (e.g., prayer, personal reflection, meditation, and nature). From an ethical perspective we cannot love God and flourish as human beings without loving our neighbor as we love ourselves. Saint John also made this clear in describing how we love God in the context of human life: "Those who say, 'I love God,' and hate their brothers or sisters, are liars; for those who do not love a brother or sister whom they have seen, cannot love God whom they have not seen" (1 John 4:20). Love of God and love of neighbor are thus inextricably bound together in ethics. Significantly, "neighbor" in the Judeo-Christian tradition does not refer to the person living next door to you or on your block. Rather, "neighbor" encompasses all members of the human family and can even be broadened to include all of God's creation.

People who cite relationships as necessary for human flourishing often do not have this in mind when they place it on their list. What we have done here was to put in theological terms what they, and perhaps you, already knew intuitively, that relationships with others (people, God, creation) provide the meaning and substance of human life and contribute significantly to our flourishing as human beings.[2] Relationships not only provide us with the opportunity to love God but it is through them that we become more truly and fully human. We are social beings by nature and have difficulty appreciating the fullness of life outside the context of relationships. This is why Tom Hanks's character in the movie *Castaway* develops a friendship with a volleyball while stranded on an island for roughly 4 years. While this appears ridiculous, it makes sense when you consider the importance of relationships. His life was not as meaningful when lived in isolation and so he sought something, anything, that could fill the void. The volleyball, which he called "Wilson," served this purpose—though not sufficiently, as we find out later in the movie when he agonizingly decides not to go after the ball, which had been swept overboard, because it would have meant leaving his make-shift boat and giving up his only chance to return home to his beloved girlfriend.

We should point out that when we talk about the link between human flourishing and relationships, we are not just talking about any relationships. We are in lots of relationships, but not all of our relationships are characterized by the love of neighbor of which Jesus speaks. For us to truly flourish and show our love of God through loving our neighbor, we need to be in what we will call "right relationships." This does not mean that we can never be in conflict with others, or that we might not get angry with others at times, or even that we have to like every person with whom we come in contact. What it means is that we need to be in relationships that are grounded in the values of love, respect, dignity, and justice. This we do by becoming virtuous people oriented to the good and by acting virtuously with the aid of moral principles that foster right relationships.

## Becoming Virtuous—The Role of Virtues

From what we have said above it may be seen that virtues—the habits, character traits, feelings, and intuitions that make up who we are as human beings—are essential for right relationships because they are the key to becoming good, virtuous people. If, as experience suggests, the way we act in relation to others is determined largely by who we are, then we must build a strong moral character through the development of virtue so that we are predisposed to do the good. In other words, if "doing the right thing" is predicated largely on "being a good person," then we have to strive to become virtuous because that is the surest way to act virtuously. It really is not possible to be in right relationships and ultimately flourish as human beings without developing virtues and striving always to become virtuous.

There is no magical formula for becoming virtuous; the only tried-and-true method is practice. Just as it takes practice to learn how to read, ride a bike, drive a car, or eat with a fork, so it is with virtue. We each may have the capacity to act virtuously, but unless we consciously and intentionally do so, day-in and day-out, virtue will never become a part of who we are as people. The more we practice acts of virtue, the more ingrained it becomes in our character and the easier it is to act virtuously. Unfortunately, as we mentioned in chapter 1, the reverse is also true. We must be careful in the choices we make because we are essentially making ourselves through our choices.

The path to becoming virtuous is less a race than a journey. It is not as if by performing one hundred acts of kindness we cross the finish line of virtue once and for all. The journey toward the virtuous life may not have an endpoint; there may not be a time when we actually "get there." If we are honest with ourselves, we have to admit that there is always room for improvement in our moral lives: we can always love more, care better, protest more strongly. Virtue, especially in Christian ethics, does not call us to live a perfect life, but rather an examined life where we constantly ask ourselves, "Who am I becoming through this action and is it consistent with who I ought to become in relation to others (people, God, creation)?" Living this type of life, an examined life directed toward virtue, gives us the best chance to love God by loving our neighbor as ourselves in each and every one of our actions.

When we think of what it means to be virtuous from a Christian perspective, we think of Jesus, who, in addition to being true God, was fully human and immersed in the human condition. For Christians, Jesus is the moral ideal of who we ought to become; he is normative morally speaking in that he perfectly embodied what it means to love God and love neighbor. Through his life, death, and resurrection, Jesus showed us not only who God is but also who we can become as human beings made in God's image and likeness. The Gospels are filled with stories portraying the virtue of Jesus. For example: Jesus showed great restraint in many situations, specifically when he withstood the temptations of the devil while alone in the desert (Luke 4:1–13); Jesus displayed great courage and fidelity to God throughout his adult life, especially while praying in the garden and contemplating his fate, which he agonizingly knew would lead to the cross (Mark 14:32–42); Jesus exhibited great compassion to the most vulnerable people in his midst, particularly to a leper who was on the fringes of society but brought back into the human community through Jesus' healing actions (Matthew 8:1-4); and Jesus practiced empathy and forgiveness to many, most notably an adulterous woman, whom Jesus protected from a hypocritical crowd that wanted to stone her to death (John 8:1–11).

Living morally as Jesus did, however, is no easy task, and we all fall short of the ideal. Yet this does not mean that becoming virtuous is unattainable. That this is true is seen in the lives of ordinary people who, despite their own limitations, nonetheless live virtuously. Some of us have been privileged to know such a person, maybe a parent, a friend, or a teacher. Most of us have at least heard of such individuals. Some of the more remarkable examples include St. Thomas More, who refused to betray his conscience by sanctioning King Henry VIII's divorce and declaring him the head of the Church of England even though he was imprisoned, separated from his family, and ultimately put to death; Rosa Parks, who stood up to racial discrimination through her simple, yet profound act of refusing to give up her seat in the "white" section of a segregated bus; Mother Theresa of Calcutta, who spent a lifetime caring for the faceless, nameless poor that were on the fringes of society; Gandhi who proved that nonviolent demonstration and resistance is a powerful tool against social injustice and the destructive forces of evil; and Martin Luther King, Jr., who called us to become more than we imagined we could be by sharing a vision of an utterly just and peaceful society.

Given that we really can become virtuous, as these individuals and numerous other figures have shown us, what virtues should we seek to develop and incorporate into our moral character? What habits, character traits, feelings, and intuitions should define us as individuals? There may not be a definitive answer to this question because any virtue that leads to our moral development as people and allows us to be in right relationships with others could be added to the list. This is why there is no universal agreement on a single list of virtues and why different virtue theorists provide different virtue lists. Nevertheless, some virtues stand out.

To be human means to be physical and material, psychological and emotional, social and relational, spiritual and intellectual, and morally free and responsible. Despite the differences that account for our uniqueness as individuals, we all participate in these basic dimensions of human life. These dimensions are interconnected and interwoven to form a complex synthesis that makes up who we are. For each of these dimensions there are corresponding virtues that ought to define us as human beings because they enable us to be in right relationships and ultimately flourish as human beings.

The main virtue regarding the physical and material dimension of human life is temperance or restraint in our pursuit of earthly and bodily goods such as eating, drinking, and sex. This virtue is essential for maintaining a proper balance between the various goods that contribute to or are instrumental for human flourishing. The main virtues regarding the psychological and emotional dimension of human life are love, empathy, and compassion. These virtues play a crucial role in our close personal relationships. The main virtues regarding the social and relational dimension of human life are justice, honesty, respect, and self-sacrifice. These virtues figure prominently in our broader social relationships and interactions with others. The main virtues regarding the spiritual and intellectual dimension of human life are faith, hope, prudence, and discernment. These virtues have much to do with how we approach human life and respond in concrete moral situations. The main virtues regarding the morally free and responsible dimension of human life are courage, integrity, and righteous indignation. These virtues pertain to how true we are to ourselves as moral beings.

This relatively short list of virtues hardly exhausts all the virtues that build up our moral character and allow us to act virtuously in relation to others. We could have listed others, such as generosity, trustworthiness, gentleness, patience, sympathy, and kindness, all of which are important. However, the virtues we have listed are some of the more vital ones pertaining to the various dimensions that make up who we are as human beings in our totality. They encompass more or less what it means to be a good person and what it takes to live in right relationships with others and ultimately flourish as human beings. They also have special relevance for health care ethics because they define what health care professionals should be and give some indication as to how they should act toward their patients. Thus they will serve us well as we move forward in the book and consider some specific cases in health care ethics.

## Acting Virtuously—The Role of Principles

The journey toward becoming virtuous requires moral principles, which are also essential for right relationships because they help us to act virtuously in concrete moral situations. Though virtue theories tend to downplay the significance of principles, they are important for three reasons. First, principles give rise to virtues and pave the way for becoming virtuous. It would be great if we were all born with a strong moral character and acted virtuously without having to consider principles. However, the reality is that we have to learn how to become virtuous and principles are useful to this end. By acting in accordance with well-established principles that foster right relationships, we learn what virtue means and progress along the path of becoming virtuous.

Second, principles specify what virtue generally demands in concrete moral situations. To say that we should be just, compassionate, and respectful means little without specific principles that articulate what these virtues require in the messiness of real life. Think about how we teach children the virtue of respect. We don't simply say, "Be respectful." Rather, we teach them concrete examples of this virtue through principles such as holding the door for others, cleaning up after themselves, always saying "please" and "thank you," and not talking about others behind their backs. These principles add color and detail to the virtue.

Finally, principles serve as a standard against which we can evaluate our choices. If we think, for example, that the most compassionate response to our dying loved one is to prolong life at all costs, we might consider this action against certain principles like beneficence, which says that we must promote the overall good of another and never harm, or equitable distribution, which says that basic social goods must be shared equally for the benefit of all. Such reflection may help us to see that the action we thought intuitively was the most virtuous is not really so, all things considered.

It is understandable that virtue theories tend to avoid principles altogether, partly because principles can take on the role of absolute rules that are always binding regardless of the circumstances, at least in some deontological theories. In this way, principles become things we *must* follow rather than simply consider as we evaluate our options. The danger of using principles in this way is that adherence to them in some situations could lead to decisions that actually undermine virtue and fail to promote our well-being and that of others. Take, for example, the case of a woman who is considering undergoing a sterilization procedure that is medically indicated because she could die if she gets pregnant again. While sterilization is not something we should ordinarily do, there are times when the principle against it must yield to the overall good of the woman and to what virtue demands in complex circumstances.

Principles are meant to serve people in their pursuit of human flourishing, not the other way around. They do not have to function in an absolute, uncompromising way. Rather, as we see it, principles should function more as action guides that complement virtue. We should use principles to get a sense of what we may be required to do in a particular situation and to evaluate the choices that we are inclined to make based on our moral character and overall orientation in life. However, in the end principles must be weighed against the total moral picture, which includes consideration of the virtues we ought to be promoting, the morally relevant circumstances surrounding the situation (including consequences), and our ultimate goal of human flourishing. When used in this way, principles offer great help as we attempt to be in right relationships through loving our neighbor as we love ourselves.

While there are numerous moral principles that foster right relationships, they all fall under the headings of two overarching principles. The first is human dignity, which refers to the inherent value and intrinsic worth of human beings. This principle is grounded philosophically in our experience of ourselves and others as basically individuals having value. Theologically, it is grounded in the belief that we are created in the image and likeness of God (Genesis 1:26–27). This alone serves as the basis for our worth as humans. It is not based on functional ability or social utility, but on the fact that God loves us and desires to enter into communion with us. We can never lose this basic dignity because we are irreversibly made in the image of God.

Flowing from the principle of human dignity are a number of other principles, some general and some specific to health care ethics, that outline some of the responsibilities we have to other people because we are inherently valuable. These include:

o *Sanctity of life:* the awareness that human life is the basis for all we do and must be treated with special care and concern at all stages

o *Beneficence:* the responsibility we have to promote the overall good of others and not harm others

o *Veracity:* the responsibility we have to be honest and truthful with others

o *Autonomy:* the freedom we ought to enjoy to choose our own way in life and to make our own decisions within moral limits

o *Informed consent:* the responsibility we have to disclose fully all relevant medical information to patients, ensure they understand the information, and allow them the freedom to make their own choices

o *Privacy/confidentiality:* the responsibility we have to protect the privacy of patients and maintain the confidentiality of their medical information o *Care for the whole person:* the recognition that human beings are not only physical but also psychosocial, social, spiritual, and moral, and must be viewed and cared for as such

o *Bodily integrity/totality:* the precedence to be given to the overall good of the person over the good of any particular body part or organ

o *Proportionate/disproportionate means:* the recognition that the duty we have to preserve our physical lives with medical means is based upon an analysis of the benefits and burdens of treatment relative to our overall situation in life (this principle will be discussed in more detail in chapter 7)

o *Principle of double effect:* a methodological principle that helps us determine whether we can proceed ethically with an action that has two effects, one good, the other bad (this principle will be discussed in more detail in chapter 5)

The second broad category of principles is justice, which refers to what we are due as human beings on the basis of our inherent dignity. Flowing from this principle are others that impose certain responsibilities on us in terms of how we structure society and how we conduct ourselves in relation to others. These include:

o *Common good:* the various dimensions of social life essential for becoming more truly and fully human and living in right relationships with others; the social structures necessary for pursuing human flourishing but also, in some contexts, the placing of limits on our individual decisions

o *Relationality:* the recognition that, as social beings fundamentally interconnected with others, our personal choices have broader social implications

o *Solidarity:* the responsibility we have to stand with our fellow human beings in times of need, for example, when natural catastrophes occur

o *Subsidiarity:* the recognition that decisions should be made at the lowest, most appropriate level, by those closest to the situation and with the best understanding of the complexities of the issue (usually applied to social-policy decisions, but with implications for clinical decision making as well)

o *Stewardship:* the responsibility we have to tend to and care for the gifts and goods available to us and to use them responsibly for the benefit of all

○ *Care for the disadvantaged:* the responsibility we have to ensure the basic needs of the most vulnerable members of society are satisfied

○ *Equitable distribution:* the recognition that the basic goods of society should be shared equitably (sometimes based on a person's effort, contribution, or need, but viewed theologically, based on a person's inherent dignity)

○ *Preferential option for the poor:* the determination to judge social policies and programs first of all from the perspective of the poor and marginalized

## Conclusion and Next Steps

This somewhat lengthy list of principles completes our normative basis (see *Figures 3A* and *3B*), which provides us with the "big picture" view of (1) what we are trying to accomplish ultimately in life (human flourishing understood as love of God, manifested through right relationships understood as love of neighbor); (2) who we should become as people (virtues necessary for right relationships); and (3) and how we should act in relation to others (principles that foster right relationships). These principles apply to all areas of ethics and should be used as a backdrop when evaluating our personal moral decisions, broader ethical issues, and cases that we study in a more academic context.

To illustrate how we use our normative basis, consider the following case.

 **Case 3A:** Ms. Hamburg is 86 years old and suffers from advanced metastatic cancer (cancer that has spread from one part to others) as well as profound dementia. Though she has been cared for in the home by family members, she was recently rushed to the hospital in severe respiratory distress (significant difficulty breathing). She was admitted to the intensive care unit of the hospital and placed on a ventilator (breathing machine). After two weeks of aggressive treatment, her doctors suggest to the family that aggressive measures should cease because they are not benefiting her and could even be increasing her suffering. Instead, they recommend focusing mainly on her comfort until she dies. The family is unsure what to do.

**Figure 3A:** Human Flourishing

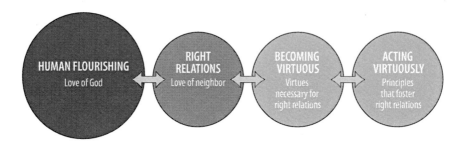

**Figure 3B:** A Normative Basis

**HUMAN DIGNITY**

Sanctity of life, Beneficence, Veracity, Autonomy, Informed Consent, Privacy/Confidentiality, Care for the Whole Person, Bodily Integrity/Totality, Proportionate/Disproportionate Means

**JUSTICE**

Common Good, Relationality, Solidarity, Subsidiarity, Stewardship, Care for Disadvantaged, Equitable Distribution, Preferential Option for the Poor

Looking at the decision to cease aggressive treatment for Ms. Hamburg against the backdrop of our normative basis gives us greater insight into what is perhaps the most ethical response in a situation that is emotionally challenging for the family. While we would like Ms. Hamburg to get better, the fact is that her overall condition cannot be improved at this point in her illness—she is dying, and medicine has reached its limits. Moreover, she is so sick that her ability to recognize her surroundings, interact with others, and pursue other basic human goods that make life worth living has been totally eclipsed. Given these and other factors, it no longer makes sense to fight with medical means to preserve her physical existence. After all, we do not live simply so that our vital physiological functions can be maintained; rather, we live so that we can pursue (at least at a minimum level and without being excessively burdened) goods that are bound up with human flourishing, especially human relationships. This view makes sense when we think about what virtues we should be exhibiting in this case and how these virtues are best lived out in light of the particular circumstances. Some of the virtues that come to mind are compassion, empathy, justice, and prudence, which seem best expressed in this case by keeping Ms. Hamburg as comfortable as possible and helping her family cope with their grief and impending loss. Such virtues are not served, however, by treating her aggressively given her poor prognosis, the additional suffering this could cause her, and the fact that the limited health care resources could be used for patients who could truly benefit from them. This view is also supported by the principles that fall under human dignity (beneficence, care for the whole person, and proportionate/disproportionate means), as well as by those that fall under justice (relationality, stewardship, and equitable distribution).

Hopefully, this brief application of the normative basis has shown how it functions in moral decision making. We should mention, though, that the use of this normative basis will not necessarily point to a single ethical response in every case. There is always a subjective dimension in ethics whereby we must account for personal, social, cultural, contextual, and other factors. Moreover, most moral matters are not black and white; in certain situations there could be a range of good or ethical options available to us, such that different, valid conclusions could be drawn by different people. The key thing for you to remember is that a normative basis does not function like a mathematical formula. We do not punch in variables and always get a single, definitive answer. Rather, it enables us to "zoom out" and put the moral situation into its total context by reflecting on the primary goal of human flourishing and its relation to our more immediate goals, what virtues we should be living out and how they would be best expressed in the particular situation, and what principles apply. In the next chapter we will discuss the role of discernment in helping us to make good moral decisions in concrete situations.

## Suggested Readings

Devettere, Raymond J. *Introduction to Virtue Ethics*. Washington, DC: Georgetown University Press, 2002.

Gustafson, James M. *Christ and the Moral Life*. New York: Harper and Row, 1968.

Harrington, Daniel J., and James F. Keenan. *Jesus and Virtue Ethics: Building Bridges between New Testament Studies and Moral Theology*. Lanham, MD: Sheed & Ward, 2002.

Rahner, Karl. *The Love of Jesus and the Love of Neighbor*. New York: Crossroad, 1983.

## Multimedia Aids for Teachers

Movies can assist students to think about a normative basis. There are several that force us to ask whether objective grounding for ethics actually exists. Below is a list of some of the more helpful ones, all of which are available on DVD or VHS through Amazon.com and other retailers.

*North Country*. Directed by Niki Caro. Starring Charlize Theron. Rated R. 2005. This movie depicts the horrible actions of male workers against fellow female workers in a Minnesota iron mine and can be very helpful for examining whether there are some actions that are simply wrong and then exploring the rationale behind this claim.

*Rashomon.* Directed by Akira Kurosawa. Starring Toshirô Mifune. NR. 1951. This movie examines the nature of truth as four people recount different versions of the story of a man's murder and the rape of his wife. While it is in Japanese with English subtitles, it can be highly effective for exploring the existence of a normative basis.

*Schindler's List.* Directed by Steven Spielberg. Starring Liam Neeson. Rated R. 1993. This movie depicts the atrocities committed by the Nazis against the Jews and can be very helpful for examining whether there are some actions that are simply wrong because they undermine the value of human life and then exploring the rationale behind this claim.

*Weapons of the Spirit.* Directed by Pierre Sauvage. Starring Pierre Sauvage. NR. 1989. This movie depicts the great sacrifices made by the people of the small French community of Le Chambon, who show through their actions what it means to love one's neighbor. At great peril to themselves, they help save hundreds of people, many women and children, from the clutches of Nazis and Nazi sympathizers.

## Endnotes

[1] For an excellent discussion of the broader moral meaning of happiness, see Raymond J. Devettere, *Practical Decision Making in Health Care Ethics: Cases and Concepts,* 2nd ed. (Washington, DC: Georgetown University Press, 2000), 28–37.

[2] For a discussion of the importance of relationships from a theological perspective, see Richard A. McCormick, "To Save or Let Die: The Dilemma of Modern Medicine," *Journal of the American Medical Association* 229 (July 8, 1974): 172–76, 174.

CHAPTER 4

# Making Good Decisions

## The Role of Discernment

Now that we have described a normative basis that gives us insight into what we are striving for in human life, who we ought to become as human beings, and how we ought to act in relation to others, we need to consider in more detail how we bring a normative basis to bear on the decisions we make in concrete moral situations. This leads us to another virtue, one that we have yet to discuss, called discernment. Discernment plays an important role in our moral lives, for it allows us to make good decisions, decisions that promote right relationships and lead ultimately to our flourishing as human beings. Yet, what exactly is discernment? How does it work? These questions will be the focus of the present chapter, in which we will describe discernment and outline a process of discernment for moral decision making that integrates the main features of our normative basis. We should point out that our description of discernment and the process that follows is rooted largely in the Christian tradition. However, we will make some modifications to the specifically Christian view of discernment to apply it to what we have discussed in previous chapters.[1]

## Discernment as a Virtue

The word "discernment" or variations of it are used often in everyday discussions. Teachers say to students, "You must discern which theory applies to the problem at hand." Counselors say to clients, "You will have to discern how best to reconcile yourself with the past." Critics say to authors, "Your analysis of the issue indicates a discerning mind." When used in such ways, discernment means more than simply noticing or seeing something. It goes beyond describing what is happening in a particular situation and engages in value-laden assessments and evaluative judgments. Discerning people perceive the subtle nuances and complexity of situations, demonstrate imaginative capacity in bringing together information and formulating responses, differentiate between available alternatives, and maintain flexibility and sensitivity in practical matters.[2] Discernment in this sense refers to the skill or virtue of perceiving and distinguishing degrees of value between diverse factors when making decisions. Traditionally, discernment has not been described in this way. However, like the virtue of prudence, we must develop the capacity to discern well so that we make good moral decisions. Discernment differs somewhat from prudence as classically defined in that discernment seeks integration of all human capacities and does not rely exclusively on our capacity to reason.

Discernment takes on a more particular meaning in ethics. As we have said, the main objective of the moral life is human flourishing understood as love of God, which comes through right relationships understood as loving our neighbor as we love ourselves in each and every situation. Discernment enables us to pursue these ends in our personal decisions by helping us to differentiate among possible options and come to the most loving and virtuous response in concrete moral situations.[3] As a virtue that we must develop through practice, discernment involves listening attentively to the inner stirrings that arise within us and consulting extensively the objective sources of morality and the accumulated wisdom of others as we face an impending moral decision. In this way, discernment is both a spiritual exercise, whereby we contemplate personal movements or stirrings, and a moral exercise, whereby we consider reasonable choices, past experiences, and other morally relevant factors against the backdrop of our normative basis.

Discernment is as much about figuring out who we ought to become as it is about what we ought to do in concrete situations. In this sense, discernment seeks to get at the heart of our relationship with ourselves, others, and God, and to help us determine the moral response most consistent with who we are as people made in God's image. Discernment goes beyond the typical action-centered questions that tend to dominate ethics to the more person-centered questions that are often overlooked: "Does this action draw me closer to God and others? Will this action contribute to my human flourishing and that of others? What kind of person am I becoming by acting in this way?"[4] In discernment, these person-centered questions precede questions that focus on what we ought to do in concrete situations.

Discernment is based on the belief that various "spirits" are present in the moral decisions we make every day. In this context, the word "spirits" refers to the various personal stirrings or movements that motivate us to act. These could be our desire to love others, be kind to others, show compassion, be faithful to God, flourish as human beings, and so on. However, they could just as easily be motivating factors that impede our growth as people and undermine our relationships with others, such as prejudices, disordered desires, self-centeredness, and so on. Discernment seeks to figure out which among the many motivating factors that cause us to act are the driving forces behind our decisions. The task of discernment is to distinguish between the diverse spiritual states that we experience and to choose the course of action that most fully expresses our love for God and our love for neighbor. The goal is always to select from the possible options the action that best promotes right relationships with others and leads us more deeply into communion with God.

As we engage in discernment, the subjective movements or spirits that arise within us are recognized and understood on a very personal level. Reason and intelligence play a role in picking up on these interior movements and in helping us to make good moral decisions in practical matters, but these skills alone do not lead us to the moral choice that best promotes right relationships and human flourishing. For this we need to engage the whole network of human capacities. This includes the intellect with its power of reason, as well as faith, feelings, emotions, intuition, and imagination. Sometimes we tend to overlook these other human capacities as if morality were purely an intellectual endeavor. However, as noted in chapter 2, this is not consistent with human experience. The fact is that in most moral matters we are guided by the heart. As the great mathematician and physicist Blaise Pascal put it, "The heart has its reasons which reason knows nothing of."[5] The word "heart" is understood here in the biblical sense as the deepest level of ourselves, where God's Spirit joins our spirit (Romans 8:16). It is at this level where we are alone with God, whose voice echoes in our depths.[6]

The heart is the focal point of discernment. "The tradition of discernment maintains that what we want in our heart of hearts will be consistent with whom God is enabling and requiring us to be and with what we are to do."[7] This does not mean that discernment is purely subjective and set against objective sources of morality such as principles, Scripture, moral teachings, and social norms. Discernment unfolds within the boundaries provided by these moral constraints and proceeds from them to concrete moral situations. Discernment builds on objective moral grounding in attending to the situation and its particularities, and in determining what is the most loving and virtuous response. It makes judgments based on what we know to be true and good in the deepest part of ourselves.

Understanding who we ought to become and how we ought to act in concrete situations through the virtue of discernment requires an adequate personal foundation. This foundation consists of three interrelated elements. First, we must be committed to growing in our relationship with God. One critical strategy in developing our relationship with God is prayer. Prayer allows us to get in touch with the voice of God and to perceive where God is leading us in our moral lives. Second, we must trust that God is with us in our everyday moral decisions. This trust provides the confidence necessary to follow those inner movements that are consistent with whom we ought to become in light of our relationship with God. Third, we must experience a certain degree of freedom from disordered passions so that we can follow the course of action that best promotes our own flourishing and that of others. Without this freedom, we are paralyzed in the face of choices for the good. These foundational elements are crucial for discernment.

## Discernment as a Process

Now that we have discussed what discernment is, we turn to how it works in everyday moral decisions. How do we go about discerning what is the most loving and virtuous response in concrete situations? This brings us to the process of discernment, which we will outline below and adapt for purposes of studying ethical issues and analyzing cases outside the context of making personal moral decisions. Before we do this, however, we should point out that the process of discerning is not like solving a problem. The practical moral reasoning of discernment is less clear, less certain, and less linear than the experimental model of reasoning designed specifically for problem solving.[8] Discernment does not operate in computer fashion and does not offer certain solutions to moral problems. Rather, discernment gives us an inner sense that we are doing the right thing. Ernest Larkin describes this well:

> [Discernment] does not tell us what to do, since it moves on a different plane from the technical. But it does indicate whether or not we are

moving in the right direction on the deepest level of our being, and in this way it enlightens our experiences, reinforces our decisions, and concretizes our desire to find God in all things.[9]

In short, discernment provides us with moral confidence, not scientific certainty, that through our actions we are promoting right relationships and ultimately contributing to our own flourishing and that of others. This may not satisfy those who want black and white answers to moral problems. Yet the unsettling fact is that life is messy and many moral situations do not have easy solutions that we can simply deduce or attain by applying principles.

The overall process of discernment consists of three interrelated components: personal reflection, contextual analysis, and critical evaluation. We will discuss these separately below but it is important to keep in mind that they work together in moral decision making.

## Personal Reflection

Discernment is about distinguishing between the inner movements that motivate us to act so we can make good moral decisions. This requires that we listen to God in prayer, and that we attain some degree of knowledge about ourselves. Prayer is an essential feature of discernment because it allows us to get in touch with the deepest level of ourselves, the place where God dwells. The prayer of discernment is not simply reciting formula prayers but, more profoundly, opening ourselves to God's presence so that we can get a sense of what is going on inside and outside ourselves.[10] Prayerful openness to God frees us from internal restraints and external pressures that affect our moral vision and our moral judgments. The interior freedom gained from prayer enables God's self-communication to be heard in our hearts and empowers us to respond to God's grace in the present moment. Meditation, contemplation, and centering prayer are just a few types of prayer that can facilitate the openness to God that discernment requires.

Self-knowledge is also a critical feature of discernment because it helps us to understand our beliefs, character, desires, experiences, motives, temperament, values, and so on. The awareness of ourselves that we gain through prayer and other forms of reflection gives us insight into the various forces that motivate us to act in moral situations. In this way, self-knowledge allows us to see the bright side of ourselves and the dark side, the positive possibilities and the limitations. Though the truth that we learn about ourselves may be painful, it is an important part of discernment because it highlights any capacity for false justification or self-deception that we may possess. Only with this truth can we discern whether our actions promote right relationships and are consistent with whom we ought to become as people made in God's image.

## Contextual Analysis

Discernment is about making good moral decisions in complex, changing circumstances. We must recognize the morally relevant features of a situation and extensively consult objective sources of morality and the accumulated wisdom of others. Responding in the most loving and virtuous way is difficult if we do not truly understand the situation in which we find ourselves. To uncover the information necessary for moral decision making we need to ask certain reality-revealing questions: "What?" "Why and How?" "Who?" "When and Where?" "Foreseeable effects?" "Viable alternatives?"[11]

"*What?*" centers on the facts and provides an initial picture of the situation ("What is going on?"). This question precedes all others because it supplies the factual information we need to move forward. "*Why?*" and "*How?*" deal with ends and means ("Why am I doing this? How am I doing this?"). Much emphasis is placed on the "*Why?*" question in ethics because it touches that which we hope to accomplish through our action and our intentions in acting (the ends). However, equally important is the "*How?*" question because it forces us to look at what we are doing (the means) to accomplish our end. Sometimes even the noblest end with the purest intention cannot justify the harmful means selected to achieve the end. Many critics of the war in Iraq have used this argument against the Bush Administration. While removing Saddam Hussein from power was a good end given the injustice of his dictatorship and the atrocities his regime committed, critics argue that the means (i.e., going to war) were not good and the end could have been accomplished in more ethical ways (e.g., diplomatic measures). Whatever your take, the point is that the means matter just as much as the ends.

"*Who?*" focuses not only on the one performing the action, but also on those whom the action will affect ("Who is doing this? Who will be affected?"). This question is important in an ethic that seeks to promote right relationships because it helps us recognize the interpersonal nature and social implications of our actions.

"*When?*" and "*Where?*" locate the event in time and place ("When am I doing this? Where am I doing this?"). These questions may seem somewhat irrelevant but they prove quite weighty in some situations. For example, to scream at church during a quiet moment in the liturgy is different from screaming after a touchdown at a football game. "*Foreseeable effects?*" concentrates on the results or consequences of our actions, both short-term and long-term ("What if I do this?"). This question deals with the ways we and others will be affected by our actions. "*Viable alternatives?*" refers to other options that may be available to us in moral situations ("What else can I do?"). This question requires a good imagination to see alternative courses of action that may not be immediately apparent. Sometimes by asking this question we come to realize that what we initially thought was the right thing to do is actually not as good as another option.

When engaging in the process of discernment and trying to figure out the moral dimensions of a situation, the reality-revealing questions must be asked. These questions may not offer definitive moral guidance in every situation, but they help us understand the total situation and draw us closer to the action that best promotes right relationships. At any one time some of the questions may be more important than others. Nonetheless, they must always be taken as a whole. They cannot be separated without sacrificing moral perspective.

Consulting objective sources of morality and the accumulated wisdom of others is also an indispensable feature of the process of discernment. Several religious and nonreligious resources are available to us when facing an impending moral decision. These resources include but are not limited to Scripture, Jesus, church, community, role models, expert authority, moral principles, and laws. The information supplied by these resources is essential to making good moral decisions that promote our own well-being and that of others.

*Scripture* is a fundamental source of morality. The Judeo-Christian story and the personal witness of the women and men of the Bible are concrete symbols that shed light on who we ought to become and how we ought to act in relation to others. Though we do not find specific answers to many of the ethical issues we face today, Scripture nonetheless gives us insight into, among other things, the values we should be promoting through our actions. *Jesus* is the moral ideal of who we ought to become. As mentioned in chapter 3, in Jesus we see what it means to be truly and fully human, and what it means to act in ways that promote right relationships. The *church* provides the theological foundations necessary for living the gospel message of love through, among other things, mediating God's grace in the sacraments. The church also guides us in moral matters through its formal teachings as well as through the moral reflections of pastors, theologians, and others. While here we have in mind particularly the Roman Catholic Church, we should point out that other religious traditions, Christian or otherwise, can also serve as important moral resources. Moral wisdom is certainly not reserved exclusively to the Catholic Church and we would not want to give that impression by our comments.

*Community* is the place where our lives unfold. The communities in which we live shape our moral character and facilitate our moral growth. The collective experience of communities also serves as a source of moral wisdom on which we can draw when making moral decisions. *Role models* give us a life-guiding moral vision. They show us how we can and ought to live morally. *Expert authority* is a critical resource in our highly technical world. Because we cannot know everything there is to know in practical matters, we have to rely on experts to fill in the gaps in our knowledge so that we can make informed moral choices. Just as we seek information from the Internet or a sales representative when we buy an iPod or a car, we often must do the same when making moral decisions. *Moral principles* are excellent sources of morality because they serve as action guides that complement virtue. As noted in the previous chapter, principles give us a sense of what we may be required to do in a particular situation and help us to evaluate the choices that we are inclined to make based on our moral character and overall orientation in life. *Laws* provide a framework for moral living. They can be helpful as moral guides in identifying personal and social values, and encouraging us to promote such values. However, laws can also fall short of fulfilling the demands of morality.

All of these sources of morality and others play an important role in the process of discernment. While discernment does not begin and end with an objective analysis of outside sources, discernment relies on the information generated from these sources in helping us arrive at good moral decisions in concrete situations.

## Critical Evaluation

Discernment is about making good moral choices that truly promote right relationships and lead ultimately to our flourishing and that of others. Since we are imperfect human beings limited in many ways, discernment can end in moral decisions that we wrongly perceive as right. To limit this possibility as much as humanly possible, we need to check our decisions against certain external and internal criteria that help us evaluate whether the course of action we take really contributes to our own well-being and that of others. Just as pilots, machine operators, and electricians have safeguards that seek to eliminate the possibility of error, so should we as moral beings, perhaps even more urgently given what is at stake for ourselves and others.

The external criteria for good discernment include Scripture and church teaching, the community and its values, and moral principles and relevant laws. We look to these criteria to see if our moral decisions in changing circumstances are in harmony or disharmony with these sources of morality. Certain questions help us measure our moral decisions against these criteria: "Is our decision consistent with the substance of Scripture and with church teaching on the matter? What is the attitude of the community toward our decision or the issue in general? Would the community support us in this decision if it became public? Is our decision consonant with moral principles and laws that apply to this situation?" If we answer "yes" to these questions, then we can be relatively confident that we are making a good decision. If we answer "no" to any of these questions, then we need to rethink the matter and try to figure out if we are not in fact proceeding in the wrong direction.

The external criteria have undoubted strength and appeal, but they also have certain limits. First, as we noted above, Scripture does not explicitly address all of the issues that challenge us in our moral lives and many scriptural texts are ambiguous and open to varied interpretations. Moreover, church teaching on moral matters is fallible and thus susceptible to error. Nor does it attend to the complexities of every moral situation. Second, the community can promote certain values and ways of acting that hinder right relationships and actually detract from our pursuit of human flourishing. As such, sometimes it may be necessary to stand against the community so that greater good can be achieved. Third, moral principles can be in conflict, as we have seen in chapter 2, and laws often are reduced to the moral minimum or can even be opposed to morality. These limits suggest that the external criteria of good discernment may not always serve as an adequate check.

To illustrate this consider the example of slavery in the United States. When slavery was an accepted social "institution," people often cited Scripture in its support and used church teaching to reinforce their position, which at the time considered slavery permissible. Furthermore, most people in the United States and in individual communities believed slavery was acceptable, at least until the abolitionist movement gained momentum. Moreover, the law permitted the trading and ownership of slaves. Now let's say you lived during this time but opposed slavery. Discernment leads you to believe that slavery was wrong, but when you consider any action against it you run smack into external criteria supporting it. What do you do? Do you go against your own best judgment

truth is disclosed, and the hospital may lose a surgeon who brings in a lot of patients if it chooses to punish the surgeon.

2. **Identify the ethical issue(s).** Sometimes this may seem pretty obvious but it is nonetheless a key step because it sets the tone for how we view the case. In describing the ethical issue(s) it is important to be very precise so we know what is at stake. In this case the main ethical issue is whether we should disclose or continue to conceal the truth from the patient who has already been lied to by the surgeon. There are also secondary ethical issues, such as whether we ought to compensate the patient in some way if we do decide to disclose the truth and how we should handle the surgeon.

3. **Consider what right relationships require and what leads ultimately to human flourishing.** Here we want to tap into the normative basis by asking who we ought to become (as individuals or communities) in terms of the virtues we should be exhibiting in the present circumstances and how we ought to act in terms of the principles that should guide our action. Recalling our normative basis we can say that the surgeon should have manifested the virtues of respect, honesty, courage, and integrity. These virtues, in the given circumstances, would best promote right relationships and contribute to the well-being of the surgeon, the patient, and the hospital. Obviously the surgeon did not exhibit these virtues. However, the hospital still has a chance to right the situation by showing respect for the patient's dignity, by being honest with the patient, by acting with courage and integrity through disclosing the truth despite the consequences. With regard to principles, we can see that veracity, which falls under human dignity, and stewardship, which falls under justice, are the main principles that apply to the case. These two principles could be in conflict since telling the truth to the patient may lead ultimately to a lawsuit that could result in a huge financial loss for the hospital, which has obligations to others (e.g., patients, employees, vendors, and the community). As such, we may have to weigh which principle is more important than the other. Is it worth losing some money if the hospital and its leaders maintain their integrity?

From a moral perspective, integrity far exceeds the value of money and so veracity would be the primary principle to consider.

4. **Brainstorm possible options.** This next step involves listing all possible options without regard for what is right or wrong—we will critically evaluate the options later. Some of the options in this case could be: (a) keep up the lie by not telling the patient and do nothing to the surgeon; (b) keep up the lie by not telling the patient but reprimand, suspend, or strip the surgeon of her credentials at the hospital; (c) disclose the truth to the patient but do nothing to the surgeon; and (d) disclose the truth to the patient, offer a financial settlement, and reprimand, suspend, or strip the surgeon of her credentials at the hospital. There are probably other options, but these are the main ones and are enough for the purposes of this illustration.

5. **Weigh options and select one.** Now we must weigh the various options by eliminating any that are simply unacceptable in light of the primary virtues and principles necessary for right relationships that we identified. Once we have done this, we need to consider the remaining options and their consequences and choose the one(s) that we believe in our heart of hearts truly promotes right relationships and contributes to our flourishing as people in a community. Given the virtues and principles we noted above, options A and B, which keep up the lie by continuing to conceal the truth from the patient, are unacceptable. These options would impair our character as individuals as well as an organization and undermine our integrity. Option C, in which we disclose the truth to the patient, might work but the surgeon would not have to account for her actions. While we can accept that errors happen and try to correct the steps in the surgical process that went awry, we cannot tolerate lying on the part of our physicians, even those that bring in a lot of money to the hospital. This leaves us with option D, which, all things considered, seems to be the best option morally. Although the patient may not accept our sincere apology and any money we offer to her and we could get sued and lose a good surgeon, this option best reflects

who we ought to become and upholds an important principle that specifies what respect for human dignity demands.

6. **Evaluate the decision against external and internal criteria.** Here we need to ask whether the option(s) we have selected stands up against the external criteria of Scripture and church teaching, the community and its values, and moral principles and relevant laws. Although Scripture and church teaching do not address the issue specifically, the values promoted through each support telling the truth and thereby preserving our integrity as well as holding the surgeon accountable. Likewise, our decision seems also to be supported by community values, moral principles, and relevant laws, all of which would favor disclosing the truth and addressing the surgeon's action of lying. What about the internal criterion? While somewhat difficult to evaluate outside of personal moral decisions, it can be reduced to certain questions when analyzing issues or cases: (a) Who are we becoming (as individuals and/or communities) through this action? (b) Is our action consistent with who we ought to become as individuals and/ or communities? (c) Will our action truly promote right relationships and contribute to the overall well-being of ourselves and others? Based on the option we have selected, we can answer all these questions positively and be able to live with the decision we have made, despite its consequences.

## Conclusion and Next Steps

This is an illustration of how we use discernment with our normative basis to evaluate cases in ethics. As we move out of the foundations section of this book and into broader issues and other cases in health care ethics, it is important that we consider them against the backdrop of our normative basis using the process of discernment that we have constructed here. This gives us the best chance of identifying the ethical concerns, seeing them in their broader context, and making decisions that truly promote right relationships and lead ultimately to our flourishing as human beings.

## Suggested Readings

Gula, Richard M. *Moral Discernment*. New York: Paulist Press, 1997.

_____. *The Good Life: Where Morality and Spirituality Converge*. New York: Paulist Press, 1999.

Maguire, Daniel C., and A. Nicholas Fargnoli. *On Moral Grounds: The Art/Science of Ethics*. New York: Crossroad, 1991.

Spohn, William C. *Go and Do Likewise: Jesus and Ethics*. New York: Continuum, 1999.

## Multimedia Aids for Teachers

There are several movies that depict good discernment skills; characters take into consideration who they ought to become and how they ought to act in relation to others by weighing, virtues, principles, consequences, and other factors in light of the circumstances. Two of the best, which are available on DVD or VHS through retailers, are listed below.

> *A Man for All Seasons*. Directed by Fred Zinnemann. Starring Paul Scofield. Rated G. 1966. While this movie is excellent for these purposes, students may not connect with it as much as a more contemporary movie. Still, it is perhaps the best cinematic depiction of discernment in light of a normative basis.

> *Scent of a Woman*. Directed by Martin Brest. Starring Al Pacino. Rated R. 1992. This movie is more current and displays good discernment skills through the eyes of a young character; as such it should resonate with students.

### Endnotes

[1] Much of the discussion of discernment that follows has been adapted from Michael R. Panicola, "Discernment in the Neonatal Context," *Theological Studies* 60 (December 1999): 723–46.

[2] For a discussion of the characteristic features of discerning people, see James M. Gustafson, "Moral Discernment in the Christian Life," in *Theology and Christian Ethics*, ed. James M. Gustafson (Philadelphia: Pilgrim Press, 1974), 99–119, at 101–9. This article first appeared in *Norm and Context in Christian Ethics*, ed. Gene Outka and Paul Ramsey (New York: Charles Scribner's Sons, 1968), 17–36.

[3] Richard M. Gula, *Reason Informed by Faith: Foundations of Catholic Morality* (New York: Paulist Press, 1989), 315.

[4] William C. Spohn, "The Reasoning Heart: An American Approach to Christian Discernment," *Theological Studies* 44 (March 1983), 30–52, at 30.

[5] *Pensées and Other Writings*, 1995 (trans. by Honor Levi, intr. and notes by Anthony Levi).

[6] Vatican Council II, *Gaudium et Spes*, no. 16, in *Proclaiming Justice and Peace: Papal Documents from* Rerum Novarum *through* Centesimus Annus, ed. Michael Walsh and Brian Davies (Mystic, CT: Twenty-Third Publications, 1994), 168.

[7] Gula, *Reason Informed by Faith*, 321.

[8] In a relatively recent book, Richard M. Gula discusses the differences between scientific reasoning and the practical moral reasoning of discernment. See his *Moral Discernment* (New York: Paulist Press, 1997), 50–52.

[9] Ernest Larkin, *Silent Presence: Discernment as Process and Problem* (Denville, NJ: Dimension Books, 1981), 58.

[10] Gula, *Moral Discernment*, 98–99.

[11] The reality-revealing questions were first proposed by Daniel C. Maguire, *The Moral Choice* (Garden City, NY: Doubleday, 1978). He further developed these questions in a book he co-authored with A. Nicholas Fargnoli, *On Moral Grounds: The Art/Science of Ethics* (New York: Crossroad, 1991). The presentation of these questions is based on the latter work, pages 49–72.

[12] For a review of the limits of Christian discernment, see Gula, *Reason Informed by Faith*, 326–28; and Larkin, *Silent Presence*, 7–8.

# CHAPTER 5

# Abortion and Maternal-Fetal Care

Clinical situations involving a threat to the health of a pregnant woman and/or her fetus represent true ethical dilemmas. In such cases, the woman (or couple) is often faced with a tragic choice between her own life and that of her fetus. In contemporary health care ethics, this tension is often resolved by focusing primarily, if not exclusively, on the autonomy of the woman, which basically means the woman has the ultimate right to decide what should be done based upon her own values. Based on this line of reasoning, the courts in the United States have essentially ruled that such decisions are private ones that the woman has the right to make. Resolving this tension is more difficult, however, in light of our normative basis, which recognizes the sanctity of human life at all stages of development and seeks to respect and protect both the mother and the fetus. The tension inherent in such situations is illustrated in the following cases.

**Case 5A:** Laura A., a 29-year-old woman who is 20 weeks pregnant, comes to the Emergency Room because her "water has broken" prematurely (preterm premature rupture of membranes). The baby's heart is still beating, and Laura is not in immediate danger. Still, she is admitted to the hospital for observation and bed rest. It is noted in her chart that she has no live children, but has lost two previous pregnancies due to miscarriage. On the fourth day in the hospital, she begins running a fever and showing other signs of infection. Her OB (obstetric) physician starts antibiotics right away. Despite the use of IV (intravenous) antibiotics, Laura's symptoms indicate that the infection continues to worsen. Her physician tells her and her husband, Keith, that she has an infection of the amniotic fluid and chorion (chorioamnionitis), and that Laura could die if they do not induce labor and deliver the baby as soon as possible. The physician also tells them that at this stage in the pregnancy, the baby will inevitably die within hours of being born because its lungs are not fully developed. Laura, however, says she does not want to consent to anything that would jeopardize the baby's life.

**Case 5B:** Sue, a 32-year-old pregnant woman, only 15 weeks and 3 days into her pregnancy, goes to the emergency department, accompanied by her husband and three young children, complaining of a persistent fever and severe back pain. After extensive testing, it is determined that Sue has a particularly aggressive form of spinal cancer that requires aggressive chemotherapy as well as radiation directed at the malignant tumor on her spine. The oncologist carefully explains to Sue that the chemotherapy and radiation will probably cause severe defects in the baby and could even cause its death. Irrespective of what the treatment would do to the baby, the pregnancy itself would put an additional strain on her body, would significantly reduce the chance of the treatment working, and would probably put Sue at risk of other life-threatening complications, such as bleeding to death. Without the treatment, however, Sue probably wouldn't even live long enough for the baby to reach viability. If Sue is to have a chance at surviving to raise her three kids she must terminate the pregnancy and begin treatment as soon as possible. The oncologist gives Sue and her husband some time to absorb all that he has told them and to think about the options.

In this chapter we will consider some of the major ethical issues related to abortion, particularly issues that come up in the area of maternal-fetal care when the life of the mother and/or the fetus is threatened. We will begin by setting the clinical and legal context and then move on to a discussion of the ethics of abortion, using as our starting point Catholic teaching in this area. While our normative basis may lead to a broader ethical analysis of the issues at hand, Catholic teaching on abortion and maternal-fetal care provides a solid basis for shaping our discussion. Catholic teaching on abortion and maternal-fetal care is rooted in centuries of the Catholic moral tradition, as are many of the values and principles that ground our normative basis, most notably human dignity and justice. As you read through this chapter, think about the cases above. How would you counsel Laura, who doesn't want to do anything that would result in the death of the fetus even at the risk of her own life? Is it morally acceptable to terminate Sue's pregnancy before starting chemotherapy and radiation or does Sue have an obligation to continue the pregnancy despite the risks to her fetus and herself? This chapter is not meant to provide you with ready-made answers to these questions, but to help you think through the ethical questions they raise against the backdrop of our normative basis.

## Setting the Context: Clinical and Legal Considerations

Induced abortion can be defined as the medical or surgical termination of pregnancy before the time of fetal viability.[1] According to a report published by the Guttmacher Institute in 1999, approximately 26,000,000 legal abortions, and another 20,000,000 illegal abortions, are performed every year worldwide.[2]

Though the number has been decreasing in recent years, approximately 1,290,000 abortions were performed in the United States in 2002.[3] Approximately 60% of abortions are performed within the first 8 weeks of pregnancy, and 8% are performed during the first 12 weeks.[4] The method of abortion depends, in part, on the time in the pregnancy at which it is terminated. That is, the type of clinical procedure used depends in part on what stage of pregnancy has been reached at the time the abortion is performed.

## Types of Abortion Procedures

In the first 12 weeks (the first trimester), vacuum aspiration (suction curettage) is the most common procedure for terminating pregnancy. This procedure consists of placing a tube (cannula) into the uterus and sucking the amniotic fluid, placenta and fetus through the cannula into a collection jar.[5] Earlier in the first trimester of pregnancy, up to 9 weeks, RU486 is also sometimes used.[6] RU486 is a combination of two drugs, mifepristone and misoprostol. The mifepristone is taken orally in the physician's office, and the misoprostol is taken a few days later by the woman at home. Mifepristone decreases the hormones that maintain a pregnancy and causes the embryo to detach from the uterus. Once detached the embryo dies. A few days later, a dose of misoprostol is taken to make the uterus contract and expel the embryo.

In the early part of the second trimester, 13 to 15 weeks of pregnancy, dilation and evacuation (D&E) is the most common procedure. The procedure is similar to vacuum aspiration except surgical instruments are used to remove larger pieces of fetal tissue. From 16 weeks of pregnancy on, the mid-second and third trimesters, several procedures can be used for terminating the pregnancy. At this stage, these procedures include: D&E (considered above); intact dilation and extraction (D&X); induction of labor and delivery; and caesarian section (C-section). Intact D&X, which is a controversial procedure, involves using instruments to turn the baby to the breech position so that its feet are facing out. Once in the breech position, the entire body of the fetus, except its head, is extracted from the woman.

The fetus's skull is then collapsed and the dead but otherwise intact fetus is removed.

Induction of labor and delivery involves administering drugs to the woman to cause contractions, i.e., to cause her to go into labor, and deliver the fetus. Nothing is done to the fetus directly, except it is expelled from the uterus along with the placenta and amniotic fluid. Most often the fetus survives the delivery, but dies shortly after being born, depending on how far along the pregnancy is at the time labor is induced, how far the baby has developed, and whether it has any life-threatening conditions. A few babies have been known to survive after being born at only 23 weeks of pregnancy (14 to 17 weeks early).[7] In these cases, the baby almost always requires aggressive neonatal intensive care (the topic of the next chapter) for the first few months of its life and has significant disabilities and developmental problems. With every week that the pregnancy can be extended beyond 23 weeks, the baby is more likely to survive and have fewer disabilities and developmental problems. A C-section is similar to the induction of labor and delivery, except contractions are not started. Rather, the baby is delivered through an incision in the woman's abdomen.

All of the above procedures are clinically accepted ways of terminating pregnancy. Which method is chosen will depend in part on the stage of pregnancy at the time the decision is made to terminate and whether that decision is elective or medically indicated. A significant similarity between the procedures of vacuum aspiration, D&C, D&E, and intact D&X is that they all result in the death of the fetus prior to its being removed from the womb. Indeed, all of these procedures require destroying the fetus as part of the process of removing it. In the cases of induction of labor and delivery or C-section the fetus is not destroyed in the process of removing it from the womb but dies as a result of being born prematurely. When the fetus dies as a "side effect" of the induction of labor and delivery or a C-section performed primarily for the purpose of saving the mother's life, this is sometimes referred to in the moral context as an "indirect abortion." Generally speaking, an indirect abortion occurs when the primary purpose of the procedure is to save the life of the mother and the fetus dies as a side effect of the lifesaving treatment. In a direct abortion, the primary purpose is ending the life of the fetus.

## The Legal Status of Abortion in the United States

Throughout most of United States history abortion has been illegal. In fact, as recently as 1965 abortion at all stages of pregnancy was prohibited by law, though 46 states and the District of Columbia allowed abortions to save the life of the mother. The legal landscape changed with the landmark case of *Roe v. Wade* (1973).[8] In this case, the Supreme Court struck down as unconstitutional almost all state laws that restricted abortion. The Court ruled that laws prohibiting abortion violated a woman's right to privacy, which is not explicit in the Constitution, but has its basis in the Bill of Rights and in the concept of liberty as guaranteed by the Fourteenth Amendment. The Fourteenth Amendment provides protection for each person regarding due process and equal protection under the Constitution. However, as part of its decision in *Roe v. Wade* the Court ruled that the unborn fetus is not a person in the "whole sense" and, therefore, not deserving of protection under the Fourteenth Amendment.

Rather than entitling the fetus to protection under the Fourteenth Amendment, the ruling in *Roe v. Wade* set limits on the laws states could enact prohibiting abortion based upon which trimester of pregnancy has been reached. Specifically, the ruling declared that during the first trimester the decision to abort is a medical judgment belonging to the woman's physician and cannot be prohibited by law. During the second trimester, states may regulate abortion as long as they allow for exceptions to protect the woman's health, as defined by the state. In the third trimester, states are permitted to regulate and even prohibit abortions, as long as they permit exceptions for protecting the woman's health and preserving her life. *Roe v. Wade* is not the only case in which the United States Supreme Court has ruled on the question of abortion.

In the case of *Planned Parenthood v. Casey*,[9] the *Roe v. Wade* ruling was affirmed and even expanded. In this case the Court stated that only a pregnant woman—not the state—has the authority to determine whether the unborn fetus should be counted as a member of the community, deserving of protection. The Court's rationale in *Casey* for giving the woman this authority was twofold. First, the "mother who carries a child to full term is subject to the anxieties, to physical constraints, to pain that only she must bear." Second, the Court ruled that the state cannot impose an undue burden on a woman's right to have an abortion by placing a "substantial obstacle in the path of the woman seeking an abortion before the fetus attains viability." Again the stage of pregnancy is given legal weight in the context of abortion insofar as the fetus is provided additional protections once it has attained "viability."

In legal contexts not having to do with abortion, however, more than half of the states consider human life to begin with conception, that is, with the completion of fertilization. Indeed, many states give the embryo legal protection outside the context of abortion either by statute, resolution, or court decisions.[10] For example, Missouri law states that "the life of a human being begins at conception," and legally defines the term "unborn child" as including embryos and fetuses "from the moment of conception until birth at every stage of biological development."[11] If someone murders a pregnant woman in Missouri that person could be found guilty of two homicides. Thus the legal status of early human life in this country represents a somewhat "schizophrenic" outlook. On the one hand, pregnant women have, as stated in the ruling in *Planned Parenthood v. Casey,* the "right to define one's own concept of existence, of meaning, of the universe, and the mystery of life," within the context of deciding whether or not to have an abortion. On the other hand, outside the context of abortion states can and do offer the embryo and fetus the same legal protections afforded to other human beings. Somewhat ironically, some states give legal protection to the embryo even earlier than most doctors would recognize a woman as being pregnant: the common medical definition recognizes "pregnancy" as beginning with implantation of the embryo.

## The Intersection of Law, Ethics, and Abortion

The United States Supreme Court used the stages of development in pregnancy as criteria for certain restrictions on what individual states could and could not prohibit. The Supreme Court later tightened restrictions on what individual states could prohibit, using the point of viability as the key consideration. The question of when viability begins and who gets to define it is truly significant from both a legal and ethical standpoint. If, for example, a fetus could survive on its own outside the womb, i.e., if it really is viable, the induction of labor and delivery or a C-section, or any method of terminating pregnancy that did not entail the destruction of the fetus, would not be considered an abortion from either an ethical perspective or a legal perspective (by implication of the ruling in *Planned Parenthood v. Casey*). These considerations illustrate how the legal and ethical questions regarding abortion intersect.

The question of when viability begins, however, is not the only significant question in both the legal and ethical contexts of abortion. As is clear from the preceding considerations of the Supreme Court's rationale, the question of whether and when human life ought to be deserving of our respect and protection has been central to the legal debate regarding abortion. For example, the decision in *Planned Parenthood v. Casey* explicitly turned on the consideration of whether or not the fetus should be considered a person deserving of the same respect and protection as other members of the community. This is not just a legal question, but an ethical question.

# Discussion: Ethical Issues and Analysis

## Respect for Autonomy and the Moral Status of Early Human Life

As in the legal context, the ethical debate regarding abortion has centered on the question of personhood and who counts as a "person." When should the product of conception (an embryo, a fetus, or an infant) be considered a person deserving of moral respect and protection? Three primary characteristics of contemporary western ethical culture have influenced the public debate regarding the moral status of unborn life: (1) relativism and legalism, (2) mind-body dualism, and (3) the supreme value of autonomy.

First, ethical relativism (the view that what is right or wrong is relative to a particular group of people or an individual) has given rise to the view that there are no moral truths that hold for everyone everywhere. As in the *Planned Parenthood v. Casey* ruling, ethics and values are defined by each individual or, at best, by social consensus. Within this framework there are very few shared normative limits, and ethics is viewed as legalistic. Accordingly, public morality is seen as primarily a matter of law. The implication is that ethics in the social realm is understood as the bare minimum of constraints on freedom necessary for individuals to be able to live together, and consent between individuals who do not share the same moral values is the foundational ethical principle.[12] As such, the role of ethics in prescribing what one ought to do in order to promote human flourishing is limited to the individual or private sphere of life.

Second, the primary underlying view of human nature is fundamentally dualistic. The idea that a human being is essentially a body inhabited by a mind dates back at least as far as Plato. A number of thinkers throughout history—including some within the Christian tradition, such as St. Augustine—have embraced this perspective. The popularity of this dualistic view in the modern period can be traced to the philosopher René Descartes, who put forth the famous adage "*cogito ergo sum*" (I think, therefore I am). The dualistic view holds that the body and the mind are two distinct and independent realities. The body is most closely associated with being human, while the mind and one's mental capacities are more closely associated with what makes someone a person.

Third, autonomy (understood as the capacity for rational thought and the ability to determine for oneself what is right and wrong, good and bad) is seen as the supreme value within contemporary western secular culture. In light of the supreme value of autonomy, human life is often seen as having value only when an individual has the capacity to act autonomously. However, within some religious traditions, such as Christianity and Judaism, the order is reversed. That is, human life is seen as having a basic intrinsic value because people are made in the image and likeness of God. Moreover, we have autonomy precisely because we are made in the image and likeness of God. Viewed theologically, life—the most basic of values, enabling all other values to be pursued—places constraints on autonomous action. In secular ethical thought, however, autonomy has been given such significance that the ability to exercise one's autonomous capacities has become synonymous with what it means to be a human person.[13] Thus the question of when personhood begins has long been the center of the abortion debate. Regarding the moral status of the fetus, two of the more predominant views are the personal position and the non-personal position.

The Non-Personal Position. The non-personal view of the fetus is influenced by and consistent with the moral relativism and dualism described above, and has been reinforced in the legal context by the Supreme Court decisions in the cases of *Roe v. Wade* and *Planned Parenthood v. Casey*. According to this position, a fetus does not deserve the same respect and protection as other members of the moral community because it is not capable of functioning in ways characteristically associated with being a person. That is, it cannot make free choices, communicate, plan for the future, participate in social life, or do anything else commonly associated with fully conscious, autonomous, rational individuals. Consequently, a fetus is not a person but only a "potential person." This view is based on a strong distinction and separation of being "human" and being a "person." As the philosopher Peter Singer writes,

> These two senses of "human being" overlap but do not coincide. The embryo, the later fetus, the profoundly intellectually disabled child, even the newborn infant—all are indisputably members of the species Homo sapiens, but none are self-aware, have a sense of the future, or the capacity to relate to others.[14]

H. Tristam Engelhardt, Jr., another philosopher, writes,

> Not every person need be human, and not every human is a person. In order to understand the geography of obligations in health care regarding fetuses, infants, the profoundly mentally retarded and the severely brain damaged, one will need to determine the moral status of a "person" and of mere human biological life, and then develop criteria to distinguish between these classes of entities.[15]

From a theological perspective, the non-personal position is inadequate for two main reasons. First, according to the view of the human person as made in the image and likeness of God, there is much more to being a human person than being fully conscious, autonomous, and rational. Rather, humans are inseparably physical and material, creative and spiritual, relational and social, as well as morally free and responsible.[16] Simply because a human being may not have the capacity to actualize or realize fully one of these innate capacities does not necessarily make that human being less than a person.

Second, the non-personal position fails to recognize the developmental dimension of human life. That is, the fact that we grow through different developmental stages at which we have different capabilities does not imply that we are not the same human being that existed as a six-cell embryo when we are eighty years old. We are, in fact, one and the same individual, just at different stages in our natural course of development. The point here is that just because we may exhibit different capacities at different stages of life doesn't mean that our underlying nature (what kind of being we are, and what form our ultimate fulfillment takes) changes in the course of those different stages. To claim otherwise is to ignore the fact that there is not only a developmental dimension of human life, but also an inherent and necessary continuity. As Stephen Schwarz has argued,

> The fact that my capabilities to function as a person have changed and grown does not alter the absolute continuity of my essential being, that of a person. In fact, this variation in capabilities presupposes the continuity

In this case, the primary purpose, or intention, of inducing labor and delivery is to rid Laura's body of the amniotic fluid and chorion containing the source of the infection, thereby eliminating the threat to her life. We can have a pretty good idea that this is the primary purpose because the physician first tried to cure or at least control the infection by using antibiotics. Thus the physician only recommended induction of labor and delivery once the only other way of eliminating the threat to Laura's life, which did not involve terminating the pregnancy, was tried unsuccessfully. We also know that the primary purpose is to cure Laura, because the physician did not recommend the induction until the infection became severe enough to present a real threat to Laura's life. We can sum up the physician's recommendation to terminate the pregnancy through induction of labor and delivery as a "last resort" for saving Laura's life.

Insofar as the physician's primary purpose is to save Laura's life, we can see that the choice to induce labor and delivery in this case is not out of any disrespect for the sanctity and dignity of the fetus's life, despite the fact that the physician foresees that it will die as a result of the lifesaving procedure. In the moral context, labor and delivery in this case is what we would call an "indirect" abortion. It is "indirect" insofar as the death of the fetus is a foreseen side effect that is only tolerated for a proportionately serious reason, namely, saving the life of the mother.

While we would have preferred that both Laura's life and the life of the fetus could have been saved, that is not a possible outcome and the physician should not be blamed or held morally responsible for the death of the fetus. In fact, not only should the physician not be held morally responsible for the fetus's death in this case, but one could make a strong case from our normative basis that it is the virtuous thing to do. If labor and delivery is not induced, both Laura and her baby will die. Thus by not inducing labor and delivery we would allow the loss of two lives. If, on the other hand, Laura consents to the induction and is saved, she and Keith can continue caring for one another and possibly try to have another baby again, if they desire. Thus, in this case, inducing labor and delivery is the course of action that best promotes right relationships and human well-being.

While this scenario provides a relatively clear example of how we might morally reason our way through a dilemma involving maternal-fetal conflict in light of our normative basis, different circumstances can give rise to more challenging questions requiring further discernment. Consider again, for example, the case of Sue, who is diagnosed with a particularly aggressive form of spinal cancer when she is only a little more than 18 weeks pregnant. In contrast to the previous case, the procedure by which the pregnancy might be terminated is not itself a cure for the condition. Whereas in Laura's case the induction of labor and delivery was a single procedure that lead to both the cure of the infection and the death of the fetus, in Sue's case the death of the fetus would result from a separate procedure that does not treat the cancer itself. In this case, the termination of pregnancy is not a "last resort," but a prerequisite that has to occur before the cancer treatment can even be started, though both the physician and Sue would rather it not have to happen. Nor is the death of the fetus a side effect of the treatment for the cancer that threatens Sue's life, but a necessary condition for that treatment to take place.

In one sense, then, we might say that the primary purpose of terminating the pregnancy is to kill the fetus so that the physicians can treat Sue—note, however, that the fetus probably will die regardless. In another sense, though, we might say that the primary purpose is still to cure Sue of her cancer, since the physician would not be contemplating terminating the pregnancy if it were not necessary to save Sue's life.

This case illustrates the complexity of situations in which the life of the mother and fetus are threatened, and how principles can only aid us so far in our moral reasoning. Does it make a moral difference whether the death of the fetus is a side effect of a curative treatment or a necessary prerequisite for the treatment? Does the sanctity of life require that Sue forego the treatment, despite the fact that both she and the baby will most likely die? How might you weigh other considerations, such as Sue's existing relationships with her husband and children, and the fact that terminating the pregnancy and starting treatment is the only chance she has at continued survival, especially given that the baby will most likely die either way? Regardless of how you answer these questions, would you be willing to say that the circumstances under which Sue and her husband must make their decision lessens the extent to which they should be held morally responsible for their decision? Do these circumstances change the moral status of the act itself?

## Conclusion

The question that has dominated the legal and ethical debates regarding abortion in this country is whether the fetus can be considered a person and, therefore, a member of the moral community. From the perspective of our normative basis, however, all human life, including the fetus, whether healthy or sick, has an inherent dignity and the right to life. If we recognize and accept this, the question becomes, under what conditions and through what procedures can terminating a pregnancy be consistent with our commitment to human life and hence morally acceptable? In rare situations, given the brokenness of human life, we will have to make fateful decisions. Nevertheless, we must always do so with an eye on what it means to live in right relationships and ultimately flourish as human beings in the context of community.

In the tragic circumstances of maternal-fetal conflict in which the life of the mother and/or fetus is threatened, principles alone will carry us only so far. At some point, virtue, prudence, and discernment must illuminate the path to human flourishing, i.e., to becoming who God is calling us to be, as individuals and as a community. In these cases, we must turn to the entire network of our human capacities to help us decide what the most loving and virtuous response is in the present circumstances.

When faced with questions regarding the best clinical approach to a life-threatening condition of a pregnant woman, we must open our hearts to God and listen for the answer. What exactly are we considering doing, and why? Is what we hope to accomplish consistent with love for our neighbor, or are the viable alternatives more consistent with such love? Of course, such discernment takes on special significance in cases involving maternal-fetal conflict because our decisions affect not one but two human lives with which we live in community. Thus we must also ask, given my obligations to both, and given all of the possible consequences, which action is most consistent with who I am as a person, who God is calling me to be, what virtue encourages, and who I will become in and through my response to this situation?

## Additional Case Studies

Case 5C: You are a nurse at a community clinic that provides prenatal services to uninsured women. The fetus of a 41-year-old woman, Stacey M., who is 15 weeks pregnant, has just been diagnosed with anencephaly, a condition in which the "higher" brain fails to develop. The baby will never be conscious and never be able to think or to talk. It has a brain stem, though, which controls bodily functions, such as breathing, heartbeat, and sucking reflexes. The doctor says that if the baby is carried to term it will die for sure within a week of being born, if not sooner. The condition poses no serious threat to Stacey's health, but the physician suggests to Stacey that it might be better to terminate the pregnancy instead of carrying it to term and having to deal with the psychological burden of knowing that her baby will die soon after it is born. The doctor offers to schedule the procedure for her there at the clinic. Some of the nurses are upset by the physician's offer to terminate the pregnancy at the clinic. These nurses argue that the fetus is a person with the right to life and should be allowed to live as long as possible, even if only for the remaining months of pregnancy. Some of the other nurses don't see anything wrong with ending the pregnancy now, given that the outcome will be the same regardless. They argue, why should the woman have to live with people asking her when she's due and if it's a boy or a girl, when she knows it doesn't matter; the outcome will be the same whether it happens now or in 6 months.

**Discussion Questions.** Do you take the side of the nurses who argue that the fetus should be given the chance to live as long as possible, even if only for the remaining months of pregnancy, or the nurses who argue that the pregnancy should be terminated, since the baby will die anyway? What would you do if you were this woman or her husband? Why?

**Case 5D:** Mary and Joe, a married couple with moderate means, have tried unsuccessfully to get pregnant for nearly 2 years. After undergoing infertility testing, the reproductive specialist suggests that Mary take fertility drugs to increase the number of mature ova expelled during each menstrual cycle. The specialist points out that these drugs increase the risk of multiple births. Despite the concerns, Mary consents and promptly begins taking the fertility medication. After three months on the drugs, Mary finds out that she has finally become pregnant. Unfortunately, it appears on ultrasound at 12 weeks' gestation that Mary is carrying five fetuses. The specialist points out to Mary that it is generally not safe to carry more than three fetuses and that she would be putting her life at some risk should she do so. The specialist points out to a frightened Mary that they could manage her pregnancy very closely' watching for and waiting to resolve any complications that may arise, but that the safest option is selective termination of at least two embryos. Being a devout Christian woman, Mary initially refuses this option but after considerable pressure from her husband, consents to the termination procedure. A nurse in the labor and delivery department feels this option is ethically unacceptable and asks for an ethics consult. Though the hospital is not Catholic it has policies against performing abortions unless absolutely necessary to save the life of the pregnant woman.

**Discussion Questions.** Do you think that a "selective reduction" procedure in this case is ethically justified? Does it make a difference that the situation arose because of the previous choice to use fertility drugs, which Mary and her husband knew could result in a pregnancy involving multiple fetuses?

Case 5E: Tammy, a 34-year-old woman who is 6 weeks pregnant, comes to the hospital due to severe cramping and mild bleeding. Through an ultrasound it is discovered that the embryo has not implanted in her uterus, where it should be, but in Tammy's fallopian tube (ectopic pregnancy). The physician tells Tammy that they need to end the pregnancy before the embryo gets any bigger or she could bleed to death. The physician suggests that they use a drug called methotrexate (MTX) to dissolve the bond between the embryo and the tube. Tammy's physician also tells her that this procedure will be less invasive than the surgical alternatives and will also have the benefit of preserving her fertility.

**Discussion Questions.** How would you define the primary purpose of using methotrexate in this case is? Would you consider this an "indirect" abortion that would be consistent with respect for the sanctity of life?

## Suggested Readings

Cahill, Lisa Sowle. "Abortion, Sex and Gender: The Church's Public Voice." *America* 168 (May 22, 1993): 6–11.

Gustafson, James M. "Abortion: A Protestant Ethical Approach." In *On Moral Medicine: Theological Perspectives in Medical Ethics*, 2nd ed. Edited by S. Lammers and A. Verhey, 600–611. Grand Rapids, MI: Eerdmans, 1998.

John Paul II. "Evangelium Vitae [The Gospel of Life]." *Origins* 24 (April 6, 1995): 689, 691–730.

Kaveny, Cathleen. "Toward a Thomistic Perspective on Abortion and the Law in Contemporary America." *Thomist* 55 (1991): 343–96.

Marquis, Donald B. "Four Versions of Double Effect." *Journal of Medicine and Philosophy* 16 (1991): 515–44.

ways of looking at these issues. Before we begin, however, the following case will serve as a helpful backdrop for the discussion.

 **Case 6A:** Baby Suzy was delivered at 24 weeks' gestational age (16 weeks premature) with a birth weight of 674 grams (about 1 pound 8 ounces, lighter than most fountain sodas). Immediately after delivery, the neonatologist did a quick test to see how Suzy was doing. The test, called an Apgar, rates the baby's activity, pulse, grimace, appearance, and respiration with a number between zero and two given for each, with 10 being a perfect score. Suzy's Apgar score at one minute was only a 1. At birth there was a faint heartbeat but no apparent respirations. Resuscitative efforts were initiated quickly. After a considerable amount of time trying to resuscitate Suzy, her caregivers were finally able to stabilize her. Suzy survived the initial onslaught of prematurity. However, she had almost every complication a severely premature baby could have:

o   hyperbilirubinemia (yellowish skin color caused by abnormally high amounts of bilirubin in the blood, which can result in brain damage depending on the severity)

o   bacterial sepsis (an infection caused by bacteria in the bloodstream, which can be fatal)

o   patent ductus arteriosus or PDA (a heart defect caused by the failure of a vessel to close after birth, which is correctable with surgery)

o   intraventricular hemorrhage (excessive bleeding inside the ventricles of the brain, which can harm the brain's nerve cells and lead to brain damage)

o   feeding problems

o   respiratory distress syndrome (difficulty breathing due to incomplete lung development, which can be fatal)

o   seizures

Suzy was connected to a variety of machines and monitors: a breathing machine (mechanical ventilator), heart monitors, intravenous infusion pumps for feeding and administering medications, intraarterial pressure gauges and temperature sensors. She was receiving numerous medications. Her physicians informed Suzy's parents that she would need surgery for a shunt to relieve the pressure caused by the bleeding in her brain, possibly another to correct the PDA, and various other treatments necessary to offset the complications that were sure to arise. Moreover, she would be in the hospital for many months—if she survived, which was still questionable. While Suzy's parents wanted nothing more than for their baby to get better, they entertained thoughts of just letting her go so she would not have to suffer any longer and they would not have to incur the huge expenses that were sure to follow. However, they kept these thoughts to themselves because they did not want Suzy's caregivers to think that they were "bad parents."

## Setting the Context: The Evolution of Neonatal Medicine

Baby Suzy's case is filled with many difficulties of a medical and ethical nature. Ironically, just a short time ago we would not have had to contend with such issues because neonatal medicine was simply powerless to intervene to save the lives of critically ill infants like Suzy. Pediatrician Clement Smith describes this well:

> So when respiration was delayed or difficult, or the infant particularly tiny and immature, or structural or neurological abnormality was apparent, we troubled ourselves far less about the quality of the infant's future life than about whether he could be given any future at all. . . . If a two pound baby of 30 weeks gestation could not survive when drained of mucus and placed in a warm isolated environment of extra oxygen, no procedure then known to us seemed very likely to increase his chances. And if he died (as he often did) we presumed he was, in simple terms, unable to live.[1]

All this has changed dramatically as neonatal medicine has developed the means to save many critically ill newborns who would have died previously. One reason for this is that neonatal medicine has become more of a science and less guesswork. Clinical and laboratory research has helped caregivers better understand diseases in newborns, how such diseases manifest themselves and progress, how they might respond to treatment, and what the outcomes might be.[2] A second reason is that neonatal medicine has become more skilled at diagnosing and treating newborn diseases. Blood gas analysis, electronic monitoring devices, and other diagnostic tools such as computerized tomography (CT) scans, echocardiography, and ultrasonography have permitted caregivers to diagnose most newborn conditions; developments in ventilation, improved resuscitation and surgical techniques, and other therapies such as total parenteral nutrition for feeding, phototherapy for hyperbilirubinemia, and surfactant replacement therapy for respiratory distress have enabled caregivers to treat many newborns who were once beyond treatment.[3] Besides these diagnostic and therapeutic advances, caregivers can now track the development and condition of fetuses through fetal monitoring and prenatal diagnosis, and treat certain fetal diseases while the fetus is still in the womb. A third reason is that neonatal medicine has become more specialized and organized. Neonatal care has shifted from general pediatric and obstetric practitioners to specially trained nurses and physicians in neonatology and perinatology.[4] These specialists work within a team setting with various consultants and support staff including obstetric ultrasonographers, obstetric endocrinologists, pediatric neurologists, pediatric cardiologists, pediatric hematologists, pediatric geneticists, respiratory therapists, physical therapists, pharmacologists, lab technicians, chaplains, and social workers.[5] Neonatal teams provide comprehensive care to critically ill newborns in organized hospital units known most commonly as neonatal intensive care units (NICUs). The first NICU in the United States was phased in at Vanderbilt Medical Center, Nashville, Tennessee, in 1962–1963;[6] today literally hundreds of NICUs exist throughout the states.

The diagnostic and therapeutic innovations of the last fifty years, coupled with improved obstetrical and perinatal care, have contributed substantially to the declining mortality rates of infants (under one year) and neonates (under twenty-eight days). In the United States, the number of deaths per 1000 live births has fallen from 26.04 in 1960 to 6.85 in 2003 among infants and 18.73

**Figure 6A:** U.S. Infant and Neonatal Mortality Rates

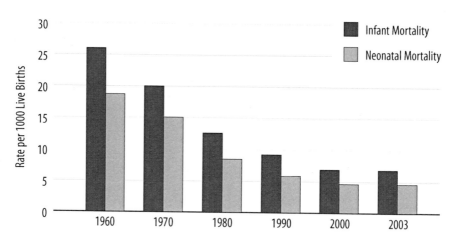

in 1960 to 4.62 in 2003 among neonates (see *Figure 6A*).[7] Reductions in mortality have been most striking for extremely small and premature newborns, who traditionally have accounted for a large number of early deaths. Not long ago few newborns weighing less than 750 grams (about 1 pound 11 ounces) were actively treated because treatment was considered futile or useless. Today, however, newborns weighing at least 500 grams (about 1 pound 2 ounces) and newborns born at 24 or more weeks' gestation routinely receive intensive care in the United States, and these limits are continually being challenged.[8]

This change in treatment philosophy is supported by outcome studies over the last several decades, which show improved survival rates for extremely small and premature newborns. For instance, Hack and associates[9] evaluated the outcomes of infants weighing less than 1500 grams (3 pounds 5 ounces or less) and reported survival-to-discharge rates of 34% (118 out of 349) for infants weighing 750 grams or less; 66% (252 out of 382) for infants weighing 751 to 1000 grams (from 1 pound 11 ounces to just over 2 pounds 3 ounces); 87% (419 out of 480) for infants weighing 1001 to 1250 grams (from 2 pounds 3 ounces to 2 pounds 12 ounces); and 93% (514 out of 554) for infants weighing 1251 to 1500 grams (from 2 pounds 12 ounces to 3 pounds 5 ounces). These results, particularly those for the extremely low birth weight infants (less than 1000 grams), are quite staggering, especially when compared with older studies

**Figure 6B:** Comparative Analysis of Neonatal Survival Rates Over Time Based on Birth Weight

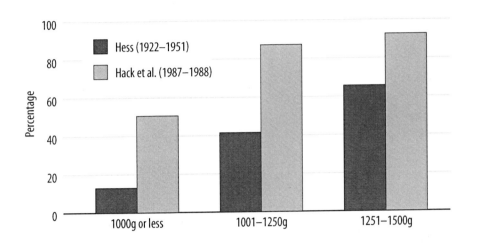

like one reported by the renowned obstetrician and early pioneer of neonatal care, Julius Hess (see *Figure 6B*).[10]

Interestingly, this study by Hack and associates may not adequately represent improvements in neonatal survivability because it occurred before surfactant replacement therapy became widely used as part of Treatment Investigational New Drug protocols in 1989 and eventually licensed for use in the United States in mid-1990.[11] Surfactant is a material normally produced by the lungs and acts by way of coating the tiny air sacs of the lungs (alveoli) allowing them to stay open, which is essential for oxygen to enter the blood and for carbon dioxide to be released from the blood. Infants who are born very prematurely have incomplete lung development and often lack this important substance. Surfactant can be inserted directly into immature lungs to lower surface tension and thus improve a newborn's ability to absorb oxygen. Since its introduction, surfactant replacement therapy has been effective in combating respiratory distress syndrome, a major complication experienced by premature newborns.

Studies analyzing survival rates of extremely small and premature infants pre-surfactant and post-surfactant have shown significant improvements since surfactant has been used. Muraskas and colleagues[12] reported neonatal survival rates of 59% (200 out of 337) for infants weighing 500 to 1000 grams (from

**Figure 6C:** Neonatal Survival Rates Over a 10-Year Period Based on Birth Weight and Gestational Age

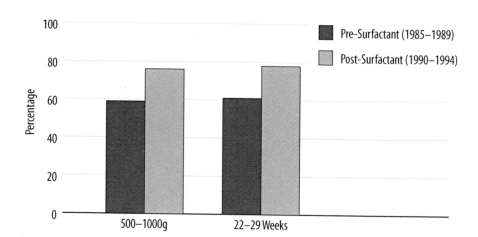

about 1 pound 2 ounces to just over 2 pounds 3 ounces) and 61% (380 out of 629) for infants born at 22 to 29 weeks' gestation during the pre-surfactant period 1985 through 1989; in contrast, survival rates were 76% (335 out of 437) for infants weighing 500 to 1000 grams and 78% (668 out of 851) for infants born at 22 to 29 weeks' gestation during the post-surfactant period 1990 through 1994 (see *Figure 6C*).

This more recent study reflects the current trend in the United States and other developed countries where newborn infants with life-threatening conditions are surviving with increasing frequency due largely to advances in neonatal medicine. Prior to the introduction and widespread use of surfactant, deaths per 1000 live births for infants born at 24 to 27 weeks' gestation hovered near 500, whereas since 1993 through 2001 the number has remained relatively static at about 300 deaths per 1000 live births.[13] Yet while improved neonatal care has resulted in better survival rates, it has not necessarily reduced the overall incidence of morbidity (diseases/complications) and disability among survivors.[14] An alarming number of newborns saved by neonatal medicine experience significant medical problems and must often contend with multiple surgeries, chronic pain and suffering, lengthy dependence on breathing machines or ventilators, prolonged hospitalization, extensive rehabilitation, and special education; this is especially true of extremely small and premature newborn survivors. These newborn infants in particular are susceptible to numerous medical complications (such as we saw with Baby Suzy in the case above) that often have long-term effects. These include but are not limited to: respiratory distress syndrome, apnea of prematurity (periodic episodes where breathing is suspended), hypoglycemia (abnormally low blood-sugar levels), bacterial sepsis, patent ductus arteriosus, intraventricular hemorrhage, necrotizing enterocolitis (a gastrointestinal disease that involves infection and inflammation that causes destruction of part of the bowel or intestine), and hyperbilirubinemia.[15]

Numerous outcome studies show this. For instance, Allen, Donohue, and Dusman[16] investigated mortality and morbidity in premature infants and reported that survivors born before 25 weeks had a higher incidence of serious medical conditions such as bronchopulmonary dysplasia (chronic lung disease), retinopathy of prematurity (an eye disorder that could result in blindness), intraventricular hemorrhage, and periventricular leukomalacia (death of white matter of the brain which results in brain damage); in addition these infants had lengthier stays in the hospital and required oxygen administration more days. In total, only 2% of the infants born at 23 weeks' gestation survived without severe abnormalities on cranial ultrasonography compared to 21% of those born at 24 weeks' gestation and 69% of those born at 25 weeks' gestation.

Studies also show that the significant medical problems extremely small and premature newborn survivors have up front manifest themselves later in life in the form of mental and physical impairments and behavioral problems. For instance, Hack and collaborators[17] compared school-age outcomes of surviving children with birth weights less than 750 grams to children weighing 750 to 1499 grams at birth and children born at term and reported that survivors in the less than 750 gram group were inferior to both comparison groups in cognitive ability, psychomotor skills, and academic achievement. Children born weighing less than 750 grams also had poorer social skills and adaptive behavior and more behavioral and attention problems; in addition these children had a higher incidence of mental retardation (IQ < 70), cerebral palsy, severe visual disability, and mild hearing loss. Hack and colleagues[18] went even further in another study whereby they compared outcomes in young adulthood for very

**Figure 6D:** Neonatal Intensive Care Costs Based on Birth Weight

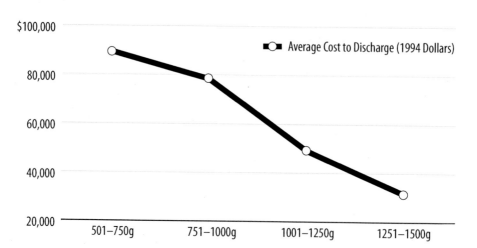

low birth weight infants (less than 1500 grams) against a cohort of normal birth weight infants. They found, among other things, that low birth weight young adults graduated from high school less frequently than normal birth weight adults (74% versus 83%), had a lower mean IQ score (87 versus 92), and had significantly higher rates of chronic conditions (33% versus 21%).

These studies are even more distressing when one considers the enormous financial costs associated with neonatal intensive care and ongoing health and educational services for surviving critically ill newborns. Families often experience significant financial burdens and society expends much by way of scarce health care resources in caring for sick newborns, especially those born extremely small and premature. Rogowski[19] measured the cost of neonatal intensive care for infants weighing 1500 grams or less and reported (in 1994 constant dollars) average treatment costs to discharge from the hospital of $89,546 for infants weighing 501 to 750 grams; $78,455 for infants weighing 751 to 1000 grams; $49,097 for infants weighing 1001 to 1250 grams; and $31,531 for infants weighing 1251 to 1500 grams (see *Figure 6D*).

This somewhat dated study of Rogowski is supported and furthered by others, such as the one conducted more recently by Tommiska, Tuominen, and

Fellman[20] in which they compared the two-year costs of extremely low birth weight infants' care against that of normal birth weight infants. In assessing the inpatient costs, outpatient costs, and costs not related to health care among the two groups, they found that the total costs for the extremely low birth weight infants were 30 times greater than those for the normal birth weight infants (104,635 Euros to 3135 Euros). While most of the differences in costs were related to hospital charges for neonatal intensive care, there were also other costs and financial burdens borne by the family in the form of loss of parental wages, expenses related to parental travel and lodging during hospitalization, and child care costs for siblings. Figures such as these have caused some to question whether the money being spent to save very sick newborns could be used in better ways, such as for education and prenatal care, especially at a time when health care costs are spiraling out of control in many developed nations like the United States.[21]

This is the historical context out of which life-sustaining treatment decisions for critically ill newborns have emerged. Before neonatal medicine had the means to prolong the lives of critically ill newborns, we did not have to concern ourselves with such decisions. All we could do was rely on the limited means available to us and hope for the best. Today, however, this is not the case. Neonatal medicine has progressed to the point that critically ill newborns are surviving with greater frequency through the application of new therapeutic and technologic innovations. Unfortunately, some critically ill newborns saved by the wonders of neonatal medicine survive only a short time despite aggressive attempts to keep them alive, while others survive only to experience severe impairments resulting from their underlying medical conditions or even from the interventions. Progress has had its dark side, and as such aggressive treatment cannot simply be presumed appropriate for every critically ill newborn. We must accept responsibility for the power we have obtained and ask the frightening question of whether what *can* be done *ought* to be done.[22]

This question assumes that survival alone is not sufficient to justify aggressive treatment, that something beyond mere physical life makes life worth pursuing. If this is true, as experience suggests it is, then we need to determine which critically ill newborns will meaningfully benefit from neonatal medicine's efforts to save them and which will not. But how do we make such determinations for these tiny little ones, for babies such as Suzy? Who decides? What ethical standards or criteria should we use to make such judgments? What role should finances and the burdens to the family and others play in the overall determination? These questions will be addressed in the next section.

## Discussion: Ethical Issues and Analysis

### Who Decides?

The first and least challenging ethical issue has to do with who should have the authority to make life-sustaining treatment decisions for critically ill newborns. The main options are parents (or legal guardians), caregivers, ethics committees, or courts. Arguments could be made for or against each group.

**Parents.** Parents are generally motivated out of profound love and a deep desire to promote the overall well-being of their newborn and protect her/him from harm. Moreover, parents have the most at stake because any decision will affect them and their family more than any of the other potential decision makers in multiple ways (emotionally, spiritually, socially, and economically). However, parents may not understand the medical aspects well enough to make truly informed decisions and could be too involved emotionally to make reasonable decisions. Additionally, not all parents seek to promote the best interests of their newborn and could be motivated by concerns that jeopardize their ability to make sound moral decisions (costs of care, burdens related to the care of their child, and social stigma of having a disabled child).

**Caregivers.** Caregivers have the technical knowledge and experience necessary to understand the medical complexities of the situation, the possible treatment options, their effects, and the potential outcomes. Moreover, they tend not to be as emotionally involved as parents and as such may be able to make more objective decisions than parents. However, caregivers could just as easily be driven by technological capacity as by a concern to promote the overall well-being of the newborn, which could lead them to seek overly aggressive treatment when perhaps more limited measures are appropriate. Additionally, life-sustaining treatment decisions have as much to do with personal values (moral, religious, social, and cultural) as they do with medical capacity and possibility. Such decisions are broad human judgments that encompass views about the meaning of life and death, the values that give life its meaning and substance, the obligations we have to others, and our relationship with God. In some instances the values of caregivers may not coincide with those of the parents or with the reality of the situation. What's more, caregivers' objectivity can be compromised just as much as that of parents if they become emotionally attached to the newborn.

**Ethics Committees.**    Ethics committees exist in most hospitals. They consist of health care professionals from diverse fields and usually some community representatives. Ethics committees have a broader perspective than either the parents or the caregivers and are less emotionally involved than either. However, ethics committees may be too distant from the situation to make good judgments (remember the principle of subsidiarity) that take into consideration the unique elements of the case as well as the value-laden aspects we mentioned above. What's more, ethics committees may not be able to mobilize quickly enough to provide a timely response to an urgent matter.

**Courts.**    Courts can apply current laws as well as legal precedent to the situation, and their judgment would be objective and not rushed. However, like ethics committees, courts may be too distant from the situation and may not be able to respond as quickly as is required for the well-being of the newborn and others.

As you can see, each group has advantages and disadvantages. So who should have the authority to decide the fate of critically ill newborns? Based on the fact that life-sustaining treatment decisions involve personal value factors as well as medical factors, we believe that the best option is a shared decision-making model in which the parents decide in conjunction with the team of caregivers. The authority for such decisions in this model would reside ultimately with the parents, who need always to be enlightened and guided by caring, competent, and compassionate health care professionals. The priority given to parents and the generally responsible action of parents will not guarantee that treatment decisions will always be morally reasonable. Therefore, caregivers and society, through ethics committees and the courts, may intervene so as to protect the well-being of newborns in certain situations. One such situation involves a parental decision opposing a treatment that would clearly benefit the newborn. Another situation involves a parental decision pursuing treatment when treatment would clearly harm or impose an excessive burden on the newborn. A third situation involves a parental decision pursuing treatment for an irreversibly ill and dying newborn who clearly would not benefit from treatment, and the use of limited health care resources would be disproportionate to any effect the treatment might have.[23] These limits to the authority of parents are simply guidelines and would need to be interpreted and applied in particular situations, but they serve as adequate checks and balances to potential parental abuses of decisional authority.

## What Criteria?

The next and most important ethical issue has to do with what ethical standards or criteria we should use when making life-sustaining treatment decisions for critically ill newborns. Over the years, as neonatal medicine increased its capacity to save newborns with devastating diseases, several standards have been proposed. The three most prominent ones are medical indications, best interests, and relational quality of life. Below we will briefly describe these standards and point out some of their strengths and weaknesses.[24]

**Medical Indications Standard.** This ethical standard bases treatment decisions on medical indications and maintains that all newborns, regardless of disability or developmental potential, possess equal dignity and intrinsic worth. Consequently, treatment decisions for such patients should not be made on the basis of disability or projected quality of life because these considerations open the door to serious abuse by those deciding. Rather, treatment decisions should be made on the more objective grounds of what is medically indicated, such as physiological or clinical data. The medical indications standard asserts that medical treatment should be provided to all critically ill newborns unless it is determined that such newborns are irreversibly or imminently dying or the medical treatment itself is judged to be medically contraindicated. For those impaired newborns who are not in the process of dying, any treatment judged to be medically beneficial, understood as the improvement of biological functioning and physical capabilities, must be provided. The leading proponent of this standard is the late Christian ethicist, Paul Ramsey.[25]

The primary strength of the medical indications standard is that it seeks to obtain the most objectivity possible by using only medical and clinical data, as opposed to subjective assessments about the newborn's projected quality of life. This does indeed reduce the possibility that parents or other decision makers will make decisions solely on the basis of the newborn's disability or development potential. This is a concern because healthy, high-functioning people often cannot imagine living with physical or mental impairments and consequently set a high bar for treatment.[26] However, the standard has several weaknesses. First, the standard is too restrictive. Quality of life considerations need to be made or else critically ill newborns would be held hostage by technology. As we have seen, neonatal medicine has the capacity to save many newborns who would have died previously, but sometimes the newborns saved must endure terrible burdens that we would not expect an adult patient to bear. Second, just because something is medically possible or that a treatment might be effective does not mean that it is beneficial and thus morally required. We can treat most complications that arise for newborns and keep many alive indefinitely but this is not the point, at least from a moral perspective. The key question is not what we can do but rather whether treatment would provide a meaningful benefit to the newborn. Third, the standard itself would cut parents out of the decision-making process: only medical information is allowed for consideration. This seems unfair and cruel. It would also eliminate values and personal/familial contexts from shaping decisions. Finally, the standard is too optimistic in regard to neonatal medicine. To say that we should treat based on clinical data assumes that medicine has all the answers about diagnosis, prognosis, treatment, and outcomes. As we mentioned above, medical uncertainty frequently shrouds the care of critically ill newborns.

**Best Interests Standard.** This ethical standard bases treatment decisions on the newborn's best interests and maintains that potential burdens to the family and society should not be considered. Rather, treatment decisions should be based on the interests of the infants in question and these interests alone. The best interests standard asserts that medical treatment must be provided to impaired newborns unless (1) death is imminent, (2) treatment is medically contraindicated, or (3) continued existence would represent a fate worse than death. This last exception is a quality of life judgment that distinguishes this standard from the medical indications standard. The leading proponent of this standard is the ethicist Robert Weir.[27]

The primary strength of the best interests standard is that by focusing on the overall well-being of the newborn it allows medical as well as quality of life and value factors to shape the decision-making process. In this way the standard recognizes that there are limits to what neonatal medicine can and should do and that some other values are at least as important as the mere preservation of physical life. However, the standard has one important weakness: "best interests" is a vague concept, and the standard itself offers little help defining it. The standard does list exceptions to treatment, which shed some light, but what is "a fate worse than death"? How do we assess this without projecting our own interests and values onto the decision? How do we evaluate our decisions to ensure that they are morally acceptable? Is this left to the parents to decide? On what grounds would they make such a determination? What limits to their judgments might apply so we can protect critically ill newborns from rash, ill-motivated judgments?

**Relational Quality of Life.** This ethical standard is really a hybrid that combines elements of quality of life with best interests. It bases treatment decisions on the relationship between the newborn's overall medical condition and the newborn's ability to pursue the goals of life, understood as material, emotional, moral, intellectual, social, and spiritual values that transcend physical life itself. The rationale underlying this standard is that human life is a good, but it is a good that needs to be protected and preserved insofar as it offers a person some hope in striving for the goals of life that make life worth living in the first place. The relational quality of life standard holds that when treatment can improve the critically ill newborn's overall condition to the point that she/he can pursue life's goals, at least at a minimal level and without experiencing excessive burdens, then it is morally obligatory because it provides a meaningful benefit to the newborn and is in her/his best interests. However, when treatment cannot improve the newborn's overall condition at all or merely maintains a physical condition in which the newborn's pursuit of life's goals will be profoundly frustrated, then it is not morally obligatory because it contradicts the newborn's best interests. In assessing the quality of this relationship, the standard maintains that the focus should be on the best interests of the newborn and these alone. The roots of this standard are found in the work of the late Catholic theologian, Richard McCormick, S. J.[28] It has been developed further by fellow theologians, the late Reverend Dennis Brodeur and James Walter.[29]

The relational quality of life standard has the same strengths as those of the best interests standard, and the additional strength of providing some insight into just what "best interests" are. The standard does this by viewing the newborn's overall medical condition against the backdrop of the newborn's ability to pursue life's goals. These goals help us to understand when treatment is truly beneficial and in the newborn's best interests. We have said throughout this book that the goal of life is human flourishing, which we pursue primarily through right relationships with others (people, God, creation). If the newborn's overall condition cannot be improved through treatment such that she/he will be able to experience life, engage loved ones, interact with others, participate in society, and fulfill personal interests at least at a minimal level, then medicine has reached its endpoint "on the basis of its own reason for existence," which is to aid us in our pursuit of human flourishing and the goals and values associated with it.[30] In such situations, treatment ceases to provide a meaningful benefit and as such the goals of care should shift to comfort and palliation. This is, of course, never an easy determination to come to, but it is one that we nonetheless must make at times if neonatal medicine is going to serve the best interests of critically ill newborns.

For these and other reasons, we believe that the relational quality of life standard is the best for making life-sustaining treatment decisions in the neonatal context. It incorporates the strengths of the medical indications standard by focusing on the newborn's overall condition and what neonatal medicine can do to improve this condition, but it does not restrict its analysis to just this. Instead it also incorporates features of the best interests standard by recognizing the limits of neonatal medicine and realizing that there are values at least as important as prolonging physical life alone. It also provides a corrective to a weakness in the best interests standard by linking "best interests" to our pursuit of life's goals, understood as material, emotional, moral, intellectual, social, and spiritual values that transcend mere physical life.

Nevertheless, the relational quality of life standard also has weaknesses.[31] First, assessing the quality of the relationship between the newborn's overall condition and ability to pursue life's goals is "not subject to mathematical analysis but to human judgment," and caregivers will need to supply concrete information and evidence for parents to make these judgments. Second, decisions based on relational quality of life considerations are not failsafe and thus parents and caregivers should proceed with "great humility, caution, and tentativeness," erring on the side of life when in doubt. Third, allowing some newborns to die based on relational quality of life considerations does not imply that their lives are less valuable than others or that their lives are not worth living. It is rather an acceptance of the fact that this valued person has come to "the end of his or her pilgrimage and should not be impeded from taking the final step."[32] Finally, decisions to withhold or withdraw treatment from some newborns should not be based on their perceived worth, social utility, or burdens to others, but on the most relevant medical and personal information available at the time. If these cautions are heeded, the relational quality of life standard can be used effectively and ethically to make life-sustaining treatment decisions for critically ill newborns.

To illustrate how the relational quality of life standard works in practice, let's go back to the case of baby Suzy. As you recall, Suzy was very sick and was looking at multiple treatments and surgeries with a lengthy hospitalization and prolonged rehabilitation—if she survived. Using this standard, the parents in collaboration with Suzy's caregivers would have to decide whether treatment could improve her overall condition so that she could pursue some of life's most basic goals, especially human relationships, at least at a minimal level without experiencing excessive burdens. To make this determination the caregivers would have to have some knowledge of the extent of brain damage Suzy sustained, the impact her other conditions will have on her overall health, and what mental and physical disabilities she will have if she survives, and would have to communicate that information to the parents.

If Suzy's parents were given reasonable assurances that further aggressive treatment could improve her overall condition sufficiently so that she will be able to pursue life's goals at a basic level without major burdens, then this standard would lead to a judgment in favor of treatment. If, on the other hand, Suzy's parents were told that all treatment could do was (1) prolong her physical life for a short time, or (2) maintain her in a condition that would not allow her to pursue life's goals at all, or (3) that she would be severely frustrated in the pursuit of these goals because of her overall condition, then this standard would lead to a judgment against treatment and the focus would switch to relieving Suzy's pain and comforting her while she was allowed to die free of invasive medical technologies. If it was simply uncertain what Suzy's prospects might be with further aggressive treatment, then this standard would lead to a judgment in favor of treatment. We do not know enough from the information given in the case to make a definitive judgment one way or the other but this is how the standard plays out.

**The Role of Costs and Burdens to Others.** The final ethical issue, which will not take long to discuss given what we have already said, has to do with what role costs and burdens to others (families and society) play in the decision-making process. As indicated above, we believe that the focus, when making treatment decisions in the neonatal context, should be on the newborn and her/his best interests. If treatment can enable an outcome where the newborn will be able to pursue life's most basic goals, at least at a minimal level and without excessive burdens, then treatment should be provided regardless of its costs and the burdens to others. While health care costs and scarce resources are an important ethical consideration (remember the principle of equitable distribution), they should not hinder us from intervening on behalf of newborns who could meaningfully benefit from treatment. There are other, more ethical, ways we can cut money from the health care budget and conserve resources (e.g., cutting waste, decreasing the amount of money we spend at the extreme end of life, reducing administrative overhead, and lowering salaries of high-paid health care professionals). Costs and resource issues, however, could be a tilting factor when parents are demanding expensive, aggressive treatment for a critically ill newborn who is imminently dying or who has no chance of pursuing life's goals (e.g., an anencephalic newborn, that is, a newborn who is born without most parts of the brain). Our health care resources are limited and need to be used wisely for the benefit of all (remember the principle of stewardship).

As for burdens to others, the most serious are those that the family must endure. Without question families of critically ill newborns suffer in many ways and must overcome terrible hardships emotionally, economically, physically, socially, and spiritually. We should be attentive to these burdens, acknowledge them, discuss them with families and, most of all, provide more social support than we do currently. We need better financial aid programs, technical assistance, and respite care for families. Nevertheless, our view of who we should become as individuals, communities, and society at large does not allow room for the burdens to families to outweigh decisions in favor of treatment for critically ill newborns who could meaningfully benefit from it. We need to attend to familial burdens as best we can, while always keeping our sights on the best interests of these little ones.

## Conclusion

Decisions about life-sustaining treatment for critically ill newborns are never easy. We have provided some insight and guidance into the ethical issues surrounding these decisions. No matter how good ethical guidelines are, however, they need always to be applied by caring and compassionate parents and caregivers whose focus should be on the newborn in need. Fortunately, this is often the case and the guidelines merely provide important moral boundaries within which good decisions can be made. As we move into the next two chapters, both of which deal with ethical issues at the end of life, we will have the opportunity to explore these guidelines in more detail and apply them to various issues around forgoing treatment at the end of life.

## Additional Case Studies

**Case 6B:** Baby John was delivered at 36 weeks and 5 days' gestational age with a birth weight of 2637 grams (5 pounds 13 ounces). Delivery was relatively uncomplicated, though at birth Baby John was cyanotic (bluish in color due to lack of oxygen) and had severe tachycardia (increased heart rate) and tachypnea (increased respiratory rate). Baby John was immediately intubated and ventilated with 100% oxygen through bag and endotracheal tube. All of this was expected, however, as ultrasonography at 17 weeks revealed that Baby John suffered from hypoplastic left heart syndrome (HLHS). HLHS is the most common cardiac defect causing death during the first year of life in the United States. The condition is fatal, but with reconstructive surgery many babies survive long-term. In fact, some institutions achieve up to 85% long-term survival rates with no significant disability. Still, there are definite risks associated with the reconstructive surgery and medical costs can be very high.

Prior to delivery, Baby John's parents told their obstetrician/gynecologist that they would seek surgery for their baby. Shortly after delivery, the surgeon scheduled to perform the procedure stops by Baby John's room and discusses things with the parents. Much to her surprise, the parents are now refusing to give their consent for the surgery. Even though the surgeon explains that they often have great outcomes for babies with John's condition, the parents do not relent, even stating that if the surgeon continues to badger them, they will get a lawyer. Dumbfounded and unsure what to do, the surgeon seeks an ethics consult to see if the parent's decision is acceptable ethically and if not, what she should do. Is the parent's decision against surgery in this case justified morally? Would it be supported by the relational quality of life standard? Why or why not? If you disagree with the parent's decision, how would you handle the situation and how would you advise the surgeon?

**Case 6C:**[33] Carol, a 26-year-old pregnant woman, went with her husband for a routine visit to the OBGYN. Much to their dismay, the ultrasound showed that the twin girls Carol was carrying were conjoined. As devout Roman Catholics, the couple refused to even consider the option of terminating the pregnancy and several months later Laura and Jeanne were born. Lying on their backs, the girls' heads and upper bodies emerged at opposite ends of a torso that was joined from the base of the pelvis to the lower abdomen. The spines were fused at the base, and their legs extended to the sides at right angles. Each twin had her own brain, heart, lungs, liver, and kidneys, and they shared a bladder that lay mostly in Laura's abdomen.

Laura was described as bright and alert; she moved her limbs, squirmed, and appeared to have developmentally normal responses for her age. Her brain appeared to be anatomically and functionally normal, and the same was true of her liver, lungs, kidneys, and heart, with one exception: Laura's aorta fed into Jeanne's, circulating blood through Jeanne's body and back into Laura through a united inferior vena cava. Jeanne's condition was less hopeful from the start. Her brain was described as "primitive" and she was unable to cry because her lungs were severely underdeveloped and virtually devoid of functioning tissue. As a result, she was incapable of breathing on her own. Her heart was abnormally large and had difficulty functioning properly. It was estimated to contribute less than 10% of Jeanne's circulatory requirements. Because of these circulatory incapacities, Jeanne relied entirely on Laura's heart and lungs to stay alive.

In the days after birth, physicians at the hospital were grim about the prognosis of the twins. They predicted that Laura's heart would fail under the excess strain in as little as six weeks. They also predicted that Jeanne would develop hydrocephalus (fluid in the brain), which would be very difficult to treat in light of her abnormal abdominal cavity and cardiac defect. The prospect of persistent hypoxia (lack of oxygen) in Jeanne increased the likelihood of further damaging her brain, and doctors also thought it could promote similar destruction in Laura. Surgeons were very optimistic, however, that Laura could survive the surgical separation, giving her at least an 85% chance. They believed that if she survived the surgery, she would be able to live out a normal life span with the most serious foreseeable complications limited to possible difficulties walking with support and controlling her bowels. They were certain, though, that Jeanne would not survive independently of her sister, and that separation would therefore lead to her demise.

Given the urgency of the situation, the surgeons waste no time in discussing the option of surgical separation with Carol and her husband. They carefully explain the benefits and risks, including the certain death of Jeanne. At first, the couple refuse to give their consent but several days later mention to one of the surgeons that they may be open to the option if they are reassured that surgical separation is acceptable morally and is not equivalent to murder of one to save another. The surgeon calls the ethics committee to review the case. Given that baby Jeanne will most likely die following surgical separation, is it morally justified to perform the surgery? If so, on what grounds and who should ultimately decide this?

## Suggested Readings

Anspach, Renée R. *Deciding Who Lives: Fateful Choices in the Intensive-Care Nursery*. Berkeley: University of California Press, 1993.

Fanaroff, Avery A., Am Weindling, and Tom Lissauer. *Neonatology at a Glance*. Blackwell, 2006.

Hauerwas, Stanley. *Naming the Silences: God, Medicine, and the Problem of Suffering*. Grand Rapids, MI: Eerdman's, 1990.

Lantos, John D., and William L. Meadow. *Neonatal Bioethics: The Moral Challenges of Medical Innovation*. Baltimore, MD: Johns Hopkins University Press, 2006.

McCormick, Richard A. "To Save or Let Die: The Dilemma of Modern Medicine." *Journal of the American Medical Association* 229 (July 8, 1974): 172–76.

Miller, Geoffrey. *Extreme Prematurity: Practices, Bioethics, and the Law.* New York: Cambridge University Press, 2006.

Sparks, Richard C. *To Treat or Not to Treat? Bioethics and the Handicapped Newborn.* New York: Paulist Press, 1988.

Weir, Robert F. *Selective Nontreatment of Handicapped Newborns: Moral Dilemmas in Neonatal Medicine.* New York: Oxford University Press, 1984.

## Multimedia Aids for Teachers

*Born Too Soon: Life and Death in the NICU.* DIA Learning. For information see http://fac.ethicsprograms.com/. This 30-minute video can be purchased separately or as part of a group of videos on select issues in health care ethics.

"Nurses: Battling for Babies." A Discovery Channel Production. 2000. This 51-minute video shows nurses in the fields of obstetrics and neonatal intensive care using their highly specialized skills to save babies at Johns Hopkins Maternity Center. It is available through www.films.com.

## Endnotes

[1] Clement Smith, "Neonatal Medicine and Quality of Life: An Historical Perspective," in *Ethics of Newborn Intensive Care,* ed. Albert R. Jonsen and Michael J. Garland (Berkeley: University of California, Institute of Governmental Studies, 1976), 32–33.

[2] Marie C. McCormick, "Survival of Very Tiny Babies—Good News and Bad News," *New England Journal of Medicine* 331 (September 22, 1994): 802–3, at 802; and E. Shelp, *Born to Die? Deciding the Fate of Critically Ill Newborns* (New York: Free Press, 1986), 82.

[3] V. L. Cassani, III, "We've Come a Long Way Baby! Mechanical Ventilation of the Newborn," *Neonatal Network* 13 (September 1994): 63–68, at 66; Hastings Center Research Project on the Care of Imperiled Newborns, "Imperiled Newborns: A Report," *Hastings Center Report* 17 (December 1987): 5–32, at 8; Mark Hilberman, "The Evolution of Intensive Care Units," *Critical Care Medicine* 3 (July–August 1975): 159–65, at 163; and Barbara Krollmann, Dona Ayers Brock, Patricia Murray Nader, Patricia Walsh Neiheisel, and Christel Schade Wissmann, "Neonatal Transformation: Thirty Years," *Neonatal Network* 13 (September 1994): 17–20, at 20.

[4] Peter P. Budetti and Peggy McManus, "Assessing the Effectiveness of Neonatal Intensive Care," *Medical Care* 20 (October 1982): 1027–39, at 1028.

[5] Michael LeFevre, Louis Sanner, Sharon Anderson, and Robert Tsutakawa, "The Relationship Between Neonatal Mortality and Hospital Level," *Journal of Family Practice* 35 (September

1992): 259–64, at 260; and Robert Weir, *Selective Nontreatment of Handicapped Newborns: Moral Dilemmas in Neonatal Medicine* (New York: Oxford University Press, 1984), 37–38.

[6] Jeff Lyon, *Playing God in the Nursery* (New York: W. W. Norton and Company, 1985), 97.

[7] Donna L. Hoyert, Melonie P. Heron, Sherry L. Murphy, and Hsiang-Ching Kung, "Deaths: Final Data for 2003," *National Vital Statistics Report* 54 (April 19, 2006): 1–120, at 95–96.

[8] Marilyn R. Sanders, Pamela K. Donohue, Mary Ann Oberdorf, Ted S. Rosenkrantz, and Marille C. Allen, "Impact of Perception of Viability on Resource Allocation in the Neonatal Intensive Care Unit," *Journal of Perinatology* 18 (September-October 1998): 347–51.

[9] Maureen Hack, Jeffrey D. Horbar, Michael H. Malloy, Jon E. Tyson, Elizabeth Wright, and Linda Wright, "Very Low Birth Weight Outcomes of the National Institute of Child Health and Human Development Neonatal Network," *Pediatrics* 87 (May 1991): 587–97.

[10] Julius H. Hess, "Experiences Gained in a Thirty Year Study of Prematurely Born Infants," *Pediatrics* 11 (May 1953): 425–34

[11] Karen C. Schoendorf and John L. Kiely, "Birth Weight and Age-Specific Analysis of the 1990 U.S. Infant Mortality Drop: Was It Surfactant?" *Archives of Pediatric and Adolescent Medicine* 151 (February 1997): 129–34, at 129.

[12] Jonathan Muraskas, Patricia A. Marshall, Paul Tomich, Thomas F. Myers, John G. Gianopoulos, and David C. Thomasma, "Neonatal Viability in the 1990s: Held Hostage by Technology," *Cambridge Quarterly of Healthcare Ethics* 8 (Spring 1999): 160–70.

[13] Michael Colvin, William McGuire, and Peter W. Fowlie, "Neurodevelopmental Outcomes after Preterm Birth," *British Medical Journal* 329 (December 11, 2004): 1390–93, at 1390.

[14] Marilee C. Allen, "Preterm Outcomes Research: A Critical Component of Neonatal Intensive Care," *Mental Retardation and Developmental Disabilities Research Reviews* 8 (2002): 221–33; Maureen Hack and Avroy A. Fanaroff, "Outcomes of Children of Extremely Low Birthweight and Gestational Age in the 1990s," *Early Human Development* 53 (December 1999): 193–218; and N. Marlow, "Neurocognitive Outcome after Very Preterm Birth," *Archives of Disease in Childhood, Fetal and Neonatal Edition* 89 (2004): F224–28.

[15] See, for instance, James A. Blackman, "Neonatal Intensive Care: Is It Worth It?" *Pediatric Clinics of North America* 38 (December 1991): 1497–1511; Maureen Hack, Linda L. Wright, Seetha Shankaran, Jon E. Tyson, Jeffrey D. Horbar, Charles R. Bauer, and Naji Younes, "Very-Low-Birth-Weight Outcomes of the National Institute of Child Health and Human Development Neonatal Network, November 1989 to October 1990," *American Journal of Obstetrics and Gynecology* 172 (February 1995): 457–64; Mary Lou Hulseman and Lee A. Norman, "The Neonatal ICU Graduate, Part I: Common Problems," *American Family Physician* 45 (March 1992): 1301–5; and Lyon, *Playing God in the Nursery*, 85–86.

[16] Marilee C. Allen, Pamela K. Donohue, and Amy E. Dusman, "The Limit of Viability—Neonatal Outcome of Infants Born at 22 to 25 Weeks' Gestation," *New England Journal of Medicine* 329 (November 25, 1993): 1597–1601.

[17] Maureen Hack, H. Gerry Taylor, Nancy Klein, Robert Eiben, Christopher Schatschneider, and Nori Mercuri-Minich, "School-Age Outcomes in Children with Birth Weights Under 750g," *New England Journal of Medicine* 331 (September 22, 1994): 753–59.

[18] Maureen Hack, Daniel J. Flannery, Mark Schluchter, Lydia Cartar, Elaine Borawski, and Nancy Klein, "Outcomes in Young Adulthood for Very-Low-Birth-Weight Infants," *New England Journal of Medicine* 346 (January 17, 2002): 149–57.

[19] Jeannette Rogowski, "Measuring the Cost of Neonatal and Perinatal Care," *Pediatrics* 103 (January 1999): 329–35.

[20] Viena Tommiska, Risto Tuominen, and Vineta Fellman, "Economic Costs of Care in Extremely Low Birthweight Infants during the First 2 Years of Life," *Pediatric Critical Care Medicine* 4 (2003): 157–63.

[21] Muraskas et al., "Neonatal Viability in the 1990s," 163.

[22] Renée R. Anspach, *Deciding Who Lives: Fateful Choices in the Intensive-Care Nursery* (Berkeley: University of California Press, 1993), 4.

[23] These situations have been adapted from Paul R. Johnson, "Selective Nontreatment of Defective Newborns: An Ethical Analysis," *Linacre Quarterly* 47 (February 1980): 39–53, at 49–50.

[24] For an excellent discussion of these and other ethical standards for making neonatal treatment decisions, see Richard C. Sparks, *To Treat or Not to Treat: Bioethics and the Handicapped Newborn* (New York: Paulist Press, 1988).

[25] Ramsey developed this standard in several of his works, namely: "The Sanctity of Life," *Dublin Review* 511 (Spring 1967): 3–23; *The Patient as Person: Explorations of Medical Ethics* (New Haven: Yale University Press, 1970); *Ethics at the Edges of Life: Medical and Legal Interventions* (New Haven: Yale University Press, 1978); and "The Saikewicz Precedent: What's Good for an Incompetent Patient," *Hastings Center Report* 8 (December 1978): 36–42.

[26] See, for instance, Saroj Saigal, Barbara L. Stoskopf, David Feeny, William Furlong, Elizabeth Burrows, Peter L. Rosenbaum, and Lorraine Hoult, "Differences in Preferences for Neonatal Outcomes among Health Care Professionals, Parents, and Adolescents," *Journal of the American Medical Association* 281 (June 2, 1999): 1991–97.

[27] Weir promoted this standard in his landmark book, *Selective Nontreatment of Handicapped Newborns*.

[28] See, for instance, Richard A. McCormick, "To Save or Let Die: The Dilemma of Modern Medicine," *Journal of the American Medical Association* 229 (July 8, 1974): 172–76.

[29] For Dennis Brodeur's work in this area, see his "Feeding Policy Protects Patients' Rights, Decisions," *Health Progress* 66 (June 1985): 38–43; and "Neonatal Ethical Dilemmas Examined," *Issues: A Critical Examination of Contemporary Ethical Issues in Health Care* 9 (November–December 1994): 1–5, 8. For James J. Walter's work in this area, see his "Food and Water: An Ethical Burden," *Commonweal* 113 (November 21, 1986): 616–19; "Termination of Medical Treatment: The Setting of Moral Limits from Infancy to Old Age," *Religious Studies Review* 16 (October 1990): 302–7; "The Meaning and Validity of Quality of Life Judgments in Contemporary Roman Catholic Medical Ethics," in *Quality of Life: The New Medical Dilemma*, ed. James J. Walter and Thomas A. Shannon (New York: Paulist Press, 1990), 78–88; and "Life, Quality of: Quality of Life in Clinical Decisions," in *Encyclopedia of Bioethics*, ed. Warren T. Reich, rev. ed. (New York: Simon and Schuster, 1995), 1352–58.

[30] Walter, "The Meaning and Validity of Quality of Life Judgments," 85.

[31] The weaknesses described here are adapted from McCormick, "To Save or Let Die," 175–76. Unless otherwise noted, any quotations in this section are from these pages of his article.

[32] Texas Catholic Bishops and the Texas Conference of Catholic Health Facilities, "Interim Pastoral Statement on Artificial Nutrition and Hydration," *Origins* 20 (June 7, 1990): 53–55, at 54.

[33] This is an adaptation of the real-life case of the conjoined twins known as Jodie and Mary, who were born on August 8, 2000, in Manchester, England. Despite protests from the parents, whose homeland is Gozo, a small Maltese island, it was decided by the British High Court that the twins be separated, which occurred shortly after the ruling on November 7, 2000. Jodie survived the procedure; Mary died during it.

# CHAPTER 7

# Forgoing Treatment at the End of Life

Forgoing treatment at the end of life is one of the most documented issues in health care ethics. Clinicians, theologians, philosophers, lawyers, and others have written extensively on it. Despite the fact that well-established medical, ethical, and legal guidelines have been in place for several decades, decisions about forgoing treatment at the end of life frequently raise ethical concerns for families of dying patients and the caregivers who attend to them. This is one reason why ethics committees in long-term care facilities and hospitals consult on this issue more than any other. To help navigate the ethical complexities of end-of-life treatment decisions, we will begin by setting the context with a set of moral considerations, a framework that will give us some perspective for understanding and thinking through such decisions. Then we will use the framework to consider three common issues associated with forgoing treatment.

## Setting the Context: Framework for Forgoing Treatment Decisions

Before we begin outlining the framework, however, we need to clarify a few things. First, when we refer to "treatment" at the end of life, we are referring to all treatments that could be employed in an effort to prolong a patient's life. This includes, among other interventions, breathing machines (mechanical ventilation), kidney machines (dialysis), cardiopulmonary resuscitation (CPR), surgical interventions, various medications and antibiotics, and feeding tubes (artificial nutrition and hydration, or ANH). In considering the ethics of forgoing treatment, all treatments are evaluated in the same way and with the same ethical criteria, which we will discuss below. ANH or IV medications in and of themselves, for example, are no more obligatory than breathing machines or surgical interventions.

Second, we use the word "forgoing" to mean either withholding or withdrawing treatment. As has been established in the law and is widely agreed upon among health care ethicists, we make no moral distinction between refusing or not initiating treatment (withholding) and removing or stopping treatment (withdrawing). Both can be permissible depending on the circumstances. Some people, however, including a fair number of health care professionals, do make such a distinction by presuming that withholding treatment is more acceptable morally than withdrawing treatment because they believe withdrawing causes the death of the patient. In some cases this may be true; in most it is not. The fact is we cannot make this determination without considering each case individually in light of the total circumstances surrounding the patient.

Distinguishing between withholding and withdrawing treatment is not only wrong morally but can be very dangerous and practically irresponsible. On one hand, it can lead to "overtreatment," in which the patient is kept alive with medical technologies well beyond what is medically and morally reasonable because one fears that withdrawing treatment will kill the patient. On the other hand, it can lead to "undertreatment," where patients who might meaningfully benefit from treatment do not receive it because one fears that once treatment is started it may not morally be stopped. Admittedly there is a physical difference between withholding and withdrawing: in one case we are doing something, in the other we are not doing something. There can also be an emotional difference: for some people, removing feels different from not starting. But there is no moral difference, at least none that can be determined in advance. The only way we can judge whether an act of withholding or withdrawing is right or wrong morally is by considering the benefits and burdens of treatment and evaluating the intention of the one performing the action.

Third, there is a moral difference between an act of killing a patient (say, with a lethal drug injection) and allowing the patient to die by forgoing treatment that is not beneficial or excessively burdensome. Although some try to collapse this distinction, particularly those in favor of physician-assisted suicide, an honest evaluation leads to a different viewpoint. The result of the two actions may be the same (the patient dies) but the cause and intention are significantly different. In the first scenario the patient dies because of the lethal injection and the intention, at least in part, is to bring about this result. In the second scenario the patient dies because of his or her underlying condition after medical technologies are removed because they have been found not to provide a meaningful benefit or they impose undue burdens. Unlike the act of giving a lethal injection, the intention here most often is not to cause death but to stop a treatment that simply is not in the patient's best overall interests. The person making the decision, whether a family member or caregiver, usually would like nothing more than for the patient to get better but decides that the likelihood of this happening is slim.

How do we know the intention in forgoing treatment is not to kill? It often happens that when treatment is withdrawn the patient does not die immediately. In our experience, when this has occurred, we have yet to witness a family member or caregiver try to kill the patient when stopping the breathing machine or removing the feeding tube does not bring about the patient's demise. If this were the primary outcome sought, then it would seem that the person would then have to take other steps to cause the patient's death.

We are obviously into a debate that borders on the theoretical. There is, however, one very good practical ethical reason why we should maintain the distinction between killing and allowing death to occur. If we were to give up this distinction, think how much more difficulty families and caregivers would have when making treatment decisions at the end of life. In many instances they are already uncertain about forgoing treatment because they fear they will be causing the death of the patient, even when it is clear that the treatment is not benefiting the patient or even harming the patient. We could only imagine that this would be much worse, to the detriment of patients, if the distinction were collapsed and every act of forgoing treatment was construed as killing.

With this background we can now move toward constructing a moral framework that can guide decision making in the end-of-life context. Much of what we will discuss here has already been said or implied in earlier parts of this book. Still, there is good reason to pull it all together specifically for purposes of looking at the issue of forgoing treatment at the end of life. While many religious traditions and secular medical associations have examined the issue of forgoing medical treatment at the end of life, the Catholic tradition has examined this issue for literally hundreds of years. What follows, then, is taken largely from the insights of that tradition, insights that have played an important part in debates over forgoing life-sustaining treatment. In what follows we will discuss the duty we have to preserve our own lives, the criteria we use for making end-of-life treatment decisions, and the meaning of benefit and burden in the end-of-life context.

## The Duty to Preserve Life [1]

The basis for our moral framework on forgoing treatment at the end of life is found in the basic Christian understanding of life and death. As Christians we believe human life is a great good that has been given to us freely out of love by God. It is through life on earth that we are able to enter more fully into communion with God by loving others as God loves us. For these reasons, we have a strong moral duty to protect and to preserve our lives. Yet this duty is not absolutely binding under all circumstances because our ultimate end lies not in this life but in eternal life with God. To hold otherwise would be a denial of a central Christian belief, namely, that new life is fulfilled through death.

This balanced view of life and death is important because it stakes a middle ground between two extreme views often present in debates on forgoing treatment at the end of life. On one side are those who claim or imply that we have complete authority over our lives and as such we can decide to do what we will, even ending our lives if we so choose. As we will see in chapter eight, this argument is often cited in support of physician-assisted suicide and euthanasia. On the other side are those who claim or imply that life is an absolute good and must be preserved at all costs regardless of the condition of the person or the medical prognosis. This argument is equally problematic because it limits human choice and often puts us at the mercy of technology. This technology may have the ability to prolong life, but in many cases it does nothing to improve the underlying condition of the patient. A more balanced Christian view holds neither extreme to be true, recognizing both a duty to preserve life and reasonable limits to this duty.

## Criteria for Making Decisions

Just what these limits are is a question that has been given considerable attention in medical, legal, and especially religious circles, most notably the Catholic moral tradition. It has been widely accepted among Catholic theologians since the sixteenth century, and subsequently by others in the fields of medicine, ethics, and law, that one needs only to use medical means that provide a proportionate hope of benefit without imposing an excessive burden or expense on one's family or community (this is what is meant by "proportionate means"). One does not have to use medical means that either fail to offer a proportionate hope of benefit or impose an excessive burden or an excessive expense on one's family or community (this is what is meant by "disproportionate means").

In assessing the benefits and burdens of treatment, the Catholic tradition has always been clear, and this still holds today in the tradition as well as in medicine, ethics, and law, that treatment must be considered relative to the person's overall situation in life. That is, the evaluation of benefits and burdens is a personal moral assessment done ideally by the patient where the patient decides whether to pursue treatment in light of how it will affect her or him holistically (physically, emotionally, spiritually, socially, and economically). In actual clinical situations this could result in one patient deciding against expensive, painful treatment because, among other things, it will only prolong life for a short time at great expense to the family. Another patient with the same condition might decide to pursue the treatment because the patient is willing to endure the burdens for a little more time and can afford it financially. This is the relativity of such decisions.

While some people may be uncomfortable with the subjective leeway afforded in this approach to treatment decisions at the end of life, the genius of it morally is that it does not just simply defer to what is medically or technologically possible. Rather, it allows for personal circumstances and values to be the driving force behind any decision made. In other words, it gives us a chance to evaluate our overall medical condition and possible treatment options against our ability to pursue life's goals and the values associated with these that give life its meaning. In so doing, this approach does not just look at the treatment itself but rather how the treatment affects the person in her or his total situation. This means that we can never say in advance that a breathing machine or feeding tube, for instance, is morally obligatory without considering the overall benefits it provides and burdens it imposes on the person. This personal approach to how we assess the obligation to use a particular medical means has been adopted by and integrated into contemporary medicine and health care ethics.[2]

## The Meaning of "Benefit" and "Burden"

If benefits and burdens are the main criteria for assessing whether treatment is proportionate and thus morally obligatory, we need to know what these mean and how they are defined in the context of forgoing treatment at the end of life. This is perhaps the most challenging question in this area because there are so many personal and contextual factors that must be considered.

Burdens are easier to define than benefits. In the medical context we think of treatment as being burdensome for the patient when it causes pain and suffering, emotional distress and anxiety, physical complications (nausea, diarrhea, constipation, unconsciousness, difficulty breathing), and when it is not easily accessible or expensive. Treatment is considered beneficial when it restores health, relieves pain, improves physical and mental status, restores consciousness, enables communication with others, and prolongs life.

From a moral perspective these truly are benefits. However, the main focus morally is not on any one specific improvement in condition. Rather, it is on the person as a whole (remember the principle of "care for the whole person") such that a treatment is considered truly beneficial when it improves the person's overall condition to the point that she or he is able to pursue the goals of life, at least at a minimal level, without experiencing excessive burdens. This is medicine's main reason for existing and any treatment must be evaluated as such.

Curiously, this perspective has fallen out of favor over the years as medicine has increased its capacity to keep us from dying. Many people now consider treatment beneficial and hence morally obligatory simply because it prolongs physical life. We saw this in the case of Terri Schiavo, the young woman from Florida who, having been unconscious for more than 15 years, died on March 31, 2005, two weeks after her feeding tube was removed. While prolonging life can be and often is a great benefit, it does not exhaust the meaning of benefit; in some situations it should give way to other concerns.

There is perhaps no better way of expressing the point about the broader moral meaning of "benefit" than by sharing a personal story. Janice, the mother of one of the authors, was diagnosed with ovarian cancer after months of nonspecific symptoms. When the cancer was finally discovered, it had spread to other parts of her body. The doctors were not optimistic about her prospects but told her that with investigational doses of chemotherapy they may be able to buy her some time, perhaps as much as a year. If sustaining life were the sole benefit Janice was considering, she would have jumped at the chance. However, as it was, she debated whether to undergo chemotherapy at all. In talking with the doctors about treatment, she wanted to know how much pain she would experience, whether her insurance covered the costs, how her relationships with her only child and other loved ones would be affected, how much time she would have to spend in the hospital, and whether she would be physically capable of working and pursuing her life's passion of painting.

Janice knew intuitively what we are saying here: sustaining life is a benefit to the extent that it enables one to pursue the goals of life that transcend physical life itself, at least at a basic level without being overly burdened. This may sound complicated, but all it really means is that we do not live life simply so that our vital physiological functions can be maintained but rather so that we can pursue values tied up with the dimensions of human life that transcend mere physical life. For Janice, and we suspect most of us, these goals included things such as pursuing personal interests, engaging loved ones, deepening her relationship with God, and contributing to society. In questioning the doctors, what Janice really wanted to know was whether treatment would give her a fighting chance to pursue these goals, or whether she would be profoundly frustrated in her pursuit of them in the effort simply to survive. After receiving some assurances of the former, she decided for treatment because she believed that it would provide, on balance, more benefits than burdens. The point is that length of life was not her primary consideration but the type of life she would live in the time that she had left. This is what we mean morally when we talk about benefit, and it is why some people may decide against treatment even it can sustain life for a time.

By way of summary, we will close out this section of the chapter by listing several moral norms that can serve as useful guidelines for treatment decisions at the end of life:

o Physical life is a basic good and as such we have a strong moral obligation to protect and preserve it; however, this obligation is not absolute—there are limits to this duty.

o The moral obligation to preserve physical life with medical means is evaluated in light of one's overall medical condition and one's ability to pursue the goals of life, understood as material, emotional, moral, intellectual, social, and spiritual values that transcend physical life.

o One should be able to make treatment decisions for oneself, given the value dimensions of such decisions; if one is unable to do this, then a person who knows and understands one's values should make the decisions in light of the values of the one in question (often called a surrogate or proxy decision maker).

o One is morally obliged to preserve physical life with medical means if one's overall medical condition can be improved to the point that one can pursue the goals of life, at least at a minimal level without major burdens.

o One is not morally obliged to preserve physical life with medical means if (1) treatment will merely sustain one's life for a short time and thereby prolong the dying process, (2) treatment cannot improve one's overall condition at all or merely maintains a physical condition in which one will be profoundly frustrated in the pursuit of life's goals, or (3) treatment imposes an excessive expense on one's family or community.

o When serious doubt exists as to the overall benefits and burdens of treatment, such doubt should be resolved by deciding in favor of treatment.

These norms and the framework out of which they arise apply to all treatment decisions at the end of life regardless of the type of treatment. We will use them as a lens through which to consider three difficult issues that arise in the context of making decisions around forgoing treatment: decisions about artificial nutrition and hydration (ANH), decisions about cardiopulmonary resuscitation (CPR), and requests for nonbeneficial (or futile) treatment.

## Discussion: Ethical Issues and Analysis

### Artificial Nutrition and Hydration

Decisions to forgo ANH are difficult for a variety of reasons. Clinically, ANH is used in complex situations, so it is hard for people to know with absolute certainty they are doing the right thing, making the right decision. In this respect, medicine and ethics are very similar disciplines because each takes place "on the ground" in concrete situations and there is often ambiguity in both. ANH is often attached to the symbolic meaning that eating food and drinking water has for us, often conjuring up indelible memories and emotions and making its use seem morally obligatory in all cases. Families and caregivers often ask, how can we withhold "food" and "water" from someone? Many believe that forgoing ANH is tantamount to starvation. Consequently it is important to demystify some of the perceptions around ANH so that the decision to forego ANH can be made properly given the relationship between the patient's overall medical condition and his or her ability to pursue the goals of life that he or she considers important for human flourishing.

Feeding tubes are used in place of the natural processes of eating: chewing, swallowing, and digestion.[3] Patients who need them have difficulty performing these natural tasks because of their medical condition. ANH is therefore a technological method of getting nutrients to individuals whose nutritional needs cannot otherwise be met, temporarily or permanently, due to their medical condition. There are several indications for using ANH. Whatever the condition, the point is to get enough nutrients into the body to help in the recovery process or to sustain life. ANH is often used in patients who have neurological deficits such as brain trauma, including coma, persistent vegetative state, stroke, or brain tumors that disrupt the natural processes involved with eating. In advanced and critical illness, ANH is often used because individuals can be too debilitated to eat. In dementia type illnesses, ANH is often used because people have forgotten how to eat. In psychiatric illnesses, ANH is often used because some people have an eating disorder of some type that prevents adequate nutritional intake. ANH is also used to prevent aspiration, which occurs when food, gastric contents, or oral secretions such as saliva enter the lungs. Aspiration can cause pneumonia and can be very serious. ANH does not prevent aspiration in some patients, such as chronically ill, debilitated individuals.

ANH should not be used when it cannot be absorbed or assimilated by the body or when there is an obstruction in the gastrointestinal tract. ANH is not indicated for patients with severe kidney, liver, or heart failure who cannot metabolize the actual contents of the feeding. Those who are imminently dying are going through natural, physiological processes and one of these processes is the complete and final cessation of eating and drinking. Using ANH in these individuals can cause fluid overload, severe breathing problems, and edema—all of which are very uncomfortable and make the dying process more difficult for the patient and the patient's loved ones.

Depending on the indications for its use, medical professionals will determine what kind of feeding tube to use. Nasogastric feeding tubes are inserted through the nostril, into the nasopharnx, down the esophagus, and into the stomach or duodenum. Nasogastric tubes are ideally used on a short-term basis because they can cause ulcers in the nostril or pharynx, sinus blockage, and infection if used beyond two weeks. Confused patients on nasogastric feeding tubes often try to pull them out because of the discomfort they experience.

Gastrostomy feeding tubes are inserted directly into the stomach and are used on a more long-term basis. The tube is inserted in a special procedure done by a surgeon or gastroenterologist called a "percutaneous endoscopic gastrostomy." This is referred to as a PEG procedure. In a similar procedure feeding tubes can also be inserted into the jejunum. PEG tube placements are normally well tolerated if used in the right class of patients. PEG tube placement requires sedation, so patients who are critically ill and those with breathing problems have increased risks during placement. While serious complications of PEG tube placement are rare, medical professionals need to watch for perforations in the gastrointestinal tract that can cause bleeding and infections either at the site of PEG tube placement or inside the abdominal cavity.

Irrespective of the route of transmission, all tube feedings have a formula that is designed to meet the nutritional needs of the patient. Registered dieticians and pharmacists will typically evaluate and then determine the specific needs of the patient. The feeding mixture is a commercial product that contains the right balance of nutrients for the patient. ANH can be burdensome, although patients' experiences vary. Common complications can include diarrhea, blockage of the tube, aspiration pneumonia, and the use of restraints to keep individuals from pulling out their feeding tubes. Thus careful monitoring of all tube-fed patients by trained health care professionals is required.

Many people are conflicted about forgoing ANH. This is why the framework outlined above is so important, for it considers ANH to be just like any other treatment. As a result, the decision to use it—or discontinue it—must be made, like all other medical treatments, in light of the proportion of benefits to burdens. Currently, many people base their argument on the means of treatment versus the ends that the treatment effects. Some suggest that any means to keep someone alive are morally required. This kind of blanket statement is difficult to accept because each situation is different and each person has a different set of values from which to make these moral determinations. Ideally, patients themselves should make the decision to forgo ANH in a shared context with their medical providers and loved ones.

At least two positions set up the moral debate concerning the practice of forgoing ANH. The decision-making framework above accepts the general tenets of one side of this debate. On the one hand, some consider ANH to be food and water and therefore basic care that should never be taken from anyone. Using the language of the framework above, there are some who consider ANH never to be burdensome except in two narrowly circumscribed conditions: (1) the patient is imminently dying (i.e., within hours) or (2) the patient cannot physically assimilate ANH. In these circumstances, forgoing ANH is morally justifiable. In this view, burden and benefit seems to be understood exclusively in physiological terms. In our view, this narrow approach neither does justice to the complexity of the clinical reality surrounding these cases, nor does it give enough respect to the importance that individual discernment has in making end-of-life decisions.

On the other hand others argue (as we have) that ANH is a medical treatment just like any other. It requires specialists to administer it, trained personnel to monitor it, and its use is contingent on a thoroughgoing benefit-burden analysis that is holistic and not simply confined to physiological parameters. Those who share this view do not agree with the assumption that ANH is food and water. They argue that a considered analysis of the ends of the treatment is a more relevant moral factor than the means of the treatment.

For this group, all means should be evaluated equally in the light of a benefit-burden analysis.

## Decisions about CPR

CPR was introduced in 1960 initially to treat sudden cardiac arrest, typically caused by events such as drowning, electrical shock, heart attack, side effects from drugs, or side effects from or during surgery. Since its inception the use of CPR has expanded to include other patients. In hospitals today, basically anybody found not breathing or without a pulse will undergo CPR, regardless of their underlying illness. There are two general exceptions to this practice: (1) a patient preference not to undergo CPR made prior to the need for CPR and, far less common, (2) a unilateral judgment made by the treating physician that the procedure would be nonbeneficial to the patient. The ethical and medical literature has focused on balancing these two exceptions. Many physicians are hesitant to withhold or withdraw life-sustaining treatment, including CPR, without the permission of patients or families, even though they may believe or know through experience that the treatment will not confer any meaningful benefit to the patient.

As practiced today CPR is a range of procedures aimed principally toward restoring or supporting pulmonary and cardiac function. These procedures can include: artificial respiration to support or restore pulmonary function, chest compressions to support or restore cardiac function, and electrical stimulation or medications to support or restore heart function.[4] Basically, CPR either replaces or stimulates the normal functions of the lungs and heart. It does not consist simply of a series of chest compressions. In the hospital setting, whenever somebody without a DNR order (do not resuscitate) stops breathing or is found without a pulse, a "code blue" is called and a specially trained team of health care professionals responds as soon as possible to initiate resuscitation procedures. Quality improvement projects track response time, the number of "successful" resuscitations, and other variables that might affect the outcome. Code teams are constantly on the lookout for process improvement opportunities and advanced technological apparatuses that can make their response better.

Survival rates for CPR are low. Its rate of success depends on when it is started and the underlying illness of the patient. The literature on the success rates for CPR is enormous.[5] With success defined as survival to hospital discharge, out-of-hospital resuscitation is successful in less than 8% of attempts,[6] while in-hospital success rates range from 14% to 18%. Many individuals survive the initial resuscitation effort, but far fewer survive to hospital discharge. This applies to patients who are ideal candidates for CPR, meaning patients who had a sudden cardiac arrest without a major underlying illness that would make their survivability less likely. The numbers change radically when the medical condition is worse. In one study of 294 patients who were resuscitated, no patients with cancer that had spread (metastasis), with infected blood (sepsis), pneumonia, or acute stroke with neurological deficit survived until hospital discharge. Low survival rates after CPR are consistently reported in patients with malignant cancer, neurological deficits, kidney and respiratory failure, sepsis, and multiple organ system failure. On the plus side, when patients who have been resuscitated survive past hospital discharge they generally do not suffer severe impairment, which is why we spend so much time, money, and effort at increasing the quality of our processes.

Given our framework for decision making, CPR is a treatment like any other. Its use must be evaluated in the light of all relevant considerations, including the patient's wishes, the diagnosis, and prognosis, while taking into account the burdens and benefits of the treatment. Since CPR has associated burdens and benefits it seems necessary that patients and physicians discuss these burdens and benefits together with the hope of arriving at a shared decision about resuscitation. It appears, however, that most physicians do not know the resuscitation preferences of their patients. Research has demonstrated that only two of ten patients with DNR orders actually discussed their preferences regarding resuscitation with a physician prior to the enactment of the DNR order. In practice, personal liberty may not be respected as much as we think.

The purpose of a DNR order is to forgo resuscitation. It does not mean that patients with a DNR order will not be appropriately cared for throughout the remainder of their hospital stay; it simply means that if the patient were to stop breathing or if her or his heart were to stop beating, the patient would not undergo CPR. All other medically indicated treatment should be offered to these patients.

As indicated, relatively few patients benefit from CPR. In the decision-making framework above, we emphasize the proportion of resultant burdens and benefits associated with the means used to sustain life. We do not focus only on the means of treatment. Therefore, the outcomes of the procedure are very important in making good ethical decisions in the end-of-life setting, as they are in every other medical setting. In this respect, CPR is not different from any other treatment, and so CPR should not necessarily be presumed. The decision requires an honest discussion between the patient and the doctor in light of two central moral concerns in medicine: (1) the freedom to make one's own medical decisions and (2) the obligation to provide treatment that offers a proportionate hope of benefit without imposing excessive burdens. With respect to CPR, the sicker someone is, the less likely CPR is to result in a successful outcome. Likewise, the more sick and frail someone is, the more invasive and potentially harmful the CPR procedure will be. Patients need to be informed more proactively if CPR may be needed so they can make informed choices given all that is at stake. All too often, CPR can become "abusive life-saving" without rendering a significantly beneficial outcome for the person as a whole. This is precisely the kind of medicine we do not want to practice.

## Requests for Nonbeneficial (Futile) Treatment

Medical practice must distinguish between (1) known beneficial treatments or therapies, (2) innovative but still experimental interventions, and (3) interventions that have empirically failed to show realistic benefit.[7] Here we deal with the third class of treatments, which are often called nonbeneficial or futile treatments. The practice of requesting, initiating, or continuing nonbeneficial treatment is commonly referred to as medical futility. Medical futility is best understood as any effort to initiate or continue a treatment when it is highly likely to fail (viewed in light of the patient's overall medical condition) and when its rare beneficial exceptions cannot be systematically explained or reproduced.[8] This understanding of medical futility rightly presumes that the moral basis for medical intervention is the notion of benefit. Moreover, in keeping with our framework in the first part of this chapter, this understanding of medical futility rightly assumes that benefit is not solely relegated to physiological benefit. Every medical intervention can have a physiological effect, but not all medical interventions have a meaningful and proportionate benefit in the broad sense of the term.[9]

> **Curative Treatment versus Comfort Care:** Every treatment has goals. These goals tend to fall into two general categories: cure or comfort. The patient's overall prognosis for recovery and the patient's personal wishes help determine whether the goals of treatment are cure-oriented or comfort-oriented. Curative therapies are generally more aggressive and invasive in nature and ideally are aimed at reversing the patient's underlying illness. Comfort therapies are aimed principally at maintaining patient comfort in the face of terminal and irreversible illness. The goal of comfort therapies is to intervene in ways that relieve suffering and improve the patient's quality of life. Comfort treatments address the symptoms associated with terminal illness (e.g., nausea, vomiting, anxiety) but do not attempt to treat the patient's underlying pathologies. The transition from curative to comfort therapy ideally takes place in a decision-making process shared by caregivers, the patient, and family.

Requests for nonbeneficial treatment usually arise in the context of providing medical care to patients who are extremely sick and are living with a serious illness that is not likely to respond to aggressive medical interventions. The overall treatment goal for this class of patients is less about cure and more about comfort. Consequently, requests for nonbeneficial treatment, which usually come from family members, can be problematic from an ethical point of view because the goals of therapy in such cases do not call for aggressive, curative therapy. It is one thing to intervene aggressively with patients who can both withstand and benefit from the therapy; it is another thing to intervene aggressively with patients who, because of their underlying illness and poor prognosis, will not proportionately benefit from curative therapies.

There are at least four reasons why requests for nonbeneficial treatment are so common. First, often there is conflict, anger, or guilt in and among the parties responsible for decision making. When this occurs, it is easy to forget that the patient's needs are of central importance. Many interventions have more to do with familial dysfunction than the overall best interests of the patient.

Second, even with well-intentioned and experienced health care professionals communication is often poor in the settings in which difficult, end-of-life decisions must be made. This can be a stressful and emotional time for clinicians and loved ones. Moreover, decision makers often have to take into account the views and perspectives of many medical personnel, including multiple medical specialists, nurses, respiratory therapists, chaplains, and others responsible for the care of the patient. All of these caregivers may not deliver a consistent message with patients and loved ones, which can make decision making very difficult. In the midst of this stress and confusion, family members sometimes request nonbeneficial therapies.

Third, loved ones often have the perception—which is in part fueled by the health care system—that they are morally entitled to every possible intervention, even those that offer little or no benefit. Because of poor communication patterns or the risk of lawsuits, physicians and health care institutions are finding it more and more difficult to say no to requests for nonbeneficial treatment. Some of the best physicians are those that have the ability to communicate in such a way that limits the range of treatment options only to those treatments that can benefit the patient's overall quality of life.

Fourth, the decision to forgo life-sustaining treatment and to allow a loved one to die from his or her underlying illness is without a doubt one of the most agonizing decisions one can be asked to make. We are never truly prepared for it. In the desire to avoid loss and prolong life, it is common for loved ones to request nonbeneficial treatment.

There are at least three main reasons why requesting nonbeneficial treatment is an important ethical issue for contemporary medicine. First, it raises important questions about who has decision-making control in the end-of-life context. What are the goals of therapy? Are they realistic? Who determines the goals of therapy—the physician, the patient, the family, some combination thereof? Should physicians have the authority to make unilateral decisions about the appropriateness of certain medical interventions? What happens if a patient or family member disagrees with the physician's assessment about what constitutes a burden or benefit? When pressured and threatened, should physicians pursue treatments they know will not work? Should patients, families, or loved ones have the right to request or, indeed, demand that nonbeneficial, life-sustaining treatments be initiated or continued? While today's medical practice has widely adopted a shared approach to medical decision making, many believe that it is the principle duty of physicians to recommend and initiate only those treatments that confer benefit. Because of this shared approach to decision making, however, more voices seek to be heard. Each voice brings its own particular value set to the conversation. Appreciating these diverse points of view is both a necessity and challenge in today's health care environment. This is particularly true in the end-of-life setting when human life is at stake.

A second reason why requesting nonbeneficial treatment is an important ethical issue for contemporary medicine is that it requires us to be more mindful of—and clear about—the implicit moral meaning and significance that the goals of medicine can have for decision making in concrete cases. A common list of the goals of medicine would include (1) relieving pain and suffering, (2) prolonging life, (3) promoting health and preventing disease, and (4) engaging in research.[10] An important ethical subtext to these goals of medicine is the notion of benefit. In this respect, medicine is explicitly tied to human flourishing. Its organizing moral force is to intervene for the overall well-being of the patient. Therefore, when people request nonbeneficial treatment they are essentially asking caregivers and caregiving institutions to consider a course of action that is contrary to the overall mission and purpose of medicine.

Requests to initiate or continue nonbeneficial treatment can be particularly disturbing when the requested intervention is likely to be harmful. For example, there is good evidence that using artificial means to feed and hydrate people with end-stage dementia is not only nonbeneficial but very frequently harmful in certain situations.[11] That is, we once thought ANH could help provide adequate nutrition, prevent aspiration pneumonia, prevent pressure sores (open wounds that develop on the bodies of those who are restricted in their ability to move or ambulate), increase quality of life, and prolong life. In fact, we now have ample evidence demonstrating that, for people with end-stage dementia and other late-stage chronic conditions such as advanced cancer,[12] ANH does not achieve these results. Yet it is commonly requested and used in patients for whom it is contraindicated.

A third reason why requesting nonbeneficial treatment is an important ethical issue for contemporary medicine is that these requests raise important social questions about medicine's part in justly distributing our human, technical, and financial resources. Health care costs are on the rise and all signals indicate that this trend is not likely to reverse itself in the near or distant future. The development and implementation of high-tech, high-cost medicine, from imaging technology to surgical equipment to medications and machines, continues to put a stress on today's health care financing mechanism. Our health care system, by reimbursing for acute care interventions, provides an incentive for hospitals to invest in, utilize, and bill for high-tech treatments even though many of these technologies may be directed at illnesses that impact relatively low numbers of the population. These may be breakthrough technologies and highly beneficial for those who need them, but they may also have deleterious financial and social effects on society as a whole.

These are social realities that cannot be avoided. Every time we intervene with a nonbeneficial treatment in the end-of-life setting—say, with a mechanical ventilator that assists in breathing, but does nothing to change the underlying illness or prognosis—we are using valuable resources that could go to others who could actually benefit from these resources. Raising the social accountability question takes health care decisions beyond individual choice. It requires us to set national priorities and place reasonable limits when and where we can. Is it necessary that numerous hospitals in the same urban centers have redundant, high-cost, low-utilization technologies? Is it necessary that health care systems succumb to every demand emerging from within the market?

# Conclusion

Ethical decisions to forgo treatments at the end of life cannot proceed without an overarching framework such as that provided in the first part of this chapter. Perhaps the most important element of this framework is that anyone faced with making decisions to forgo treatment must consider the likely benefits and burdens associated with the treatment.

Good ethical decision making in medicine is tied very closely to good medical decision making. That is, ethical decision making cannot proceed without a healthy respect for the unique clinical reality facing each patient. To evaluate morally the means of treatment independently from a particular person's concrete circumstances is to elevate unnecessarily the moral status of the means of treatment. It misses the important point about what benefits the treatment might confer.

We want you to get a sense as to how you might apply the decision-making norms set forth in the framework in the first part of this chapter. The three case studies that follow will help you toward this end.

## Additional Cases Studies

Case 7A: Mrs. Neil is a 58-year-old school teacher. She had a stroke six weeks ago that left her with some severe deficits. Her doctor has told her family that because of her injury, she will not be able to walk on her own, feed herself, or be independent from full assistance for the rest of her life. Currently she is still in the hospital and has not communicated with her family in any way since her stroke. She is breathing on her own but will most likely experience unpredictable bouts of respiratory distress for the rest of her life, requiring future mechanical ventilation. She is receiving nutrients through a feeding tube, which has been inserted surgically in her stomach. Her husband wants the doctor to remove the feeding tube and allow the effects of the stroke to take their natural course. He is sure this is what his wife would want, especially given the grim diagnosis. He knows this not only from what she has told him in the past, but also because of her free and independent character. She would not want to exist like this. The doctor has told the husband that she does not feel comfortable removing the feeding tube because she believes it to be necessary to sustain her life.

**Discussion Questions.** Do you think the husband's request is reasonable? What do you think about the doctor's response? If you were the husband, how would you proceed? Do you think you can remove this feeding tube and still honor the sanctity of Mrs. Neil's life?

**Case 7B:** Ms. Right is 79 years old and has end-stage renal disease and liver failure. She also has congestive heart failure. She is very sick and her medical situation is critical. She also has pneumonia and has been on and off the breathing machine during her 4-week stay in the ICU. She was admitted with mental status changes. Her doctor has been talking with her and her family about CPR if she should stop breathing or if her heart should stop beating. Her doctor believes she is not a candidate for CPR. Given her medical situation, she is not likely to survive the resuscitation attempt. The family wants the doctor to attempt resuscitation. One night, late on his shift, the doctor is called to Ms. Right's room because she went into pulmonary arrest. Against the family's wishes, he does not proceed with CPR.

**Discussion Questions.** Are you comfortable with this decision? Did the doctor make the right choice? What would you say to him if you were Ms. Right's son or daughter?

**Case 7C:** Mr. Stanley is 83 years old. His cancer has recently spread to his brain. He has been admitted to the ICU with respiratory distress and pneumonia. He has been hospitalized four times in the past two months for similar reasons. Given his overall medical condition and very poor prognosis for a meaningful recovery, his doctor recommends forgoing mechanical ventilation in favor of an approach directed toward comfort. Mr. Stanley's wife disagrees with this plan. She wants everything done to keep him alive. She tells the doctor that it is criminal to suggest not using a breathing machine to keep her husband alive. She threatens to file a lawsuit against the hospital and the attending physician if they refuse.

**Discussion Questions.** Knowing that a breathing machine will only prolong his death and will not offer any overall benefit to the patient, the doctor wants to deny Mrs. Stanley's request. Can the doctor do this? Should the doctor do this? How should doctors handle requests for treatments they know will not benefit patients?

## Suggested Readings

Brody, Howard, Margaret L. Campbell, Kathy Faber-Langendoen, and Karen S. Ogle. "Withdrawing Intensive Life-Sustaining Treatment." *New England Journal of Medicine*, 336 (February 27, 1997): 652–57.

Hamel, Ronald, and Michael R. Panicola. "Must We Preserve Life?" *America* 190 (April 19, 2004): 6–13.

McCormick, Richard A. *The Critical Calling: Reflections on Moral Dilemmas since Vatican II* (Washington, DC: Georgetown University Press, 1989). See especially the chapter "Nutrition-Hydration: The New Euthanasia," pages 369–88.

Miles, Stephen H. "Informed Demand for 'Non-Beneficial' Medical Treatment." *New England Journal of Medicine* 325 (August 15, 1991): 512–15.

Slomka, Jacquelyn. "What Do Apple Pie and Motherhood Have to Do with Feeding Tubes and Caring for the Patient." *Archives of Internal Medicine* 155 (June 26, 1995): 1258–63.

Panicola, Michael R. "A Catholic Guide to Medically Administered Nutrition and Hydration." In *A Catholic Guide to Health Care Ethics*, edited by Ronald Hamel, 109–26. St. Louis: Liguori Publications, 2006.

## Multimedia Aids for Teachers

"The Death of Nancy Cruzan." PBS *Frontline*. March 24, 1992. For information see www.pbs.org/wgbh/pages/frontline/programs/info/1014.html. This 90-minute video documenting the case of Nancy Cruzan may be hard to obtain but many university libraries, especially those with medical or law schools, have copies.

*Persistent Vegetative State: To Live... or Let Die.* DIA Learning. For information see http://fac.ethicsprograms.com/. This 30-minute video can purchased separately or together with other videos on select issues in health care ethics.


## Endnotes

[1] Much of what follows is adapted from Michael R. Panicola, "A Catholic Guide to Medically Administered Nutrition and Hydration," in *A Catholic Guide to Health Care Ethics,* ed. Ronald Hamel (Liguori Publications, 2006)., 109–26; and Ronald Hamel and Michael R. Panicola, "Must We Preserve Life?" America 190 (April 19, 2004): 6–13.

[2] See, for example, the Hastings Center, *Guidelines on the Termination of Life-Sustaining Treatment and Care of the Dying* (Briar Cliff Manor, NY: Hastings Center, 1987); Cynthia B. Cohen, ed., *Casebook on the Termination of Life-Sustaining Treatment and the Care of the Dying* (Briar Cliff Manor, NY: Hastings Center, 1988).

[3] The medical information in this section comes from Myles Sheehan, "Feeding Tubes: Sorting out the Issues," *Health Progress* 82 (November-December 2001): 22–27.

[4] See: http://www.rwjf.org/newsroom/featureDetail.jsp?featureID=893&type=3&print=true (accessed August 3, 2006).

[5] Unless otherwise noted, the data presented here on CPR come from the Council on Ethical and Judicial Affairs, American Medical Association, "Guidelines for the Appropriate Use of Do-Not-Resuscitate Orders," *JAMA* 265 (April 10, 1991): 1868–71.

[6] Marcus Eng Hock Ong, Joseph P. Ornato, David P. Edwards, et al., "Use of an Automated, Load-Distributing Band Chest Compression Device for Out-of-Hospital Cardiac Arrest Resuscitation," *JAMA* 295 (June 14, 2006): 2629–37.

[7] Lawrence J. Schneiderman and Nancy S. Jecker, "Is the Treatment Beneficial, Experimental, or Futile?" *Cambridge Quarterly of Healthcare Ethics* 5 (1996): 248–56, at 249–50.

[8] Lawrence J. Schneiderman and Nancy S. Jecker, *Wrong Medicine: Doctors, Patients, and Futile Treatment* (Baltimore: Johns Hopkins University Press, 1995), esp. chapters 1–3.

[9] Lawrence J. Schneiderman, Nancy S. Jecker, and Albert R. Jonsen, "Medical Futility: Its Meaning and Practical Implications," *Annals of Internal Medicine* 112 (1990): 949–54.

[10] Mark J. Hanson and Daniel Callahan, eds. *The Goals of Medicine: The Forgotten Issues in Health Care Reform* (Washington, DC: Georgetown University Press, 1999).

[11] Ina Li, "Feeding Tubes in Patients with Severe Dementia," *American Family Physician* 65 (April 15, 2002): 1605–10.

[12] Thomas E. Finucane, "Tube Feeding in Patients with Advanced Dementia: A Review of the Evidence," *JAMA* 1999; 282: 1365–1370.

# CHAPTER 8

# Controversies in the Care of the Dying

Perhaps no other area in health care ethics has held the attention of Americans more than that of the care of the dying. From the very beginning of time, ethical issues in the context of death and dying have held a primary place in moral and cultural debates. One of the main reasons is that death hits home. Each of us has been, or surely will be, affected by the loss of someone close to us. The manner of a loved one's death leaves a lasting memory on family and friends, especially if it comes prematurely or under tragic circumstances. We all experience human finitude, and no matter how much we try we cannot escape the fact that we have a limited life cycle just like any other living organism. We are born, we live, and we die. This fact of life—perhaps the ultimate fact of life—can and often does haunt our existence, especially as we grow older and experience more of life's uncertainties and tragic realities. It comes as no surprise that some of the most heated ethical debates within and among families, professions, religious denominations, legislatures, and courtrooms revolve around the extent to which one can be "assisted" in the dying process by health care professionals.

In this chapter we examine some of the central ethical debates around how we care for the dying. These debates are important because nobody has ultimate control over the dying process. Moreover, these debates are not abstract but arise from within the particularities of individual and social experience. Most people have a simple goal as it relates to the dying process: to die well free of any unnecessary pain and suffering and, despite the inevitable hurdles brought on by the dying process, enhance relationships with loved ones in a way that contributes to human flourishing.

As you ponder the various issues we discuss, consider some of the following questions: What does dying mean to you? What experience do you have with the loss of loved ones? Were they able to die well and in a way that was consistent with their personal values and beliefs about life, death, and human flourishing? Did the process of dying as well as the institutional and social structures they confronted throughout the process contribute to their integral well-being? Do you believe that individuals should have the right to choose euthanasia or assisted suicide at the end of life? How do euthanasia and assisted suicide affect health care institutions and the healing professions? Are they consistent with the ethical and professional duties of caregivers? From an ethical perspective we must address these difficult questions if we are going to uphold the ideal of a good death for the dying while keeping our sights on individual and collective human flourishing. They are also important questions on a more personal level because one day, sooner or later, we will confront our own mortality.

One of the most contentious ethical debates in the United States revolves around the desire, among some individuals and groups, for the legalization of euthanasia and assisted suicide.

---

**Euthansasia and Assisted Suicide:** The basic difference between euthanasia and assisted suicide centers on the person or group responsible for the "death act." The definitions below will help clarify the difference.

o   Euthanasia: Greek for "easy/good death," classically referred to an easy or painless death. Today, euthanasia generally denotes an action or omission that is deliberately intended to cause the death of somebody who is suffering from an illness.

o   Voluntary Euthanasia: Direct and intentional termination of a person's life at the request of someone who wishes to die

o   Involuntary Euthanasia: Direct and intentional termination of a person's life without that person's consent

o   Assisted Suicide: A death act in which a third party (usually a physician) provides the means for ending life while the person who wishes to die performs the action

---

Some have made the claim that euthanasia and assisted suicide should be options of last resort in those rare cases in which physical pain and existential suffering (extreme psychological or spiritual suffering) cannot be eliminated. Others have suggested that if care at the end of life were better and if it were directed to the holistic needs of the dying in more comprehensive ways than it currently is, then support for the legalization of euthanasia and assisted suicide would diminish. We believe that euthanasia and assisted suicide should not be options for the dying and their caregivers; they are unnecessary in the vast majority of cases, and they ultimately can cause more harm than good within the institutional and social dimensions of health care. Moreover, they fundamentally alter the nature of the moral relationship that exists between dying patients and their caregivers.

## Setting the Context: Underlying Distortions in Contemporary End-of-Life Care

We are now able to do things in medicine that were once unimaginable. The evolution in medicine has served people well, but has not occurred without internal and external factors pushing it to become what it is today. These factors represent a context for understanding where medicine has been, where it is now, and where it will go in the future. In this section we examine three interrelated and underlying distortions that affect contemporary medicine in the end-of-life context. Each distortion has had a role to play as medicine has evolved. The issues we examine have contributed positively to human flourishing and should not be dismissed outright. However, over time they have been applied and interpreted in extreme ways, thereby creating the conditions of concern for the multitude that rely on end-of-life care to be humane in its approach and balanced in its application. These distortions have roots in American culture, medical ideology, and moral reasoning.

### Cultural Distortions

The "death with dignity" movement, which began roughly in the early 1970s and continues today in various forms, represents a cultural movement that gave rise to calls for increased individual control of decision making at the end of life and demands for the legalization of euthanasia and assisted suicide. It is important to clarify that "death with dignity" is primarily a slogan, much like other slogans such as "right to life" or "pro-choice." Different people understand such slogans differently. Though slogans often cannot capture the essence or the complexities of the range of issues that fall within the scope of a movement, they have staying power. This is the case because slogans are often connected to vocal and well-positioned interest groups that cling to certain shared cultural and moral values that the particular movement holds dear. The death with dignity movement has given undue influence to one of the most cherished values in American life: personal autonomy.

The death with dignity movement makes three basic points that appeal to certain cultural and moral values within the United States. First, it claims that human beings are autonomous and free and, as a result, individuals are best suited to make their own moral judgments concerning the manner and timing of their death. Second, it submits that individuals have a right to refuse any medical treatment, even if the decision runs counter to medical advice and may result in death. Third, some of the more vocal elements within this movement argue for the right to euthanasia or assisted suicide and urge their legalization.

Movements like this typically evolve as a response to a certain set of personal and social experiences. Many claimed that the death with dignity movement arose because there was something wrong with the delivery of end-of-life care, particularly as it related to the role of personal choice in treatment decisions. While the deeply embedded value of individual choice has always been an American virtue, Americans began to experience first-hand how this virtue was being stymied in the medical context. That is, Americans began to react to paternalistic forms of medical decision making in which medical professionals (primarily physicians) were making treatment decisions for individuals without necessarily seeking adequate input from them or their families. Real cases in the recent past have entered into popular culture and have remained in the headlines. The American reaction to these and other cases lead to the call for increased decision-making rights for individuals in the end-of-life context. The legalization of euthanasia and assisted suicide were among the choices many Americans sought to have as available options.

Culturally, Americans are firmly rooted within the liberal philosophical tradition. "Liberal" here does not refer to liberal political positions (the liberal left versus the conservative right). Rather, the "liberal philosophical tradition" refers to a set of deeply embedded cultural and moral values that center around the primacy of individual liberty and individual rights in moral matters. As it relates to health care ethics, liberal values such as autonomy, privacy, and equality have played a very important historical role in shaping the moral perspectives of many Americans, particularly in the end-of-life context.

Perhaps the most beloved of all liberal values is personal autonomy. Autonomy comes from the Greek and means "self-rule." Many refer to autonomy today as self-determination. It is understood to be the capacity to make decisions for oneself without interference from others according to a self-prescribed plan of life. Autonomy is a chief source of human dignity in the liberal tradition. Max Charlesworth, an Australian philosopher, summarizes well the connection between autonomy and human dignity in that tradition:

> I cannot abdicate or de-emphasize my personal autonomy since that would be tantamount to abdicating or de-emphasizing my status as a moral agent or person. In fact, to complain of the "absolutisation of autonomy" is rather like complaining of absolutising personhood. Autonomy is not something one can have too much of.[1]

Here one's status as a moral agent, one's very worth and dignity as a person, is contingent upon the possession of autonomy. Autonomy can be considered the conceptual foundation for the death with dignity movement. Whether this is the most secure grounding for the movement is another question and not one we will take up in this book. Regardless, while autonomy is important for the moral life, giving it the prominence it has enjoyed in moral debates represents an idealistic, and often simplistic, overvaluing of its place in the moral life. The point here is that the death with dignity movement brought the cultural value of autonomy into end-of-life decision making in a way that had not been done previously. Where you see or read about arguments in favor of euthanasia or assisted suicide, you will invariably see some kind of reference to autonomy or self-determination as one of its foundational concepts.

The very public cases of Karen Ann Quinlan, Hugh Finn, and Terri Schiavo, to name just a few, wrestle with the delicate moral sensibilities that many people have around the fact that individuals can be kept alive by technical means that in ways seem to eclipse the power of nature.[2] As a result, the death with dignity movement represents a kind of cultural backlash against (1) paternalism in contemporary medicine and (2) the power of technology to keep people alive in ways that can offend their personal dignity. The value of personal autonomy in the medical context can become distorted precisely because at some point, whether for long or short periods, illness itself places a natural limit on autonomy. Dependence on others is inevitable, especially during the dying process.

## Medical and Moral Distortions[3]

Daniel Callahan, a noted philosopher and health care ethicist, has written for many years about how medical ideology has a distorted view of its role in conquering nature:

> In its press to master mortality, medicine has come to distort its understanding of nature, a distortion aided and abetted by public expectations, nicely feeding medicine's own confusions. That distortion can be simply stated: *medicine has come, in its working research, and often clinical agenda, to look upon death as a correctable biological deficiency.* This stance has thus introduced into the practice of medicine and public attitudes a profound and often destructive self-contradiction. *We have been left fundamentally uncertain whether death is to be accepted as part of life or rejected as a repairable accident.*[4]

Callahan believes that medicine has become, over time, confused about its relationship to nature. Instead of working with a healthy respect for one of the most certain parameters of human nature—human finitude—medicine has come to believe that one of its fundamental goals should be the eradication of death. In other words, rather than being merely an instrumental good for our pursuit of human flourishing, medicine has come to see itself in our technological age as a good unto itself with one of its primary goals being prolonging life and forestalling death. Many of the most critical debates in health care ethics today, in one way or another, revolve around this lofty goal. It has arisen, for example, in the stem cell research debate, in the debates over how the information from the Human Genome Project can and should be used, and in the debates over embryo sex selection and selective termination of multiple fetuses. To be sure, technology has a role to play in crafting the distortion that medicine can conquer nature.

In medicine and other parts of life technology is often associated with progress. Along with autonomy, progress also happens to be another liberal value that, when left unchecked, can have its own set of problematic consequences. We often fail to ask the important question, what price do we pay for progress? Technology in and of itself is not evil. Albert Einstein knew that nuclear technology could be used for good and bad. Likewise, technology in the medical realm can be used well or poorly. Therefore, it is the responsibility of scientists, health care professionals, and society to debate how technology should progress and how it should be applied to serve the best interests of individuals as well as promote the common good.

The ideological basis for technological progress within medicine merges nicely with one of most deeply held ethical notions within the Western moral tradition: the sanctity of life ethic. Whether grounded in philosophical or theological sources, the sanctity of life ethic provides a moral basis for using technological means at our disposal to maintain life. If, as some versions of the sanctity of life ethic hold, human beings are sacred and have inestimable value, then the moral obligation for doing all that we can to fight disease and death becomes stronger, and for some even absolute. Some suggest that if we have the technology to sustain life, then we must use it.

The view that medicine can conquer death and the view that the sanctity of life ethic requires us to do everything we can to sustain life are distortions that can do more harm than good. They represent extreme views. Unfortunately, each distortion has found its way into medical practice and moral discourse. Medically, in most of our hospitals we have a very difficult time managing the dying process. In medical language, we have not learned how to integrate comfort care with aggressive, curative treatment or when we should switch from curative treatment to comfort care only or transfer patients from hospitals to home or hospice settings where they can be free of invasive medical technologies and all the barriers that impede loved ones from getting the most out of their final days. Callahan refers to our tendency in modern clinical medicine "to push technology as far as possible to save life" and "to go as close to that line as possible before the cessation or abatement of treatment" as "technological brinkmanship."[5] In our hospitals the dying are often taken to the "brink" before decisions are made that truly promote their integral well-being and respect their dignity as people made in the image of God. What's worse, from the moral perspective, they are taken to the brink grounded precisely on a distorted understanding of the practical requirements of what it means to offer due respect to the sanctity of life. The medical and the moral distortions fit hand and glove.

The problem here is not that technology is evil; it often is used toward morally proper ends. Rather, the issue is more about the illusion that modern medicine can master the use of medical technology in ways that give it ultimate power over nature and an authoritative voice in questions related to human flourishing. The unfortunate by-product of such a view is that the modern technological artifice takes the place of "old-fashioned" human compassion as we journey with the dying. Callahan makes this point well:

> Because of the focus on technological intervention human relationships are often neglected or judged less important, more dispensable than high-quality technical work. Machines and lab results become the center of attention and replace conversation with the patient.[6]

Morally, we have become captivated by technology's perceived ability to uphold the sanctity of life in stronger ways than in days past. We all want to demonstrate respect and reverence for life. However, as discussed in chapter 7, the belief that human life has inestimable value does not mean that there are no limits to what we can and should do. It is precisely because of these medical and moral distortions that many people have sought more extreme ways to assert control over their wishes in the end-of-life setting, up to and even including euthanasia and assisted suicide. At the end of the day, ethics is about drawing lines in the sand. In order to draw the line in the sand in a reasonable and acceptable place, we must consider the underlying distortions and value assumptions that inform our perspectives and concrete choices.

The story of Terri Schiavo is a case in point.[7] How many times did you hear someone say that removing her feeding tube would represent yet another instance of how our culture devalues life? How many times did you hear someone say that removing her feeding tube would be crossing the line? Perhaps another way to think about these questions is to consider how removing her feeding tube might be an instance of demonstrating the value of her human life and an acceptance of the limitations of medicine—and life. How many times did you hear someone say that removing her feeding tube would be the same as murder? There was a time when we did not have feeding tubes, breathing machines, and sophisticated, high-powered drugs that help sustain life. By what standard were end-of-life decisions made at that time? Surely not all cases of forgoing treatment were acts of murder and therefore intentional choices to devalue human life. Was life any less sacred without these treatments? Technologies do not exist in a moral vacuum. Technologies do not relinquish those caring for dying patients, and deciding on their behalf, from the responsibility of making end-of-life decisions. In fact, technology increases the likelihood that all of us will someday have to face these decisions.

## Discussion: Ethical Issues and Analysis

With this context in mind, in this section we turn our attention to euthanasia and assisted suicide and offer an overview of both. Because the drive toward physician-assisted suicide (hereafter, PAS) is outpacing the call for euthanasia, we will concentrate on PAS and the arguments for and against PAS. Because many believe strongly that personal autonomy demands that euthanasia and assisted suicide should be viable options for any competent dying person, it seems difficult to imagine a time—even if end-of-life care were the best we could make it—in which interest in legalizing these actions would entirely disappear.

## Euthanasia and PAS

The word euthanasia is taken from the Greek and means a good or noble death (*eu* = good or noble, *thanatos* = death). Francis Bacon, an English philosopher who is best known for revolutionizing scientific method in the seventeenth century, was the first to use the English word "euthanasia." He used the word to refer to an easy, painless, or happy death.[8] Today many draw a distinction between voluntary and involuntary euthanasia. Voluntary euthanasia is giving a lethal dose of medication to a seriously ill or dying person who has given free and open consent. Involuntary euthanasia is giving a lethal injection to a person—who may or may not be terminally ill—who has not given free and open consent.

In the Netherlands voluntary euthanasia began to be commonly practiced without fear of legal prosecution in 1993, although it was technically illegal. In 2001 the Netherlands legalized voluntary euthanasia in certain conditions. Case reports, surveys, and studies suggest that involuntary euthanasia is practiced in the Netherlands as well.

In the United States PAS is gaining more momentum for legalization than euthanasia. This is the case because many health care professionals recognize a moral difference between actively injecting a seriously ill or dying person to bring about their death and merely assisting them by writing a prescription so that a terminally ill person could take the lethal medication if and when he or she chooses to take it. Though we agree that technically euthanasia and PAS differ (in terms of the actions necessary to bring about death), we find it very difficult to discern a moral difference between the two. In each act the intention of the physician is to help to cause death. The physician participates in the dying process in ways very different from merely forgoing the treatment of a dying person because that treatment no longer confers any meaningful benefit or imposes excessive burdens. This is why we urge an alternative, more constructive approach to end-of-life care that we believe better respects the inherent dignity of the dying, contributes more fully to their pursuit of right relationships and human flourishing, and maintains the ethical foundations of medicine.

In this country euthanasia is illegal. However, PAS is legal in Oregon. The Oregon Death with Dignity Act (hereafter ODDA) was first passed as a ballot measure (measure 16) in 1994.[9] A ballot measure is a law that comes before all eligible voters in a state; it is not introduced, debated, and voted upon only by elected representatives. Many consider the ballot measure procedure to be the most direct form of democracy we have in the United States because it gives all eligible voters an opportunity to initiate ballot measures on their own provided they meet certain conditions. Because the initiative for a ballot measure originates with the eligible voters of a state, it often has grassroots appeal among that state's citizens.

The ODDA passed by a slight margin in 1994, 51% in favor and 49% opposed. Implementation of the proceedings was delayed by legal injunction until the Ninth Circuit Court of Appeals lifted the injunction in 1997. A second ballot measure (measure 51) on the legalization of PAS was put before the eligible voters of Oregon in 1997. This time, the ballot measure sought to overturn the ODDA. This was the first time in its history that the citizens of the state of Oregon voted twice on a single issue in the ballot measure process. The second ballot measure was rejected by a margin greater than that which the first ballot measure passed, with 60% opposed to overturning the ODDA.

As a result of these political and legal proceedings, physicians in Oregon have been assisting in the deaths of dying patients since calendar year 1998. According to the latest annual report on the practice, which was issued on March 9, 2006, by the Oregon Department of Human Services, a total of 246 people have died under the terms of the act since 1998. *Figure 8A* charts the numbers of those who received lethal prescriptions since 1998, those who died under the terms of the act since 1998, and the ratio of PAS deaths per 10,000 deaths in the state of Oregon since 1998.

**Figure 8A:** Prescriptions Written, Number of Deaths, and Ratio of PAS Deaths

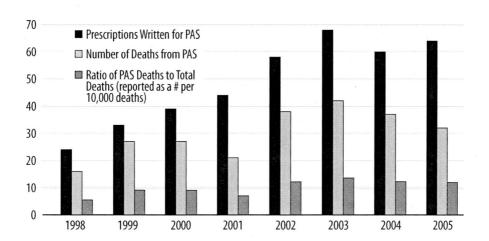

Physicians who assisted dying patients in their suicide indicated that eight of ten of their patients had at least three overriding concerns that lead them to choose PAS: (1) inability to participate in life's enjoyments, (2) loss of personal dignity, and (3) loss of autonomy. It is interesting to note that these overriding concerns are existential in nature and that they do not necessarily relate to intractable physical pain. Since this information comes from physicians and not people who actually chose PAS, they may not be accurate enough to permit the drawing of firm conclusions as to why people chose PAS. We will explore in more detail the reasons why dying people choose PAS below. As *Figure 8A* indicates, the number of lethal prescriptions written for PAS does not correspond to the number of deaths from PAS. This is because some patients who received the lethal medication chose not to take it, whereas others died before they had the chance to take it. Others are still living.

Demographically, certain patterns and trends have emerged with respect to the characteristics of those choosing PAS in Oregon. Males and females are about equally likely to opt for PAS. The vast majority of people choosing PAS are white (97%). Divorced and single people are more likely to choose PAS. Educated people (people with at least a bachelor's degree) are more likely to request a lethal medication. In the order listed, the three most likely diagnoses for people requesting PAS in Oregon are: malignant cancers, amyotrophic lateral sclerosis (ALS), and HIV/AIDS. Eighty-seven percent of people choosing PAS in Oregon had been enrolled in hospice programs at home, and 99% had either Medicare or private health insurance.

Under the terms of the ODDA, a number of conditions must be met in order to obtain a prescription for a lethal dose of medication. Dying people must

1. Be 18 years of age and a resident of Oregon
2. Have decision-making capacity
3. Have a terminal illness that will lead to death in six months
4. Make two oral requests for PAS to their physician, separated by at least 15 days
5. Provide a written request to their physician, signed in the presence of two witnesses
6. Have confirmation of the diagnosis and prognosis from their prescribing physician and a consulting physician
7. Have their prescribing and consulting physicians determine that the dying person has decision-making capacity
8. Be referred for a psychological exam if their prescribing or consulting physician believes the dying person's judgment is impaired by a psychiatric or psychological condition

Since this decision is not made solely by the individual, other conditions of the law involve those with a part in it, such as physicians and pharmacists.

1. Prescribing physicians must inform dying patients of alternative options, such as comfort care, hospice care, and pain control
2. Prescribing physicians must request, but cannot require, that the dying notify their next-of-kin of their request for PAS

3. Prescribing physicians must report all prescriptions for lethal medications to the Oregon Department of Human Services

4. Pharmacists must be informed of the prescription's intended use

5. Physicians and pharmacists are under no obligation to participate in a person's request for lethal medications

We have listed these data and these requirements for two main reasons. First, they will serve as a model and benchmark for other states that attempt to legalize PAS. Other states that have attempted, through various political measures and proposals, to legalize PAS include Alabama, Arkansas, California, Colorado, Maine, Maryland, Michigan, Nebraska, New Hampshire, Vermont, and Wisconsin. Second, and this is in particular reference to the actual requirements of the law, they represent a good example of the tension between procedural ethics and substantive ethics.

Procedural ethics refers to the notion that agreement functions as the governing factor in deciding whether something can be considered morally acceptable. This notion has great appeal in pluralistic societies precisely because it gives personal autonomy and informed consent high priority. In a pluralistic society such as ours, if people cannot agree on a single approach to resolve moral disputes, then agreement or consent becomes the default moral parameter for moral decision making in state or federal policy.

Substantive ethics considers the morality of the action in question before it makes any kind of determination that the particular action should be open and available to all people. The ODDA is a fine example of this tension. The act simply creates a process—grounded morally on personal autonomy and consent—for obtaining a lethal prescription to end one's life. The substantive moral debate about the passage of the act took place prior to the votes on the measures, though some have questioned whether such debate ever actually occurred.

## Arguments in Favor of PAS

The arguments for and against PAS emerge from what has been presented above. We can characterize these debates as being philosophical, medical-professional, and existential in nature, and will examine each in turn. We do not offer a comprehensive analysis of each and every argument in the case for and against the morality of PAS. Rather, we examine those that are most often cited or are the most plausible.

**Philosophical.**  By far the most common philosophical argument in favor of euthanasia and PAS is the self-determination argument. In the liberal worldview, as noted above, autonomous choices ideally reflect the authentic values of a free individual. They come from within and therefore, at least ideally, reflect the truest picture of the self. In a worldview in which respect for individual liberty reigns supreme over the moral commitments that arise from our relational nature, intentional acts of coercion that limit the free expression of the self are not viewed favorably. Thomas Preston and his colleagues employ the argument from self-determination for PAS:

> There is a moral reason to respect others' autonomous choices, and this reason gains strength as the importance of the choice under consideration increases. An autonomous decision to hasten one's death is a profoundly important decision for a terminally ill person that involves his or her most significant values. There is therefore an extraordinarily strong moral reason not to restrict such a decision. This reason becomes even stronger when provisions are in place to ensure that the choice is indeed highly autonomous and not coerced.[10]

A critical feature of this argument is its sliding-scale view with respect to the level of importance of the choice at hand. If the choice at stake does not have a high degree of significance to one's values, can the justification for trumping one's autonomy be weaker? And who gets to decide how significant a choice is? Implicit in the above quote from Preston is the view that the circumstance of terminal illness makes requests for PAS morally different from other forms of suicide—for example, the suicide of the scorned lover, or the adult pedophile whose life of predatory crime has now become public knowledge. Terminal illness can bring with it terribly excruciating circumstances. Why, the reasoning goes, should we prevent free and autonomous individuals from acting on their authentic desires and self-made moral projects?

**Medical-professional.** Perhaps the most controversial argument for PAS revolves around claims concerning how PAS falls in line with the virtues and duties of health care professionals to promote the best interests of their dying patients (the principle of beneficence). Health care professionals take seriously the moral virtues and lofty goals of their profession. One of the time-honored goals of medicine is the prevention and relief of suffering. Virtuous physicians, therefore, seek to act compassionately toward their patients, doing only what is in their best interest. Many within the medical community believe strongly that when medical providers cannot provide relief of suffering it is a professional duty to assist actively in the death of dying patients. Not to do so, some argue, would be abandonment, which is anathema to a good physician. Sherwin Nuland, a respected physician and author, describes the medical-professional element of the argument in favor of PAS in this way:

> If the prevention and relief of suffering are the aims of the medical profession—and not only the preservation and the prolongation of life—it seems imperative to rethink our profession's reluctance to participate in euthanasia or even be present during an assisted suicide without the legal guarantees of protection. . . . Physicians who believe that it is a person's right to choose death when suffering cannot otherwise be relieved must turn to their own consciences in deciding whether to provide help in such a situation. Once the decision to intervene has

been made, the goal should be to ensure that death is as merciful and serene as possible.[11]

The medical-professional argument in favor of PAS, as Nuland suggests, goes to the heart of what it means to be a caregiver. There are times when, at the end of life, pain cannot be adequately controlled and intractable suffering persists. In these cases, a medical intervention does not exist to eliminate these realities and so the question arises: what professional responsibility do physicians have in participating, in an ultimate and final way, in the death of their dying patients? Surveys show that physicians, much like the rest of the general population, have mixed views about legalizing PAS. In the United States a majority of physicians tend to think that patients should have a personal right to PAS, but a majority of physicians also maintain that they would not assist their patients in suicide. Likewise position statements from professional organizations are either against legalizing PAS (e.g., American Medical Association) or are neutral about the practice (e.g., American Academy of Hospice and Palliative Medicine). When you find health care professionals arguing in favor of PAS, it generally stems from what they believe to be their professional duty to stand by their patients and not abandon them in their time of need. Timothy Quill, perhaps the most eloquent and balanced physician-advocate of PAS as an option of last resort for the dying, understands the duty of nonabandonment this way:

> Nonabandonment reflects a continuous caring partnership between physician and patient. . . . It acknowledges and reinforces the centrality of an ongoing personal commitment to caring and problem solving between physician and patient. . . . Nonabandonment also reflects an obligation to respond to vulnerable persons whom we contact in our daily clinical work.[12]

The obligation of nonabandonment is the principle argument of some that, while good end-of-life care should be the norm, PAS should be an option of last resort for those who cannot benefit fully from all that contemporary end-of-life care has to offer.

**Existential.** In their study in Washington State of (1) people who seriously pursued PAS and (2) surviving family members of people who either pursued PAS or had assistance in their death, Pearlman and Starks were able to glean three motivating factors for PAS.[13] The first set of motivations is illness-related factors. These factors include both problems associated with the symptoms of the terminal illness and problems associated with the effects of the treatment. The second set of motivating factors, threats to sense of self, extend beyond the impact of acute depression and reach more into the realms of coping with the losses brought on by the dying process. Specifically, those in the study associated the motivation to pursue PAS with loss of control over one's life and inability to engage in meaningful relationships with one's family, friends, and community members. Such losses contribute to an overall sense of isolation and meaninglessness about life's significance and purpose. The third set of motivating factors, fears about the future, are deep-seated fears about the dying process itself. Specifically, many in the study were afraid that the dying process would lead to states that were worse than death itself.

Taken together, these three sets of motivating factors lead the individuals in this study to seek a hastened death through PAS. The point here is that these are not necessarily motivations that stem from the physical assaults of the dying process. Rather, they are deep-seated existential factors that give rise to concern among these dying people. Because of these factors many inside and outside the medical community believe that PAS should be a viable option of last resort for those who have profound existential suffering associated with their terminal illness (we do not know the exact number of those that would fall into this category). It is clear from the Oregon experience with PAS that most people who go through PAS do so on existential grounds, not necessarily because their physical ailments cannot be adequately addressed. The moral debate, at this point, should perhaps center on how to address the root problems that give rise to these existential concerns and whether PAS and euthanasia should be viable options in resolving these problems.

The fundamental concern of dying people is to die well. We know from studies with patients, families, and medical providers that the elements of a good death are primarily, though not exclusively, existential in nature. For instance, Karen Steinhauser and her colleagues found that there are six components of a good death: (1) pain and symptom management, (2) clear decision making, (3) preparation for death, (4) spiritual completion and meaning-making (5) contributing to others during the dying process, and (6) affirmation of the whole person.[14] Again, these are largely existential issues. Many have raised the question, as we will below, whether it is sound ethically, medically professionally, and socially to engage in PAS as a means of eliminating existential suffering. Indeed, researchers and caregivers are developing innovative treatment strategies to help address the existential realities of the dying process.[15]

## Arguments Against PAS

The arguments against PAS follow much the same path as those for it. That is, many who argue against PAS use some of the same concepts or themes as those who argue for it.

**Sanctity of Life.** One of the historical moral threads found in virtually all societies, whether grounded in philosophical, social, or theological arguments, has been a belief that human life is sacred and valuable. In the most general and conceptual sense, the sanctity of life argument against PAS starts from the moral premise that there exists a set of moral claims on individuals, institutions, professions, and societies to uphold the sacredness of life. John Collins and Edmund Pellegrino argue against PAS from the lens of the sanctity of life:

> When a society sanctions killing an innocent person, it abandons a longstanding tradition of its interest in human life. Sanctioning their killing devalues all life, especially the lives of certain vulnerable citizens.... To sanction their killing suggests that their lives are of low quality and that they are expendable, socially useless and a burden to society.[16]

We have debated and will continue to debate precisely the substance and practical import of sanctity of life claims, as well as their grounding from a moral perspective. But individuals, institutions, professions, and societies must not deny, so the thinking goes, that human lives have value. To do so through a social policy legalizing euthanasia and PAS would be tantamount to denying one of the bedrock principles of an enlightened society.

We saw above how this position can be distorted and how it can actually bring harm to people if not applied in a reasonable way. This is a problem of application, not necessarily a conceptual problem with the value itself. To be sure, there continue to be examples of disrespect for human life. For most, these flagrant violations of humanity provide the justification for increased emphasis on respecting the sacredness of human life. It is interesting to note that the 1919 constitution of the German Weimar Republic contained no references to the view that humans have inviolable dignity, while the 1947 German constitution—written after the downfall of Nazism—states as its first clause that humans have inviolable dignity. Experience tells us something important, if we are open to its lessons.

Those who argue against PAS on the grounds that it is an affront to the sanctity of life are basically arguing for a proportionate application of the means by which we demonstrate reverence for the sacredness of human life in concrete situations at the end of life. In other words, in the end-of-life setting, as in all other areas of applied ethics, the values we try to uphold can be undermined by the way in which we try to uphold them. With respect to PAS, it seems inconsistent to hold that life is sacred while intentionally helping to bring about a dying person's death on the grounds that this is the only way, given the circumstances, to respect a dying person's sanctity of life.

**Medical-professional.** If we examine PAS only from the perspective of individuals who request PAS, many would find it reasonable to want to do everything in their power to alleviate the pain and suffering of the dying—up to and perhaps including assisting them in their death. Ethical practice and understanding, however, transcends the individual realm and enters into institutional and social realms as well.[17] Therefore, limiting ethical practice only to the concerns of individuals is short-sited. From our normative basis, which includes a broader institutional-social ethics point of view, PAS raises serious issues for the moral integrity of institutions that deliver end-of-life care and for the trust we place in professional caregivers to do what is in the best interests of the dying.

People go to health care institutions and engage their caregivers for healing. People enter into relationships with caregivers with a view toward wellness. Lois Snyder and Daniel Sulmasy, writing for the Ethics and Human Rights Committee of the American College of Physicians-American Society of Internal Medicine, conclude that one of the strongest arguments against PAS is the medical-professional argument:

> One can raise serious questions about whether medicine should arrogate to itself the task of relieving all human suffering, even near the end of life. ... The medical profession might better serve patients by acknowledging that the elimination of all human suffering is also a false goal that, if pursued, will ultimately lead to bad medical care. ... Assisting in suicide carries with it the danger of compromising the patient-physician

relationship and the trust necessary to sustain it. It also undermines the integrity of the profession and diverts attention from the real issues in the care of the dying, subverting the social role as of the physician as healer, and altering the meaning of beneficence in medical practice.[18]

Two important points related to the medical-professional argument against PAS flow from this quote. The first is related to the proper and realistic goals of medicine, one of which traditionally has been the alleviation of pain and suffering. Yet, most of us understand that not all suffering, especially suffering that has existential sources, can be fully relieved. Therefore, they call on the medical profession to admit its own limits and consider an alternative strategy of journeying compassionately (literally "suffering with") with their dying patients rather than eliminating those whose existential suffering cannot be relieved.

The second point is related to the notion of right relationships, an idea familiar to you by now and very important to the virtue-based moral foundations of this book. The doctor-patient relationship is perhaps the most distinguishing feature of medicine's moral foundations. The bedrock of this relationship is trust, the basis for the medical profession's entire disposition toward the pursuit of a patient's human flourishing. Without it, the conditions for a right relationship between the doctor and patient cannot exist.

The points raised above ought not to be dismissed as old-fashioned and pious accounts of the mythical and symbolic practice of medicine in a bygone era. Perhaps now more than ever, when the moral foundations of medicine are jeopardized by the financial demands of managed care and the volatility of market capitalism, when over 40,000,000 people have no health insurance (most of whom are women, children, and the working poor), and when there are ethnic and socio-economic disparities endemic in our health care system, it seems absurd that we could honestly and with a straight face be debating whether PAS should be legalized in this country.[19] How can we not think PAS would be abused? This is not meant to dismiss the plight of those who suffer at the end of life. To be sure, the concerns of the dying are very real. We believe that because of these circumstances, there is no better time than the present to address our core priorities in the delivery of medical care. One of the ways we can do this is by making universal access to quality end-of-life care a national priority.

**Palliative Care.**[20] In the United States, care for dying patients is inadequate. Very often it is characterized by a lack of pain and symptom control and an inability to meet the total needs of the dying. It proceeds with conflicts about who should make end-of-life decisions and about how far we should go with the life-prolonging technologies at our disposal. Moreover, family caregivers of the dying often experience significant impairments in their financial, physical, and psychological well-being.

A primary problem is that our health system pursues two parallel tracks when treating the dying: either an aggressive, curative approach, or a comfort care approach. The two tend not to be integrated, as we noted above. The comfort care approach often takes place after a decision has been made to discontinue all aggressive, curative treatments—usually only after they have proven to be of absolutely no benefit and excessively burdensome to the patient. All of this, of course, typically comes at great expense to the patient, the family, the health care facility, and society, due largely to the way we reimburse for health care at the end of life. In a classic move of short-sightedness on the part of our legislators, Medicare, the federally-administered health plan for U.S. citizens 65 and older, only pays for comfort care or hospice benefits after patients have made a decision to cease all curative, aggressive treatments. This means, essentially, that health care professionals and facilities are not paid directly for providing comfort care services when dying patients need them most, which experience shows is at the time of diagnosis of a serious illness (e.g., cancer, lung disease, congestive heart failure) that will eventually result in death.

This whole situation is complicated by demographic projections that will put increased financial and resource strain on our health care system. By the year 2030, 20% of the U.S. population will be over 65 years old. Most adults who die in this country have one or more chronic illness. As people live longer, their health care needs become increasingly complex. We need to come to grips with these realities and find a way to deliver care at the end of life that is more holistic in its approach, respectful of the values and aspirations of the dying, consistent with the properly understood goals of medicine, and not unduly expensive.

As we have stated throughout this book, we are seeking to understand medicine as a means of promoting human flourishing; there is no justifiable reason that dying patients and their families should be hindered in their pursuit of that goal. Palliative care is geared toward relieving suffering and improving quality of life for the dying. It treats them holistically, focusing on interventions that are directed to their whole being—physical, psychological, social, and spiritual. It seeks to treat not only the physical burdens that accompany the dying process but also the existential and spiritual burdens that the dying inevitably experience. It relies on team care, with various professionals working in a coordinated fashion with the twin goals of relieving suffering and improving the quality of life for the dying so that they have the time and opportunity to die well and with dignity.

Ultimately, palliative care seeks to reclaim the traditional goals of medicine—which, prior to the advent of modern medical technology, were providing comfort and improving quality of life—and to integrate these with the more modern goals of curing and prolonging life. Only when these goals are held together and put on equal ground will we be able to care for the dying in a way that respects their inherent dignity as people created in God's image and allows them to enhance relationships and find meaning at the end of life. A shift of this magnitude in medicine will only occur gradually. Nevertheless, palliative care is facilitating this shift by promoting, for example, better pain and symptom management; better communication with patients, their families, and their caregivers; more attention to the holistic needs of dying patients and their families; and smoother and more timely transitions from hospitals and other institutional settings to more appropriate sites of care, such as the home or hospice facilities. These are important elements in the care of the dying that for too long now have gone overlooked, despite the good intentions of health care professionals.

Palliative care is an important step in the right direction in our quest to care better for the dying. Nevertheless, palliative care cannot and does not totally eliminate the main reason people pursue PAS, namely, existential suffering and the anxiety that comes with exiting this world. This is impossible, since suffering is part of the human condition; it would be deceptive to suggest that palliative care does this. Still, palliative care does attempt to address this problem in a more humane, ethical, and compassionate way than does PAS. Whereas palliative care promotes companying and suffering with the dying, PAS buys into a modern notion of compassion that might actually be the ultimate form of abandonment, seriously threatening our ability to live in right relationships with others and flourish in the context of community. Allen Verhey, the Protestant theologian and ethicist, speaks to this new, "modern" view of compassion that often grounds the case for PAS as a way of eliminating existential suffering:

> Modern "compassion" wants to stop the crying. Instead of being willing to suffer *with* another, modern "compassion" wants to put an end to suffering—and by whatever means necessary. Modern "compassion" insists that suffering be eliminated, even if that means eliminating the sufferer.... Modern "compassion" is formed of the expectation that the world should be, right now, the sort of place where suffering can be avoided, where we need not suffer for anything or with anyone.... The most obvious failure of modern "compassion" . . . is the simple truth

that technology does not provide an escape either from our mortality or altogether from our suffering. "Compassion," then, prompts us to use technologies against pathologies and ends up, ironically, blinding us to the suffering of people.[21]

Embedded within Verhey's message is a challenge to all of us to find a way, difficult as that way may be, to journey with dying patients. Palliative care seems like the best way to us because it offers a more holistic approach to caring for the dying and upholds the deeply held canons of medicine and morality that require us to accompany the dying throughout the entire dying process, from diagnosis of illness to its natural conclusion in death. The challenge for our modern and technologically driven society will be to incorporate this utterly traditional way of caring for the dying into the more dominant modern approach that seeks to cure and prolong life, often at great costs to the dying patient, their family, and others.

## Conclusion

Human flourishing is possible even in the dying process. Many dying patients, with the support of family, friends, community, and caregivers, have found a way to die well. This should be our goal as we continue to seek to understand what we need to do as the dying embark on their final journey.

## Case Studies

Case 8A: At age 60, Mrs. Thomas had become severely disabled by cardiac failure due to a damaged heart. In an attempt to restore her quality of life to what it was prior to the cardiac failure, she underwent cardiac surgery. Twelve hours after the surgery, however, her heart became weak once again—as the surgeon had feared would happen. Despite attempts at employing a variety of aggressive attempts to help reverse her situation, treatments in the ICU did not restore her cardiac output to a sustainable level. With appropriate informed consent, Mrs. Thomas had an experimental cardiac assist device implanted in her chest. A few hours after this surgery, her cardiac output began to fall again. Though she was on a respirator and receiving fluids, everyone involved in her treatment agreed that Mrs. Thomas would not survive through the night. Since Mrs. Thomas was conscious and vaguely alert, she was able to consent to additional morphine to control her pain. Four hours later, another dose of morphine was needed to control her pain. When Mrs. Thomas continued to show signs of pain, her surgeon had the nurse draw up a "heavy" dose of potassium chloride and injected it into her intravenous line. Both the nurse and the surgeon knew that this dose would likely result in the death of Mrs. Thomas. Within minutes, Mrs. Thomas lay still and the cardiac monitor showed no heartbeat. She was dead.

**Discussion Questions.** What do you think of the surgeon's actions in this case? What do you think of the nurse's actions in this case? Is this an instance of physician-assisted suicide or euthanasia? Is euthanasia justifiable if the patient wants it and agrees to it?

**Case 8B:** Dr. Smith has been in private practice for 22 years. She has extensive experience caring for terminally ill patients; her peers consider her a specialist in the field. She views patient nonabandonment as the most important ethical value in her work, but she often feels conflicted about what it means in concrete cases.

Dr. Smith is morally ambivalent about actively assisting a patient to die. Though she has never done it, she thinks there are times when it may be justifiable.

Mrs. Stone, a patient of Dr. Smith's for 15 years, has end-stage breast cancer that has spread to her bones. Mrs. Stone has been living with cancer on and off for the past 5 years. Dr. Smith has told Mrs. Stone that her death could come in the next one to three weeks. Despite all efforts, she is in extreme physical pain. Unable to bear the physical pain and existential suffering any longer, she asks Dr. Smith to write her a prescription for medication that Mrs. Stone can take to end her life.

**Discussion Questions.** What should Dr. Smith do in this case? What would you do in this case? If she does not comply with the patient's request, would Dr. Smith be abandoning her patient? Why or why not? Should physician-assisted suicide be a viable ethical, legal, and medical option when caring for dying patients?

**Case 8C:** Nearly eight months ago, Mr. Michaels was diagnosed with a large brain tumor. After pursuing curative treatment initially, he elected for a purely symptom-oriented approach. Even though his internist tried to persuade him to continue curative therapies, Mr. Michaels was clear that his greatest concern was not death but becoming physically dependent on his family and intellectually impaired. His main goal at the time was to manage his symptoms so that he could have quality time with his wife and children. To help with his symptom control, Mr. Michaels is taking dexamethasone to relieve inflammation and pain as well as anti-seizure medications. Initially, his right-side weakness and headache improved for several weeks as he and his family worked to achieve closure together.

Unfortunately, Mr. Michaels abruptly developed right-side weakness and intermittent confusion due to reemerging seizures and his symptoms continued to worsen despite aggressive symptom management. Sensing his physical and intellectual deterioration, Mr. Michaels told his internist he wanted to "get on with it before I can't do anything for myself." Further mental and physical deterioration became more frightening to him than death. As a physician, he thought he would die quickly by stopping steroid therapy. The internist urged Mr. Michaels to continue his medications for symptom relief, but Mr. Michaels did not want to take anything that could in any way prolong his life. At his internist's insistence, Mr. Michaels agreed to a single visit with a psychiatrist, who confirmed that Mr. Michaels understood his treatment options and was not clinically depressed. After saying his good-byes to friends and family, Mr. Michaels discontinued dexamethasone therapy.

To his consternation, Mr. Michaels did not become comatose or die. Instead, his right-side weakness worsened and his seizures became more frequent. Mr. Michaels found his situation intolerable, physically and emotionally. He did not explicitly request medication that could be taken in a lethal dose, but his desire for a hastened death was clear. "I just want to go to sleep and not wake up," he said.

All members of the team were committed to relieving his distress but had different views about deliberately assisting death. They searched for common ground while continuing to adjust his seizure medications and attempting to support his family and bring some quality to his remaining days. Despite their best efforts, Mr. Michaels clearly did not want to continue living under his current circumstances.

He discussed with his internist the option of voluntarily refusing food and fluids and being sedated until he died. The internist was ambivalent about pursuing this option because Mr. Michaels could live a fair amount of time with a reasonable quality of life if more aggressive palliative measures were taken. Still, Mr. Michaels insisted on this course of treatment. Unsure whether this would be a case of patient-directed palliative care or euthanasia, the internist asked for an ethics consult.

**Discussion Questions.**   Name every individual and every entity that has a stake in the outcome of this case; of these people and entities, whose position holds the most moral significance? Is there such a thing as "rational suicide"? If yes, is it justifiable? If you were on the ethics committee at this hospital, how would you address this case? What is the relationship between existential suffering and physical pain, and how does the relationship between the two come into play in this case?

## Suggested Readings

Callahan, Daniel. *The Troubled Dream of Life*. New York: Simon & Schuster, 1993.

Foley, Kathleen, and Herbert Hendin, eds. *The Case against Assisted Suicide: For the Right to End-of-Life Care*. Baltimore: Johns Hopkins University Press, 2002.

Jennings, Bruce, Gregory E. Kaebnick, and Thomas H. Murray, eds. *Improving End-of-Life Care: Why Has It Been So Difficult?* Garrison, NY: Hastings Center, 2005.

Kelly, David F. *Medical Care at the End of Life: A Catholic Perspective.* Washington DC: Georgetown University Press, 2006.

Pence, Gregory E. *Classic Cases in Medical Ethics: Accounts of Cases That Have Shaped Medical Ethics, with Philosophical, Legal, and Historical Backgrounds,* 3rd ed. Boston: McGraw Hill, 2000.

Quill, Timothy E., and Margaret P. Battin, eds. *Physician-Assisted Dying: The Case for Palliative Care and Patient Choice.* Baltimore: Johns Hopkins University Press, 2004.

## Multimedia Aids for Teachers

*Dad.* Directed by Gary David Goldberg. Starring Jack Lemmon. Rated PG. 1989. This movie, which deals with the issues that people face when losing a spouse after many years and facing their own health crises, is available on DVD or VHS through Amazon.com and other retailers.

*Assisted Suicide and End of Life Care: Dying Well.* DIA Learning. For information see http://fac.ethicsprograms.com/. This 30-minute video can be purchased separately or with a group of videos on select issues in health care ethics.

*On Our Own Terms: Moyers on Dying.* Program 2, *A Differernt Kind of Care.* 2000. This video, originally a PBS broadcast, provides an in-depth look at how caregivers are helping patients cope with the physical, psychological, social, and spiritual realities of serious illness and death. For more information see http://www.films.com/id/398/On_Our_Own_Terms_Moyers_on_Dying_in_America.htm or call Films of the Humanities at 1-800-257-5126.

*Whose Death Is It Anyway? Tough Choices for End of Life.* Directed by Kit Lukas and Produced by Alvin H. Perlmutter. Featuring Nancy Schneiderman, M.D., and Betty Rollin. The Independent Production Fund. 2005. For more information and to purchase, see www.whosedeathisitanyway.com.

*Wit.* Directed by Mike Nichols. Starring Emma Thompson. Rated R. 2001. This movie, which spotlights a woman facing her own mortality, is available on DVD or VHS through Amazon.com and other retailers.

## Endnotes

[1] Max Charlesworth, *Bioethics in Liberal Society* (Cambridge: Cambridge University Press, 1993), 34.

[2] More information about all these cases can be found online. For more information about the Karen Ann Quinlan case, go to http://www.csulb.edu/~jvancamp/452_r6.html. For more information on the Hugh Finn Case, go to http://www.pbs.org/wnet/religionandethics/week738/cover.html#. For more information on the Terry Schiavo case, go to http://reports.tbo.com/reports/schiavo/.

[3] The ideas and concerns raised in this section come from Daniel Callahan, *The Troubled Dream of Life: In Search of a Peaceful Death* (New York: Simon & Schuster, 1993), 57–90.

[4] Callahan, *Troubled Dream of Life*, 58, emphases added.

[5] Ibid., 40–41.

[6] Ibid., 41.

[7] For a comprehensive analysis of the ethical, legal, and medical issues related to the controversy surrounding Terry Schiavo see Arthur L. Caplan, James J. McCartney, and Dominic A. Sisti eds., *The Case of Terry Schiavo: Ethics at the End of Life* (Buffalo, NY: Prometheus Books, 2006).

[8] Harold Y. Vanderpool, "Death and Dying: Euthanasia and Sustaining Life," in *Encyclopedia of Bioethics*, ed. Warren T. Reich, rev. ed. (New York: MacMillan, 1995), 1:554–61.

[9] The information reported on the ODDA in this section comes from the 2005 annual report on PAS issued by the Oregon Department of Human Services. To see the full annual report for calendar year 2005, go to: www.oregon.gov/ph/pas (accessed August 4, 2006).

[10] Thomas Preston, Martin Gunderson, and David J. Mayo, "The Role of Autonomy in Choosing Physician Aid in Dying, in *Physician Assisted Dying: The Case for Palliative Care and Patient Choice,* ed. Timothy E. Quill and Margaret P. Battin (Baltimore: Johns Hopkins University Press, 2004), 39–54, at 40–41.

[11] Sherwin Nuland, "Physician-Assisted Suicide and Euthanasia in Practice," *New England Journal of Medicine* 342 (February 24, 2000): 583–84, at 584.

[12] Timothy E. Quill, "Nonabandonment: A Central Obligation for Physicians," *Annals of Internal Medicine* 122 (March 1, 1995): 368–74, at 368, 369, 370.

[13] Robert A. Pearlman and Helene Starks, "Why Do People Seek Physician-Assisted Death," in *Physician Assisted Dying: The Case for Palliative Care and Patient Choice*, ed. Timothy E. Quill and Margaret P. Battin (Baltimore: Johns Hopkins University Press, 2004), 91–101.

[14] Karen E. Steinhauser, Elizabeth C. Clipp, Maya McNeilly, et al., "In Search of a Good Death: Observations of Patients, Families, and Providers" *Annals of Internal Medicine* 132 (May 16, 2000): 825–32. See also Betty R. Ferrell, "Overview of the Domains of Variables Relevant to End-of-Life Care," *Journal of Palliative Medicine* 8 Supp. 1 (2005): S22–S29.

[15] See, for example, Harvey Max Chochinov and Beverly J. Cann, "Interventions to Enhance the Spiritual Aspects of Dying," *Journal of Palliative Medicine* 8 Supp. 1 (2005): S103–15.

[16] John Collins and Edmund Pellegrino, "A Response to Euthanasia Initiatives," *Health Progress* (March 1994): 36–39, 53, at 39.

[17] This point comes from Jack Glaser, *Three Realms of Ethics: Individual, Institutional, Societal* (Kansas City: Sheed & Ward, 1994).

[18] Lois Snyder and Daniel Sulmasy, "Physician-Assisted Suicide," *Annals of Internal Medicine* 135 (August 7, 2001): 209–16.

[19] Snyder and Sulmasy, "Physician-Assisted Suicide," 211.

[20] Unless otherwise noted, the information within this section comes from R. Sean Morrison and Diane E. Meier, "Palliative Care," *The New England Journal of Medicine* 350 (June 17, 2004): 2582–90.

[21] Allen Verhey, "Suffering and Compassion: Looking Heavenward," *Perspectives* (February 1995): 17–20, at 17, 18.

# CHAPTER 9

# Reproductive Technology and the Quest for Offspring

## • Ethics at the Intersection of Technology
## • and Procreation

As discussed in earlier chapters, technology has greatly increased medicine's capacity to diagnose and treat human disease and as a result extend the lives of patients who would have died previously. Another area where technology has had a major impact on medicine is human reproduction. Whereas in the not too distant past we were subject to the whims of nature when it came to getting pregnant, today we now have a variety of means to enhance or even substitute for natural processes in an effort to have children. Many of us have been touched by these technological breakthroughs, either directly or indirectly. Some of you reading this may have been born through the wonders of this technology or know of a friend or family member who has had recourse to this technology in one form or another. If not, you probably have at least heard of fertility treatments and reproductive clinics, read ads in magazines or newspapers seeking sperm and egg donors, or have seen stories on television about couples or individuals who have had five, six, even seven children after undergoing reproductive intervention. While reproductive technologies (RTs) are fascinating and make for compelling news, they also give rise to important ethical issues that are not resolved as easily as some would have us believe—either by saying these are simply matters of personal choice or by reciting absolute prohibitions against any "technological intrusion" into human reproduction.

To avoid this trap, we would like to consider RTs in light of human flourishing and right relationships. Only by putting reproductive interventions into this broader context can we get beyond slogans and adequately reflect on the ethical issues to which they give rise. Because we will be focusing solely on the ethics of RTs, we will not address the issues of contraception and sterilization, which are often included in discussions of human reproduction. While these are indeed important subjects in health care ethics, much has been written on them over the years and there is little we can add to the discussion.[1]

Good ethics is based on good facts, so we will begin by setting the context, offering a brief description of select reproductive technologies, and highlighting some of the ethical issues to which they give rise. Then we will discuss the ethics of RTs in more detail against the backdrop of our normative basis.

# Setting the Context: The Science of Reproductive Technology

The most common and frequently used RTs are artificial insemination (AI), and in vitro fertilization (IVF).[2] Although there is some variation in each of these methods, all separate human reproduction from the act of sexual intercourse.

## Artificial Insemination (AI)

The least "technological" of all RTs, AI was the first major intervention into reproduction. Developed over two hundred years ago, AI has become a popular means of achieving pregnancy outside of normal reproduction, particularly in the last fifty years or so. In its simplest form, AI involves collecting sperm from a male (usually by means of masturbation) and injecting the sperm directly into the woman's uterus. Special techniques have been developed over the years to increase the likelihood of AI's success (e.g., detecting the precise timing of ovulation, giving the woman fertility drugs, and "washing" the sperm) and a new name has been given to this technique, intrauterine insemination (IUI). AI is perhaps the most accessible RT because it is relatively simple and inexpensive, about $300–$700.

Originally, AI was used to combat the ill effects of infertility in married couples when the couple could not have sexual intercourse or when the husband had a low sperm count or poor sperm motility (sperm lack the ability to make the long journey to the egg). The simple intervention offered such couples hope of having a baby of their own. This seemed fine enough to most people, but a relatively short time ago third parties in the form of sperm donors, often anonymous, were thrown into the equation. This opened the door for married couples to use another man's sperm to get pregnant when the husband's sperm was deficient. It also opened the door for others to use AI outside the context of marriage, even if infertility was not an issue. Heterosexual women without male partners and lesbian women, for instance, have used AI successfully to achieve pregnancy.

While AI has helped married couples and others overcome infertility troubles and have children, the technique itself raises ethical issues and its expanded use further complicates matters, especially when a donor is involved. What happens to married couples when they have recourse to a donor's sperm? How does this affect their relationship and the way they view resultant offspring? How does it affect the offspring, who may later learn that their genetic (or biological) father is not the person who has raised them all these years? Is it acceptable for men to sell their sperm anonymously and to have no responsibility for their genetic offspring? What are we to make of the use of AI outside the context of marriage? Is this an acceptable application of the technology or should it be limited to married couples? Are some relational settings more appropriate than others for raising children? How are offspring affected when they are born to unmarried mothers or people in nontraditional relationships? On a more fundamental level, is infertility a disease that medicine and its technologies are meant to fix? Should we use AI on women who do not have infertility problems?

## In Vitro Fertilization (IVF)

With the birth of the first "test-tube baby," Louise Brown, in 1978, IVF has become an oft-used reproductive intervention, particularly when infertility issues are more complicated than simply low sperm count or poor function in the male. IVF entails (1) harvesting eggs from a woman's ovaries (this could be either the woman seeking to have a baby or a donor); (2) collecting sperm from a male (husband, partner, or donor), usually obtained through masturbation, though other procedures offer options for such collection; (3) bringing the egg(s) and sperm together in a small laboratory dish (i.e., in vitro); (4) facilitating fertilization of the egg(s) outside the body; and

(5) transferring one or more of the resulting embryo(s), after they have incubated for 3–5 days in a culture medium, into a woman's uterus (this could be either the woman seeking to have a baby or a surrogate who will carry the baby and then give it up at birth).[3]

Unlike AI, IVF is anything but simple. Egg harvesting is a complex process and can be very burdensome for the woman. First the woman must receive fertility drugs so that her ovaries will produce an abnormally large amount of eggs, which can cause serious mood swings as well as physical complications, including abdominal cramping and nausea. Then the woman must have her blood tested every other day to measure hormone levels, and she must have periodic ultrasounds. Prior to egg retrieval, the woman must receive a hormone shot of human chorionic gonadotrophin (HCG) to prepare the eggs for release. The actual retrieval is done under anesthesia, using a long needle to suck out from 10–20 eggs.

There are also potential risks to the woman. In rare situations the fertility drugs can cause the woman's ovaries to hyper-stimulate, requiring hospitalization until the ovaries return to normal. In extremely rare situations the woman's ovaries can rupture, resulting in permanent infertility or even death.[4]

Also unlike AI, IVF can be very expensive. Although wide variation exists, each fertilization cycle costs roughly $10,000–$13,000; most women go through two or three cycles before pregnancy occurs. As mentioned above, to provide the best chance of success at minimal cost to the person or couple multiple eggs are often fertilized (10–20). Fertilized eggs are then transferred into the woman's uterus for implantation—usually one or two, depending on the age of the recipient. From a simple economics basis, this seems the most beneficial and cost-effective route. However, there are limits to this cost-benefit analysis. If more than three fertilized eggs are transferred at one time, the likelihood of multiple pregnancies dramatically increases, which proportionately increases the likelihood of fetal loss and premature birth, with all its associated costs (see chapter 6).[5] Moreover, multiple pregnancies can lead to selective termination, where one or more fetuses are destroyed to reduce the risks to the woman, who cannot safely carry all the fetuses, or to improve the odds of successful development for the remaining fetuses.

To eliminate the need to harvest eggs multiple times and thus reduce the burdens and risks to the woman supplying the eggs, the remaining fertilized eggs not transferred in an IVF cycle are often saved through a technique known as cryopreservation.[6] This involves freezing the "excess" or "spare" embryos at appropriate temperatures so that they can be used later if needed. Consequently, when an early treatment cycle succeeds, there may be leftover embryos in cryopreservation. What can or should be done with them? Should they remain in a state of suspended animation? Should they be donated to another person or couple? Should they be donated and used for research purposes? Should we simply discard them?

With a success rate of 20%–50%, IVF has helped thousands of women achieve pregnancy and have children. The technique itself and some of its uses raise significant ethical concerns, however. Some of these concerns are similar to those related to AI, while many go further. Is IVF an acceptable means of achieving pregnancy in the first place, since (unlike AI) it goes beyond assisting natural processes and actually replaces them with a technology in which fertilization occurs outside a woman's body? Does IVF impose disproportionate burdens on women who, among other things, have to endure the difficult egg harvesting process and potentially carry multiple embryos to term, thus increasing the risks associated with pregnancy? What are we to make of sperm and egg donation and the use of surrogates? Is it acceptable to pay these third parties for their "services"? Does this third party involvement cheapen and degrade human reproduction and result in the commercialization of baby-making and the exploitation of potential donors? Is it wise to separate the components of parenting—genetic, gestational, and social? What is the affect on children born through IVF? What impact does this have on our views of marriage, childbearing, childrearing, and parenting? Is it acceptable to fertilize more embryos than can be safely transferred into a woman and then freeze the "extras" that are not used? Does this undermine the value of early human life and further weaken our view of it? What about the use of genetic screening techniques that are often employed prior to transferring embryos into the woman's uterus? Can we discard those embryos with genetic anomalies or even those who may not be the "right" sex? Finally, what about the issues of access and equitable distribution? Is it acceptable that IVF, given its expense, is only available to select members of our society, namely, those who have significant financial means or generous health care coverage? Ought we to be spending our money on IVF when the basic needs of so many go unmet?

## Discussion: Ethical Issues and Analysis

Having briefly reviewed the science involved, we now move to an ethical analysis of the issues related to RTs. We have already spent a considerable amount of time listing these issues in the form of questions. Since there are so many, we cannot do justice to them all in this short chapter. We will have to be content with looking at some of the more pressing issues, starting with the question of whether it is morally acceptable to intervene in reproduction.

### Intervening in Reproduction

This may not seem like an important issue, especially since we are so accustomed to babies being born as a result of reproductive interventions. However, when AI and, especially, IVF first became widely available, the main ethical question was whether we could use these budding technologies at all. The concern was that we could be overstepping natural limits by creating life apart from sexual intercourse within marriage, and that by doing so the "humanness" of reproduction could be lost as technology replaces the generative, life-giving act of the spouses. To put it more simply, the concern was that babies would be created through technological means as opposed to natural means, and that this could cheapen the reproductive process and undermine the good of marriage as well as the dignity of those born through the use of such technology.

This discussion unfolded mostly within Christian religious circles, but rapidly spilled over into the public debate. Interestingly, apart from the Roman Catholic Church, most Christian religious traditions ultimately decided that interventions into reproduction, such as AI and IVF, could be morally acceptable despite the so-called "unnatural means" of achieving pregnancy. Although there were some reservations as to how the interventions might be used, there was general agreement that their use within marriage could be justified morally. A brief survey of various Christian perspectives demonstrates this:

- *Church of England.* The responsible use of IVF to remove the disability of childlessness within marriage will not threaten to undermine the interweaving of procreational and relational goods in general within marriage. In fact, in specific marriages, it may offer an enrichment of the marriage relationship, which both partners gladly accept.[7]

- *Lutheran.* Procreation within marriage is viewed as a positive blessing and divine commandment. As such, treatment for infertility is strongly encouraged. So long as remedies for infertility take place within the context of marriage, they are viewed as morally acceptable. Therefore, there is no objection to AI where the husband's sperm is used or to IVF when using the gametes of the married couple and the womb of the married woman, and no embryos are destroyed.[8]

- *Episcopalian.* AI and IVF within the context of marriage using the gametes from a married couple are morally acceptable. Assistance with infertility utilizing donor eggs and sperm is considered highly controversial. Surrogate motherhood is generally opposed as well.[9]

- *Methodist.* Although there is an insistence on a connection between procreation and marital sexuality, the insistence is only insofar as procreation is to grow out of the love of the married couple. Therefore IVF is approved when utilized by husband and wife and their respective gametes exclusively.[10]

- *Baptist.* No necessary connection exists between procreation and individual procreative acts. Children are a blessing, and a biblical reading approves of attempts to utilize technology to assist where biology has created limitations. Use of donor gametes is an open question and dependent on further biblical analysis specific to the set of circumstances.[11]

- *Reformed (Presbyterian and United Church of Christ).* Responsible procreation within marriage is viewed as an important religious value. Consequently, recourse to reproductive technologies within the marital context is generally viewed as morally acceptable. Use of donor gametes faces greater scrutiny, but may be morally justified in certain circumstances.[12]

- *Seventh Day Adventist.* Human reproduction is part of God's plan (Gen. 1:28), and children are a blessing from the Lord (Ps. 113:9; 127:3). Medical technologies that aid infertile couples, when practiced in harmony with biblical principles, may be accepted in good conscience. Christians may seek medically assisted reproduction only within the bounds of the fidelity and permanence of marriage.[13]

The thinking behind these various Christian viewpoints is that procreation is a great good of marriage. As such, remedies to correct infertility, within the context of marriage, are encouraged and welcomed. Just as we use technological means to overcome biological limitations caused by illness, so too can we when it comes to the problem of infertility, especially since it enables couples to bring their love to fruition and to grow in relationship with one another. There is nothing that says procreation has to be achieved solely by "natural means" of conceiving and "life-giving." We can get an assist from technology as we do in many other areas of our lives.

A steadfast opponent of this viewpoint is the Roman Catholic Church, which holds to this day that reproductive interventions, such as AI and IVF, are not morally permissible when they go beyond assisting natural processes and instead substitute for them in an effort to help married couples achieve pregnancy. While procreation within the context of marriage is indeed a good, the integrity of the marriage and the dignity of the child demands that pregnancy be achieved through natural means as the marriage partners express their love for one another in the intimate act of sexual intercourse ("marriage act") and cooperates with God in the creation of a new human being. This viewpoint is summarized well in the introduction to part 4 of the *Ethical and Religious Directives for Catholic Health Care Services:*

> With the advance of the biological and medical sciences, society has at its disposal new technologies for responding to the problem of infertility. While we rejoice in the potential for good inherent in many of these technologies, we cannot assume that what is technically possible is always morally right. Reproductive technologies that substitute for the marriage act are not consistent with human dignity. Just as the marriage act is joined naturally to procreation, so procreation is joined naturally to the marriage act.[14]

Unlike the other Christian traditions that we have reviewed, the Catholic tradition presents a unique Christian perspective in that the moral evaluation of reproductive interventions is concerned primarily with the intervention or individual act itself, and only secondarily with the couple's intentions or any good consequences that might arise (i.e., having a baby). This we see in a statement of the Second Vatican Council:

> When there is question of harmonizing conjugal love with the responsible transmission of life, the moral aspect of any procedure *does not depend solely* on sincere *intentions* or on an evaluation of motives. It must be determined by objective standards. These, based on the nature of the human person and *his acts,* preserve the full sense of mutual self-giving and human procreation in the context of true love (emphasis added).[15]

According to Catholic teaching, then, any intervention into reproduction that substitutes for the natural act of sexual intercourse within marriage is absolutely prohibited, no matter what good may come out of it. IVF, in particular, necessarily moves procreation from the purview of the married partners into a laboratory, where fertilization occurs outside the woman's body. In this way, procreation is deprived of its essential "total self-giving" of the partners as manifest through the natural act of sexual intercourse. Catholic teaching does hold, however, that "certain artificial means designed only to facilitate the natural act or to enable that act, performed in a normal manner, to attain its end" are not necessarily off limits or forbidden.[16]

So what are we to make of RTs? Are they a morally acceptable means of achieving pregnancy or do they represent an unwarranted technological intrusion into reproduction? Considering this question against the backdrop of our normative basis, it seems to us that the objection raised by the Catholic Church focuses too heavily on the intervention itself and whether pregnancy is achieved through natural means as opposed to technological ones.[17] This is certainly a concern, because we are dealing with the delicate area of human reproduction and there is always the potential for abuse of the technology. Yet our normative basis, grounded as it is in human flourishing and right relationship, would consider RTs in a much broader context by reflecting on whether reproductive interventions can help married people grow in their relationship with one another and progress on the path of human flourishing through the life-giving role of becoming parents.

In saying this, we do not mean to give the impression that people have an absolute right to have children regardless of the means used, or that having children of one's own is necessary for human flourishing. We agree with Maura Ryan that "as a dimension of human flourishing, the opportunity to conceive or bear a child of one's own can be called basic without being necessary, central without being essential."[18] Rather, we are saying that any moral evaluation of RTs must go deeper than merely looking at the intervention itself and include an assessment of how the intervention contributes to the overall development and flourishing of the married couple. It just might be that, when viewed in this way, we come to the conclusion that *in certain circumstances* reproductive technology is a morally acceptable means of enhancing the relationship of married people who are committed to one another and to expressing their love in the creation of a new human being.

All this assumes that marriage is the normative or ideal context for having children. With no disrespect to single parents or parents within nontraditional relationships, experience seems to suggest that, all things considered, marriage offers a certain level of stability for the raising of children that other relationships may not. This, of course, is not always the case. Additionally, the use of RTs outside the context of marriage often involves donors or surrogates and this, to us, is unacceptable for three main reasons. First, it seems to cheapen and degrade human reproduction, as the baby that results is not the fruit of the love between two committed individuals but the choice of individuals who contract with third parties and pay for their "services" (whether it be eggs, sperm, or uterus). Second, it seems to distort our collective view of human reproduction and responsible parenting. While AI using donor sperm raises concerns, IVF has an added layer in that you can have a sperm donor, an egg donor, and a surrogate mother, all with the possibility that the person or couple who eventually raises the baby had no part in any of this. In effect, a baby produced through IVF could have five "parents": the genetic parents (those who donate the eggs and sperm), the gestational parent (the woman who carries and delivers the baby), and the social parents (those who rear the baby). Third, the possibility exists that it can negatively affect offspring who must, if the truth is told, deal with the fact they were conceived through the use of a donor or donors and carried by a surrogate whom they most likely will never know. Empirical evidence is mixed on this. You might try an experiment: ask yourself how you would feel if you found out that you were born through the use of eggs bought over the Internet after a careful screening process that involved selecting just the "right" woman with just the "right" traits.

## Disproportionate Burdens to Women

An often overlooked issue that arises with RTs is that women, not men, tend to bear most of the burdens, whether it is the burdens associated with egg harvesting, with the actual intervention, with carrying and delivering the embryo, and with raising any resulting children. Is it fair that the woman must undergo this grueling process, especially if it is not the woman's infertility issue but the male's? To some extent we cannot do anything about this. The burdens are what they are and unfortunately they fall disproportionately to women. And women always have a choice to participate or not—or do they? Society has a way of telling women that they must have children, that they can only be complete through this experience. Psychologically and spiritually this can have devastating effects on women. Is there not subtle coercion, then, for women to use reproductive technologies in an effort to get pregnant when infertility gets in the way?

What about egg donors and surrogates, who do not even get a baby in the end? Is it fair to them that they have to participate in this process and endure the burdens, which can be quite significant with egg harvesting and with surrogacy, especially if multiple embryos are transferred? Of course, they do not have to participate. They, too, have a choice—or do they? Surrogacy arrangements can be quite lucrative, as can payment for eggs (on average about $3000–$5000, but sometimes higher for the "right" eggs). How enticing do you think it is to women who may be struggling financially to offer themselves up so that another person or couple can achieve their dream of having a baby? What do they have to go through when they are being screened for their eggs or picked for surrogacy, having to answer sensitive questions, submit health records, and be looked over physically? Is this how we want to treat women? Does it not objectify them and exploit them for the personal gain of others?

These are all difficult questions and none of them have easy answers. It is hard to say outside the context of a particular case whether the burdens of reproductive interventions that women are made to endure undermine their dignity and threaten their integral well-being. Nevertheless, as we consider the ethics of RTs against the backdrop of our normative basis, we must keep these questions in mind because they can have a significant impact on our overall moral evaluation. In the end it may come down to a matter of consent on the part of the woman. Still, we must be mindful of this overarching issue, too, often cast aside in ethical discussions of reproductive interventions.

## Access and Equitable Distribution

Another issue that gets too little attention when considering the ethics of RTs is that of access and equitable distribution of health care resources. As noted above, IVF is quite expensive, prohibitively so for many people in the United States and people in many other parts of the world where access to even basic health care services is lacking. Is it fair that IVF is available to some but not to others? We could fix this problem perhaps, at least in developed nations, by requiring all health insurance plans to provide coverage for it. Currently some do, but most do not. Adding this coverage, however, would significantly increase overall health care spending, which is already quite high (2006 estimates indicate over $2,000,000,000,000 in the United States) and continues to rise at a furious pace. Is IVF important enough that we are willing to make it accessible more fairly than it is presently? Probably not, since there are more basic areas of health to which we need to attend (e.g., immunization, clean water, and preventative health programs for chronic illness), and the option of adoption is always available.

Even if we did add IVF coverage to health plans, however, it would not solve the problem totally, given that over 40,000,000 Americans are presently uninsured. This brings us to the question of whether we should be doing IVF at all when so many of our fellow Americans lack even minimal health care coverage. Even though the costs of all RTs are high (about $2,000,000,000 a year in the United States alone), they are assumed mostly by individuals, not by health plans or the federal government. Thus a dollar saved on IVF or some other reproductive technology does not necessarily mean an extra dollar for basic health care for the uninsured. Still, we do dedicate health care resources to technological reproduction in the form of time, money, equipment, research, and personnel. Wouldn't such resources be better used in other ways that improved more significant health problems? What is more, is it ethical for a society to pursue expensive, elective interventions when so many people, mostly women, children, and the working poor, have to rely on emergency rooms or overcrowded free clinics for their care or go without.

Unfortunately, in our society the market tends to dictate access to health care services and distribution of health care resources. In effect, if you have the money, you can get the services. This is largely how the reproductive technology industry works. Put simply, those with the means can have the babies. While this may satisfy economists, it is obviously not the best system from an ethical perspective. Health care should be more coordinated and if we were prioritizing in terms of basic health requirements, reproductive technologies might fall far down the list. Given these concerns, particularly when they are viewed in light of human flourishing and right relationships, it seems inconceivable that we could look upon RTs favorably. But given the fact that interventions are available and will continue to be so in the future, we have to make more prudent and discerning choices regarding their use. Rather than letting the market make our decisions for us and assuming that we have unlimited procreative liberty, we need to recognize our responsibility to the common good. Although the leap from the individual to society may not seem natural, our normative basis demands it insofar as we are social beings connected to others in our pursuit of human flourishing.

## Value of Early Human Life

The last issue that we need to consider involves the treatment of embryos in reproductive interventions where fertilization occurs outside the woman's body, such as IVF. Though it is clear from the abortion and stem cell debates that many people do not consider the 4–5 day old embryo a person, no one can reasonably deny that it is human life at a very early stage of its development. Everyone reading this book passed through this stage of human development. However we may view embryos individually or collectively, the least we can say is that it is valuable and deserves respect as a beginning form of human life. If this statement is true, then we have to ask whether our current handling of embryos in our attempts to achieve reproduction technologically is morally acceptable.

Wouldn't it be more respectful to human life to develop only the amount of embryos that could be safely transferred into the woman without having to submit "extra" embryos to the cryopreservation process, which is not without its risks? Admittedly this would be more expensive because a failed intervention would mean starting over again and not just utilizing excess embryos. Yet how much more respectful is this of human life than creating excess embryos that need to be stored in freezers, that are often discarded because they are no longer needed, or are donated for research where they are manipulated and dissected for the "good" of science? By instituting this change, wouldn't we be saying that human life matters, and wouldn't this translate into a deeper respect for all life that spills over into all our relationships and to our views of creation? At least it would be better than what we are currently doing.

There are also concerns about genetic screening techniques (e.g., pre-implantation genetic diagnosis) prior to embryo transfer to weed out undesirable embryos that might have a genetic mutation or, even worse, might simply be the "wrong" gender. What does this say about who we are as individuals and as a society? Does this practice undermine the gift of life by turning embryos into products for which we can select traits, as we do when we purchase a new car? If we are serious about pursuing human flourishing and fostering right relationships, then we have to be more respectful of early human life in all its dynamism. We ought to find the treatment of embryos in reproductive interventions simply unacceptable when viewed against this larger backdrop.

## Conclusion

We have spent a lot of time describing the science of RTs and discussing the ethical issues to which they give rise. By way of conclusion, let's consider some case studies that allow us to apply some of our reflections.

**Case 9A:** Sam and Camory, happily married for over eight years, have been trying to have children for some time now without success. Examination by a physician reveals that Camory has blocked fallopian tubes and surgery will not be able to rectify the condition—quite simply, they are not able to have children via conventional means. They strongly desire to have a child that is a genetic offspring of theirs, and although their insurance does not cover reproductive interventions other than fertility drugs, they are willing to make the financial sacrifice. Sam and Camory's deep longing for children leaves no reason to doubt they will be loving parents. To a certain extent they also feel that their marriage is lacking because they are not able to have children. Faced with this situation, IVF seems like the best solution. Camory is a prime candidate for the intervention because her uterus and ovaries are healthy. Also, Sam has an adequate sperm count and the sperm function properly. Thus neither a donor nor surrogate will be necessary. IVF seems to offer them a really good chance at having genetic offspring.[19]

This is a typical and common situation in the context of reproductive technology. Like so many other individuals and couples, Sam and Camory's deep longing for children and feelings of emptiness stem from problems related to infertility. IVF offers them some hope of overcoming these challenges. The question is whether it is morally acceptable for Sam and Camory to pursue this reproductive intervention in an effort to a have a child. The first thing to consider as we think about this case is how having a child through technological means will affect their relationship. Will it bring them closer together in their love for one another? Will it satisfy the deep longing and emptiness that they have? What kind of parents will they be? Will their love for one another be reflected in how they care for the child, should the procedure be successful? Given what we know it seems that Sam and Camory's relationship could be enhanced by having a child. Though happily married for eight years, they long to have a child, which they would very much welcome into their lives and for which they would take full parental responsibility. Yet is this adequate? This would suggest that any committed, married couple experiencing infertility could pursue reproductive technologies if they are willing and able. Our normative basis requires us to look deeper.

The use of a donor or surrogate is not an issue here. If they were going to have recourse to a donor or surrogate, we would have to object given the potential negative impact on the marriage, offspring, and society at large.

We also must consider whether the burdens on Camory are acceptable. Is Camory aware of what IVF entails in terms of fertility drugs, egg harvesting, the transfer of multiple embryos, and the possibility of multiple pregnancies and associated risks? If her physician explained all this to her and she is willing to accept the burdens, it is hard to argue from this basis, especially since she will not be asking another to carry these burdens for her (through egg donation or surrogacy).

How will Sam and Camory's decision affect their financial well-being and the common good? Since their health insurance does not cover IVF, they are going to have to assume all the costs. We don't know what impact this will have on them, but if they can reasonably afford it without undermining their overall well-being, then it would be hard to deny them this opportunity on these grounds. If they were receiving help or coverage from their health plan, one could argue that their use of IVF could drive up the overall costs of the plan and result in increased premiums for all members, but that is not the case here.

Will Sam and Camory elect to create multiple embryos and choose to freeze any that are not transferred in the first cycle of treatment? Respect for early human life demands that they only create the amount of embryos that could be safely transferred for implantation without having recourse to cryopreservation. If they insist upon this point we would have no objections on these grounds.

Finally, we must consider whether there are any viable alternatives for Sam and Camory, such as becoming foster parents or adopting. Would one of these options satisfy their deep longing to have a child? Either of these options would allow Sam and Camory the opportunity to be parents while at the same time providing a safe, loving home for a child in need. For many people with problems of infertility, though, these are options of last resort because of their strong desire to have children of their own. Though ideal, these options seem to demand more from Sam and Camory than we can reasonably expect.

The case of Camory and Sam reveals again that one must not isolate individual decisions about reproductive interventions from the broader context of human flourishing and right relationships. We may not have satisfied your desire for definitive answers to the ethical questions raised by RTs, but hopefully through the discussion of the ethical issues and the analysis of the case we have shown what needs to be considered. Perhaps the most we can say about reproductive interventions outside of concrete situations is that there are certain circumstances in which their use may by morally permissible. Like many of the Christian religious traditions noted above, the circumstances that we would find acceptable would be within the context of a loving, committed marriage, where there is no recourse to donors or surrogates, where the health and safety of the woman is protected, where embryos are not destroyed, where financial burdens are borne by the couple, and where the common good is not negatively affected. The use of RTs in such a context and under these circumstances would be conducive to fostering right relationships and ultimately contributing to the well-being of the married couple and their children without undermining that of others.

**Case 9B:** A 35-year-old female contacts you regarding a letter she received from an infertility clinic where she contracted services for in vitro fertilization some 15 years ago. The letter states that she has five embryos frozen in cryopreservation and her agreement is due to expire in six months. The infertility clinic is asking what she would like to have done with the embryos at the expiration of the contract. The contract stipulated that she could continue the cryopreservation process on a year-to-year basis at $300 annually. The woman was unaware that she had any embryos still in cryopreservation and is stunned to find out that she is now responsible for determining their fate. She is currently divorced from the man whose sperm was used in the in vitro fertilization process, and has sole custody of the children.

At the same time, the former husband received the same letter due to legal stipulations in the informed consent process at the time of the in vitro process. The letter states that the mother has the right to determine what to do with the embryos (which includes donation for research purposes), unless she chooses to have the embryos destroyed. In the latter case, the partner's consent would be necessary as well, regardless of marital status. Further complicating the matter is the fact that the ex-husband's visitation rights had been taken away due to allegations surrounding child neglect and abuse, and the woman does not want to re-open a custody battle in the courts for fear that her ex-husband might gain visitation rights. Also, she had recently lost her job and, although she has found new employment, it pays substantially less. She says she is barely getting by as it is, and is not financially prepared to handle the $300 fee to keep the embryos in cryopreservation.

The woman tells you that she is a Roman Catholic. She has not gone to church in quite some time, but is well aware of the Catholic Church's position on abortion and does not feel it is right to simply dispose of the embryos. Furthermore, destruction of the embryos would require the husband's consent, and she does not want to reestablish contact if avoidable. Despite financial hardship, does the divorced couple (or at least the woman) have obligations to maintain the embryos in cryopreservation? Or should the woman simply offer the embryos for adoption in order to avoid reestablishing contact with her former husband and the corresponding risks to her children should contact occur? Is there another ethically permissible option?

**Case 9C:** John, a 22-year-old man who has been married just under a year, has just been diagnosed as brain-dead after a severe car accident. His wife, Dana, who has the legal right to make decisions for him, agrees to multiple organ donations to be coordinated by a local organ procurement organization. Dana also makes an unusual request: can sperm be obtained from John so that she can become impregnated through IVF? Dana states, "This is one way that John can live on." John's primary physician is obviously uneasy about this request and probes into the situation further. The physician finds out that John never really discussed having kids with Dana. Nevertheless, Dana insists, "This is what John would have wanted." Should the sperm be retrieved from John so Dana can have his baby? Why or why not? Does this formulation call into question the nature of family? What role should society have in answering that question?

## Suggested Readings

Congregation for the Doctrine of the Faith. "Donum vitae." http://www.vatican.va/.../congregations/cfaith/documents/rc_con_cfaith_doc_19870222_respect-for-human-life_en.html.

Diekema, Douglas S. "Involuntary Sterilization of Persons with Mental Retardation: An Ethical Analysis." *Mental Retardation and Developmental Disabilities Research Reviews* 9 (2003): 21–26.

Kelly, Kevin T. "What the Churches Are Saying about IVF." In *Readings in Moral Theology No. 8*, edited by Charles Curran and Richard McCormick, 267–294. New York: Paulist Press, 1993.

Kohl, Beth. *Embryo Culture: Making Babies in the Twenty-First Century*. New York: Farrar, Straus, and Giroux, 2007.

Sontag, Sherry. *One in a Million: The Real Story of IVF and the Fight to Forge a Family*. New York: PublicAffairs, 2007.

Spar, Debora L. *The Baby Business: How Money, Science, and Politics Drive the Commerce of Conception*. Boston: Harvard Business School Press, 2006.

Spencer, John R., and Antje du Bois-Pedain, eds. *Freedom and Responsibility in Reproductive Choice*. Oxford: Hart, 2006.

Robert Winston. *The IVF Revolution: The Definitive Guide to Assisted Reproductive Technologies*. London: Vermillion, 1999. Excerpts at: http://www.pbs.org/wgbh/pages/frontline/shows/fertility.

## Multimedia Aids for Teachers

"Making Babies: An Examination of the Booming Infertility Business." PBS *Frontline*. 1999. Excerpts at: http://www.pbs.org/wgbh/pages/frontline/shows/fertility.

## Endnotes

[1] For further reading on these topics, see, among others: Charles E. Curran and Richard A. McCormick, eds., *Dialogue about Catholic Sexual Teaching: Readings in Moral Theology No. 8* (Mahwah, NJ: Paulist Press, 1993); Michel Foucault, *The History of Sexuality*, vol. 1, An Introduction, trans. Robert Hurley (New York: Penguin, 1978); John T. Noonan, Jr., *Contraception: A History of Its Treatment by the Catholic Theologians and Canonists* (Cambridge: Harvard University Press, 1986); and Jael Silliman, Marlene Gerber Fried, Loretta Ross, and Elena R. Gutierrez, *Undivided Rights: Women of Color Organize for Reproductive Justice* (Cambridge, MA: South End Press, 2004).

[2] There are other reproductive interventions, such as gamete intrafallopian transfer (GIFT), and zygote intrafallopian transfer (ZIFT), intravaginal culture (IVC), uterine lavage embryo retrieval (ULER), partial zona dissection (PZD), and intracytoplasmic sperm injection (ICSI). We will not discuss these due to space limitations.

[3] For an excellent source on the process of in vitro fertilization, see: Robert Winston, *The IVF Revolution: The Definitive Guide to Assisted Reproductive Technologies* (London: Vermillion, 1999), 1–12.

[4] This discussion of egg retrieval is based on the excellent article by Jessica Cohen, "Grade A: The Market for a Yale Woman's Eggs," *The Atlantic* 289 (December 2002): 74–78.

[5] Evangelos G. Papanikolaou, et al., "In Vitro Ferilization with Single Blastocyst-Stage versus Single Cleavage-Stage Embryos," *The New England Journal of Medicine* 354 (March 16, 2006): 1139–46; Ann Thurin, et al., "Elective Single-Embryo Transfer versus Double-Embryo Transfer in In Vitro Fertilization," *The New England Journal of Medicine* 351 (December 2, 2004): 2392–2402.

[6] F. Nawroth, et al., "Cryopreservation in Assisted Reproductive Technology: New Trends," *Seminars in Reproductive Medicine* 23 (November 2005): 325–35.

[7] See Church of England Board of Social Responsibility Personal Origins (2nd Edition), CHP, 1996.

[8] Commission on Theology and Church Relations, Lutheran Church-Missouri Synod, *Human Sexuality: A Theological Perspective* (St. Louis, MO: Social Concerns Committee, 1981); Division of Theological Studies, Lutheran Council in the U.S., *In Vitro Fertilization* (New York, NY: 1983).

[9] General Convention of the Episcopal Church, Statements on Abortion, In Vitro Fertilization, Control of Conception, and Genetic Engineering (obtainable from the Episcopal Church Center, New York, NY).

[10] W. B. Neaves and P. Neaves., "Moral Dimensions of In Vitro Fertilization," *Perkins Journal* (Winter 1986): 10–23.

[11] Christian Life Commission, Southern Baptist Convention, *Issues and Answers: Biomedical Ethics* (Nashville, TN, 1981).

[12] Office of the General Assembly, Presbyterian Church, Covenant and Creation (New York, NY: Office of the General Assembly, 1983); Office of the General Assembly, Presbyterian Church, *The Covenant of Life and Caring Community* (New York, NY: Office of the General Assembly, 1983).

[13] General Conference of Seventh-day Adventists Administrative Committee (ADCOM), Silver Spring, Maryland, July 26, 1994. http://www.adventist.org/beliefs/other_documents/other_doc10.html

[14] *Ethical and Religious Directives for Catholic Health Care Services*, 4th ed. (The United States Conference of Catholic Bishops) available on-line at: http://www.usccb.org/bishops/directives .shtml. See also: *Donum vitae*, On Respect for Human Life in its Origin

[15] Cf. Second Vatican Council, *Gaudium et Spes*, 51.

[16] Pius XII, "Address to the 4th International Convention of Catholic Physicians," in *Readings in Moral Theology No. 8*, ed. Charles E. Curran and Richard A. McCormick (New York: Paulist Press, 1993), 224.

[17] Congregation for the Doctrine of the Faith, Donum vitae. http://www.vatican.va/.../ congregations/cfaith/documents/rc_con_cfaith_doc_19870222_respect-for-human-life_ en.html.

[18] Maura A. Ryan. *The Ethics and Economics of Assisted Reproduction: The Cost of Longing* (Washington, DC: Georgetown University Press, 2001), 172.

[19] This case is an adaptation of one found in Craig Paterson, "A Case of Misdirected Love? In-vitro Fertilization and the Quest for Fertility," *Health Care Ethics USA* 8 (2000): 4–5.

# CHAPTER 10

# Stem Cell Research and Human Cloning

## What Cost a Cure?

In 1877, Louis Pasteur discovered antibiotics. In 1929, antibiotics were first used as a medical therapy with the discovery of penicillin. By 1946, antibiotics had been credited with saving countless lives and extending the average human lifespan.[1] In 1998, human embryonic stem cells were isolated (found) and cultured (grown outside the body) for the first time by scientists working separately at the University of Wisconsin and at Johns Hopkins.[2] Like antibiotics, stem cell research offers the promise of relieving the suffering and saving the lives of millions of people, and possibly extending the human lifespan even more. Broadly, the potential benefits of stem cell research include generating cells and tissues in the lab for transplantation and creating replacement cells and tissues in the body to cure diseases such as Parkinson's, Alzheimer's, heart disease, cancer, and arthritis. The actual and potential medical uses of stem cells and the types of ethical issues raised by stem cell research and human cloning can be illustrated by a few cases:

**Case 10A:** Molly Nash was a six-year-old girl with Fanconi anemia, a rare genetic disorder that prevents bone marrow from being made by the body. This condition is often fatal at a very young age. A bone marrow transplant from a matching sibling can offer an 85% rate of success for treating this disease. Because Molly did not have a sibling, her parents decided to have another baby with the hope of using the placenta and umbilical cord blood after its birth for a stem-cell transplant for Molly. The parents used in vitro fertilization (IVF) combined with preimplantation genetic diagnosis, a type of genetic screening on embryos created through IVF, to ensure that the baby did not have the same disease as Molly, and that the baby would be a genetic match for the transplant. Of the thirteen embryos created, two were suitable genetic matches for the stem cell transplant and were implanted in Mrs. Nash. One survived. On August 29, 2000, baby Adam was born. A few weeks later, and after further screening, his six-year-old sister received a transfusion of stem cells from his umbilical cord blood and placenta. The stem cell transplant was successful, and both Adam and Molly are healthy.[3]

**Case 10B:** In 1971, David Vetter was born with no immune system due to a rare genetic condition known as severe combined immunodeficiency syndrome (SCID). Only 20 seconds after being born, he was placed in a special bed in a germ-free enclosure in the hospital. Due to his condition, David could only be handled using special gloves that reached inside the enclosure. David lived to be 12 years old, but was never able to leave his germ-free "bubble" or experience a human touch. Scientists in France have been able to use stem cells from other children to cure nine children suffering from SCID.[4] Many of them later developed a rare but treatable form of cancer as a side-effect of the stem cell treatment. With the cancer in remission, all of the former SCID patients are now considered to be healthy, normally developing children, though it is uncertain whether the cancer will ever return.

**Case 10C:** Twenty years from now, you find yourself staring blankly at your mother's physician as she tells you that the genetic tests they have just run confirm that your mom's severe headaches are the first symptoms of Alzheimer's disease. The doctor explains that the prognosis is not as bad as it once was. Because they caught the disease early enough, they can take the stem cells of a cloned human embryo and inject them into your mom, and the brain cells being destroyed by the Alzheimer's disease will be replaced. There is, however, a 90% chance your mom will have to receive these injections several times a year for the rest of her life, and because they involve destroying a new cloned embryo every time she receives an injection, the treatment is very expensive. Thankfully, she and your father can afford to pay for a supplemental health insurance plan that will cover the cost of the treatment.

Stem cell research has already begun to save lives, and the potential to cure other currently untreatable diseases is even greater. Some types of stem cell research, however, are ethically controversial. For example, some people question whether research on human embryonic stem cells should be done at all. Moreover, human cloning is highly controversial and there are many—including some who are advocates for embryonic stem cell research—who oppose attempts at human cloning. Embryonic stem cell research and the possibility of human cloning raise many different ethical questions about the value of human life in its earliest stages, the goals and limits of medicine, and who we, as a society, are becoming through the use of medical technology. In this chapter we will consider some of the primary ethical questions raised by embryonic stem cell research and the possibility of human cloning. But first, we must familiarize ourselves with some of the basic science.

## Setting the Context: The Science and Politics of Stem Cell Research and Human Cloning

### What Are Stem Cells?

Stem cells are "blank slate" cells that have not yet developed a specialized function within the body or have not yet become a specific type of cell.[5] Stem cells are therefore referred to as *undifferentiated*. Stem cells are also capable of dividing and renewing themselves through a process termed *proliferation*. Stem cells can proliferate many times over in order to replenish other specialized cells that are lost due to the normal aging process of the body or due to injury or disease. This ability to divide and renew themselves allows stem cells to be grown continually for an almost indefinite period of time in a Petri dish. When a group of stem cells is cultured in this way, the result is known as a stem cell line. As stem cells replenish other cells within the body that die off due to normal wear and tear or due to disease or injury, they become specific types of body cells or tissues, such as heart cells, skin cells, blood cells, pancreatic cells, or nerve cells, through the process of differentiation. Like the stem of a plant out of which the leaves grow, stem cells give rise to the other cells of the body.

### Types of Stem Cells

There are two main classifications of stem cells: embryonic and "adult." Embryonic stem cells (ESCs) are obtained from 4–5 day old embryos (called *blastocysts* at this stage of development), very early embryos consisting only of an inner cell mass made up of stem cells and a thin outer membrane (called the *trophoblast*, which makes up all the extra-embryonic material such as the placenta). In order to obtain ESCs a needle is inserted into the trophoblast and the stem cells are sucked out, thereby destroying the embryo. Today, the most common source of ESCs are "spare"—that is, unwanted—embryos left over from in vitro fertilization. According to current estimates, there are roughly 400,000 such embryos in fertility clinics in the United States, though the utility of all of these embryos for stem cell research may be limited.[6] ESCs are so attractive to research scientists because they are *pluripotent,* which means that they can, at least theoretically, become any type of cell or tissue in the body. Because they are pluripotent, it is believed that ESCs will be more useful than other types of stem cells for treating more diseases, once scientists figure out how to make them become what they want them to be (such as cardiac muscle cells for heart attack victims or pancreatic islet cells for insulin-dependent diabetics).

Adult stem cells (ASCs) are found in the human body once it has developed beyond the blastocyst stage. The term "adult" stem cell is actually somewhat misleading, because it suggests they are only found in adults, as the concept of adulthood is generally understood. Actually, ASCs can be found in the bodies of adults, children, and infants, in umbilical cord blood (which can be retained after the umbilical cord is removed from a newborn baby), and in the placenta (or afterbirth). ASCs have been found in the bone marrow (the spongy tissue inside bones that makes blood cells), peripheral blood, the eyes, the brain, skeletal mucscle, teeth, liver, skin, the lining of the gastrointestinal tract, the pancreas, and even belly fat. Historically, most ASCs have been considered to be *multipotent* rather than pluripotent, though there is new evidence that suggests that some ASCs may be capable of transdifferentiation much like pluripotent ESCs.[7] *Multipotent* means that ASCs are believed to be limited to becoming only the type of cell of the tissue in which they are found. For example, an ASC taken from bone marrow, though still undifferentiated, will only be capable of becoming a bone marrow cell, at least theoretically. For this reason ASCs were generally thought to offer less therapeutic promise for the treatment of disease, though new scientific evidence is raising questions about that.

## The Scientific Debate

The potential therapeutic usefulness of ESCs and ASCs has been at the heart of the scientific debate regarding stem cell research. Many scientists argue that, because ESCs are pluripotent, they offer the greatest potential for advances in the treatment of disease. Another advantage of ESC research over ASC research put forth by some in the scientific community is that ESCs are more readily available, more easily found, and can proliferate outside the body much longer than ASCs. Consequently, many scientists want unfettered access to ESCs. However, currently there are no proven uses of ESCs in treating human disease, while it has been reported that ASCs have been used in 72 different therapeutic applications.[8] Before any therapeutic uses of ESCs are realized, scientists still need to understand better how undifferentiated cells become differentiated and how to control or direct this process. There are also safety issues associated with ESCs that ASCs do not have. For example, ESCs have been shown in mice to grow uncontrollably into cell and tissue masses making up benign tumors known as *teratomas*.[9]

Contrary to previously held beliefs, some ASCs have shown evidence that they might have the ability to "cross over" and differentiate into cells found in organs and tissues other than those from which the ASCs were derived.[10] For example, bone marrow stem cells have been known to differentiate into brain cells, skeletal muscle cells, and liver cells. Brain stem cells have also been known to differentiate into blood cells and skeletal muscle cells. This ability to cross over from being a stem cell of one tissue or organ to a differentiated cell of another tissue or organ is termed *plasticity*. The fact that more recent research has shown that some ASCs do have the capacity to be reprogrammed into various cell types calls into question the scientific arguments of those who favor ESC research, but the scientific debate continues.

One reason for this debate is the concern that, because we have fewer and fewer ASCs in our bodies the older we get, a person may not have a sufficient supply of ASCs for certain therapies that might be developed in the future for devastating diseases, such as Alzheimer's disease and Parkinson's disease. Why not just use someone else's ASCs in that case? As with organ transplantation, there are concerns that if ASCs come from someone else, the recipient's body might attack and reject the cells, mistaking them for the cells of a disease. One possibility for avoiding this scenario, some scientists argue, could be to take ESCs from a cloned embryo, an embryo that shares most of its DNA, with the exception of its mitochondrial DNA, in common with the person from whom the embryo was cloned. Recall the hypothetical scenario in *Case 11C*. By taking a stem cell from a cloned embryo, the body would recognize it as one of its own cells. Thus, some scientists argue that ESC research combined with human cloning is the most effective and safest way to develop new treatments for especially devastating diseases that are currently incurable.

## The Science of Human Cloning

Cloning is the process of replicating genetic material and even whole organisms. Cloning is an asexual method of reproduction in which offspring are created from a single "parent." In 1997, Scottish scientists successfully cloned a sheep.[11] Dolly, as she was called, was genetically identical to her "mother." The scientists obtained the DNA and were able to get it to grow into Dolly, a living, breathing genetic replica of another sheep, through a process known as Somatic Cell Nuclear Transfer (SCNT) . Though Dolly was born only after 300 unsuccessful attempts, many people now believe that SCNT could be used to clone human beings.[12] In SCNT, a non-reproductive (somatic) cell, such as a skin cell, is taken from an individual. The nucleus (the part of the cell containing the person's entire genetic code) is then extracted from that cell. That nucleus is then inserted into an ovum (egg) that has had its own nucleus and DNA removed. The egg with the nucleus from the somatic cell is then mixed with chemicals and given a small electric shock to start it growing. The result is a living embryo with the exact genetic make-up of the individual from which the somatic or non-reproductive cell was originally obtained. The embryo then could develop for a short time in a Petri dish or could be implanted in the womb of a surrogate mother or gestational carrier.

Human cloning (SCNT) can be categorized as either therapeutic or reproductive, depending on its intended purpose. In reproductive cloning, the purpose is to implant the embryo in the uterus of a woman who would later give birth to a child. In therapeutic cloning, the purpose is not to create a child (i.e., the purpose is not reproductive) but to create an embryo that will be allowed to develop only to the blastocyst stage (3 to 5 days) and then be destroyed for its stem cells. To call cloning for this purpose "therapeutic" is a little misleading for two reasons. First, there is nothing therapeutic about it for the embryo that has to be destroyed in order for its stem cells to be obtained. Second, as we have pointed out, ESCs have yet to yield any proven medical therapies. While it would be more accurate to call it "research cloning," the prevailing trend is to refer to SCNT for the purpose of obtaining ESCs for use in research as "therapeutic" cloning. The emphasis is on the hope that medical therapies might one day be derived from research on ESCs taken from 3–5 day old cloned human embryos, and that cloning would provide an almost endless supply of ESCs for use in those therapies.

Reproductive cloning has been widely rejected by mainstream society, though some fringe groups do continue to advocate for it, and some have claimed—without substantiation—to have done it successfully. Therapeutic cloning, however, is advocated by many scientists and politicians who support ESC research. Therapeutic cloning is even legal in some countries and seems to be gaining support in the United States. In addition to the rejection issue related to ESCs, the push for therapeutic cloning is also being driven by the human thirst for knowledge, by the desire to remain scientifically and commercially competitive in the global context, and by the desire for prestige.

## U.S. Public Policy, Human Cloning, and Stem Cell Research

The science of stem cell research and human cloning gives rise to complex public policy questions. Should ESC research be allowed, regulated, or even encouraged by the government? Should taxpayer money be used to fund ESC research? Should therapeutic cloning be legal? These are not only public policy questions, but ethical questions at the macro or societal level.

**The Politics of Human Cloning.** While there is wide agreement at the federal and state legislative levels that reproductive cloning should be banned, opinions are mixed regarding therapeutic cloning. For example, while Iowa, Louisiana, Maine, Minnesota, North Dakota, South Dakota, and Rhode Island have passed laws banning therapeutic cloning, California has passed a law allowing it.[13] At the federal level, the U.S. House of Representatives has twice passed a bill banning both reproductive and therapeutic cloning, but the Senate has yet to debate the issue formally. Two competing bills have, however, been introduced in the Senate. The "Human Cloning Prohibition Act of 2003" (S.B. 245) would ban both therapeutic and reproductive cloning, while the "Human Cloning Ban and Stem Cell Research Protection Act" (S.B. 303) would ban reproductive cloning but permit therapeutic cloning. Though President George W. Bush has openly stated that he would support a total ban on all human cloning, many Republican and traditionally pro-life senators have crossed party lines on the issue of therapeutic cloning. Likewise, the President's Council on Bioethics has publicly supported a prohibition of reproductive cloning, but stopped short of supporting a total prohibition of therapeutic cloning, supporting a moratorium on the practice instead until sufficient regulations can be worked out.[14]

**Stem Cell Research in the Public Arena.** There is even more variation in the views of politicians regarding ESC research. Several senators who traditionally hold pro-life positions have advocated for the unfettered and publicly funded pursuit of ESC research. This shift can be attributed largely to their views regarding the moral status of unwanted embryos in fertility clinic storage units as somehow different from other human life. For example, Senator Orin Hatch has asserted that a frozen embryo in a refrigerator in a clinic is not the same as a fetus developing in a mother's womb.[15] Likewise, former Senator Connie Mack has gone on record as supporting ESC research based on the view that as long as an embryo is destined not to be placed in a uterus, it cannot become life.[16]

While such reasoning can be persuasive, it embraces an inconsistent ethic of life. It is true that an embryo that remains in a cryopreservation tank in a fertility clinic is not actually progressing through its developmental stages like a fetus in the womb. It is also true that an embryo destined not to be implanted cannot become a person. However, limiting moral standing to the developing fetus in the womb implies that the moral worth of life is ultimately attached to achieving a particular developmental stage of growth rather than the inherent value of human life itself. This view either posits the accidental circumstances of individual lives as the basis of moral worth, or assumes the right to life is conditioned on the actual or potential capability to function as a person rather than on life itself. Ultimately, such views undermine the arguments that pro-life politicians have put forth in different contexts. If an embryo, even one in a cryopreservation tank, is not human life, then what is it? How could it become human life simply by being placed in a uterus, if it is not a human life to begin with?

A more consistent approach to the issue is reflected in the second Bush Administration's approach to the question of using federal funds for ESC research. At the time that human ESCs were first isolated and grown by private researchers, federal regulations did not allow federal money to be used for funding any research that involved the destruction of human embryos. In 1999, during the Clinton Administration, the National Institutes for Health (NIH) published draft guidelines outlining the conditions under which it would allow for the first time federal funds to be used for ESC research.[17] However, the Clinton Administration did not approve the guidelines until September of 2000, just before the president's final term in office ended. No government funds were dispensed for the purpose of ESC research before

President George W. Bush came into office. The guidelines were subsequently put on hold until the Bush Administration could review them and make a decision as to whether or not they should stand or be revised.

In August of 2001, in his first Address to the Nation, President Bush announced the creation of new stem cell research guidelines that would permit federal funding to be used for ESC research, but only on existing ESC lines and not for research that would further contribute to the additional destruction of existing embryos. In order to ensure that federal funds would not be used for research that entailed the destruction of existing embryos, the Administration created a Stem Cell Registry consisting of 64 ESC lines worldwide. Many in the scientific community questioned the feasibility of using these ESC lines. Advocates of ESC research questioned whether U.S. researchers would be given access to ESC lines in foreign countries, whether the existing cell lines would be sufficiently genetically diverse, whether they would be reliably capable of differentiation, and whether they would be reliably capable of proliferation. Despite these questions and growing political support for ESC research, President Bush vetoed a bill passed by both the House and Senate in July of 2006 that would have allowed funding for ESC research to create new stem cell lines from additional embryos. According to President Bush, such a bill "would support the taking of innocent human life in the hope of finding medical benefit for others. . . . It crosses a moral boundary that our decent society needs to respect."[18] President Bush's stem cell decision was not limited to the issue of federal funding for ESC research; he also dedicated $250,000,000 in federal funds to go toward ASC research and created the President's Council on Bioethics to provide guidance on public policy matters related to stem cell research and many other ethical issues in health care and the life sciences.

While the Bush Administration's approach to the question of federal funding for ESC research actually expanded the scope of research for which federal funds could be used, it did not go as far in permitting the use of federal funds for ESC research as the original NIH guidelines proposed under the Clinton Administration. In the end, President Bush's approach constitutes a compromise position on the question of federal funding for research that involves the destruction of human embryos as well as the primary ethical considerations underlying the competing ethical views.

## Discussion: Ethical Issues and Analysis

The first thing to note about the ethical issues raised by stem cell research is that ASC research is not as controversial as ESC research. While there are ethical issues related to ASC research, these issues are very much the same as the ethical issues raised by any other type of research involving human subjects. ESC research is clearly more controversial because obtaining the ESC entails the destruction of human embryos. As the political debate illustrates, there are three main ethical questions raised by ESC research, in addition to the medical and scientific questions about ease and effectiveness:

1. Is a 4–5 day old embryo deserving of moral respect and protection?
2. If unwanted embryos in fertility clinics are going to be destroyed anyway, why not harvest their stem cells first and reap the potential benefits?
3. If we don't use these embryos for research, how do we respond to those patients, now suffering from diseases, who might have benefited from such research?

### The Moral Status of the Pre-Implantation Embryo

As we saw in chapter 5 on issues related to maternal-fetal care, there are competing views regarding the moral status of prenatal human life.

According to one view, consistent with our normative basis, human life has an inherent human dignity and is deserving of the moral respect owed to all human beings from the moment it comes into existence. At the other end of the spectrum is what can be termed the non-personal view, which holds that the fetus is not deserving of the same respect and protection as other members of the moral community. Also recall that this view is based on the fact that early human life is not yet capable of functioning in ways characteristically associated with being a person; it is not capable of making free choices, communicating, planning for the future, or participating in social life, nor does it share other characteristics commonly associated with fully conscious, autonomous, and rational individuals. As the previous discussions of this chapter illustrate, this view also holds with regard to the pre-implantation embryo. In this context, however, a third view emerges.

In contrast to the personal and non-personal positions, there is the pre-personal position.[19] According to this view, the embryo is deserving of the respect and protection due to other human beings at a stage of development long before it has developed the capability to function in ways commonly associated with fully functional, autonomous individuals. However, according to this view, the embryo is not in fact due such respect and protection from the moment it comes into existence. Rather, the human embryo is deserving of respect and protection only once it reaches the biological point of development in which twinning is no longer possible (i.e., once the embryo has implanted in the uterus and there is no chance that it would separate into two identical but distinct embryos). Accordingly, being a unique individual member of the human species rather than being a person is the factor that determines who is deserving of moral respect and protection by the community.

The morally relevant consideration here is that individual members of the human species have an innate and ordained natural end to which all human life is inherently and developmentally oriented, and thus have a right not to be subjected to interference in their biological and personal development toward this end. However, because a certain biological stability oriented toward that fulfillment is not present until the point of development at which twinning is no longer possible, pre-implantation embryos would not be included as full members of the moral community. Hence this position can be called "pre-personal" regarding pre-implantation embryos, which—though human—cannot be said to be unique individual human lives.

The pre-personal position is much less arbitrary than the non-personal position insofar as it grounds moral worth in being a member of the human species rather than being a "person." This view is less arbitrary in the sense that being a living member of the human species is a matter of biological fact, whereas "personhood" is an elusive and variable philosophical category. However, the pre-personal position can still be criticized for overemphasizing the moral relevance of individuality. The fact that twinning is still a possibility at a very early stage of development does not necessarily mean that the pre-implantation embryo is not an individual human being. When twinning does occur, it is invariably preceded by the biological development of a single organism. Thus, "the fact that a group of cells is able after separation to develop independently into a second individuated organism in no way refutes the prior existence of an individual organism, but confirms it."[20] The pre-personal position can also be criticized for being arbitrary in a different way than the non-personal position. In particular, if human life, rather than personhood, is the basis for membership in the moral community, then what basis is there for granting this moral status only to *individual* human lives? In the end, the primary difference between the pre-personal and non-personal views is that the pre-personal position associates moral status with "individuality" rather than with "personhood." Both views still preclude, however, certain members of the human species, namely, pre-implantation embryos, as being deserving of moral respect and protection.

**Responding to the Questions of ESC Research.** According to the view of the human person at work in our normative basis, we as rational beings created in the image and likeness of God have both the capability and responsibility to participate in God's ongoing act of creation. In other words, we have a moral responsibility to use our intelligence and freedom to help create a human community in which the basic human needs of individuals are met and flourishing is made a real possibility. From this perspective, stem cell research in general is not necessarily ruled out or forbidden as "playing God." Indeed, stem cell research can be a valuable tool for helping people to pursue human flourishinge, if the associated ethical issues can be resolved. Rather than an outright rejection, our normative basis provides a framework for responding to the ethical questions raised by stem cell research, both adult and embryonic, and for placing limits on stem cell research in general.

Clearly, one limit that arises from the personal view of the moral status of the pre-implantation human embryo is the moral rejection of ESC research. This limit would apply to all forms of ESC research, whether using embryos left over from infertility treatments or those that are the direct result of "therapeutic" human cloning. The source of the embryo is not the problem. From the perspective of our normative basis the problem is that systematic, socially sanctioned destruction of one category of human life is the basis for medical treatments to save other human lives. This is morally inconsistent with the concepts of the sanctity of life, solidarity, right relationships, and human flourishing in community. These concepts also give rise to other limits on stem cell research related specifically to the goals of medicine.

From our perspective, the value of medicine is achieved when it helps people function better as human beings and more closely achieve human flourishing. Simply stated, medicine should serve the good of human life and of the human person; neither human life nor the human person should be used in the service of medicine, that is, for the advancement of medicine. Giving priority to the goals of medicine over the good of a human life suggests that society has its priorities backwards. While the advancement of medical technology and the discovery of new cures for devastating diseases are in themselves noble goals, they should be supported only to the extent that they are truly done in service to the goals of human life. We as a society must not allow medical research and science in general to be driven by other factors—such as political or economic interests—that potentially lead to the devaluation, commercialization, or instrumentalization of human life.

While a great good in and of itself, the finding of new ways to cure devastating diseases is not the only way that medicine can serve right relationships and human flourishing. Even when a cure is not possible, other appropriate goals of medicine include preventing illness and finding other ways of alleviating the suffering that is an inevitable result of our being part of the created world. For example, pain management, spiritual care, and emotionally comforting those who suffer are reasonable goals of medicine, when we acknowledge the dignity of the spiritual, social, and emotional dimensions of the human person in addition to the physical and material dimension. Indeed, these goals are not only appropriate, they are ways that medicine can help to make the sick or dying person more whole and thereby foster right relationships and human flourishing even in the face of human frailty. Focusing our energies and resources on overcoming the inevitable reality of death, an impossible task, will likely lead us to overlook other opportunities to alleviate suffering—ways that promote the value of human life rather than devalue it.

To be sure, this line of reasoning goes against the grain of the prevailing consequentialist view in our society that the potential cure of millions of people suffering from devastating diseases justifies the use of early human life for the purpose of ESC research. The consequentialist justification of ESC research is not only put forth by politicians and medical scientists, as we discussed previously, but it is also espoused by some medical ethicists. Art Caplan and Glenn McGee have argued in favor of ESC research:

> It is the moral imperative of compassion that compels stem cell research. The stem cell research consortium Patient's Coalition for Urgent Research estimates that as many as 128 million Americans suffer from diseases that might respond to pluripotent stem cell therapies. . . . More than half of the world's population will suffer at some point in life with one of these three conditions [cancer, heart disease, Parkinson's disease], and more humans die every year from cancer than were killed in both the Kosovo and Vietnam conflicts. Stem cell research is a pursuit of known and important goods. . . . [There] is no need more obvious or compelling than the suffering of half the world at the hand of miserable disease.[21]

Though our normative basis would not lead us to share in this conclusion, the argument raises an important question that needs to be addressed, namely, how should we reply to the accusation that we are failing to respond to the needs of those who suffer from diseases that potentially could be cured through ESC research? Gilbert Meilander, a Protestant theologian who also rejects the consequentialist justification of ESC research, provides us with a starting point for responding:

> Only by supposing, as modernity has taught us, that suffering has no point other than to be overcome by human will and technical mastery—that compassion means not readiness to suffer with others but a determination always to oppose suffering as an affront to our humanity. We could have helped you only by destroying in the present the sort of world in which both we and you want to live—a world in which justice is done now, not permanently mortgaged in service of future good. Only in short, pretending to be something other than the human beings we are.[22]

In his own way, Meilander has articulated one of the sentiments at the very heart of our normative basis regarding right relationships, the social virtues, and the principles of justice, including solidarity, relationality, and the common good.

## Practical Implications

Consider again the cases with which we opened this chapter. Given the normative foundations we have laid out, how should we evaluate the case of Adam and Molly Nash. Is it understandable that her parents wanted to save Molly's life? Yes, of course. Did they feel incredible pressure to do so? Obviously. Would you or I do the same as they did? Maybe. It is impossible to know for sure until one is actually in such a situation. Can we say, though, that what they did should be considered a model for how we as a society and our medical community should respond in all similar cases? Working from our normative basis, we would have to say, "No." While one irreplaceable and invaluable life was saved and another brought into being, this state of affairs was made possible only by using other human lives as a means to that end. While some great good did come from this, devaluing and destroying some human lives in favor of other human lives undermines the value of the good being sought and would not be consistent with our understanding of right relationships characterized by love of neighbor, as we have described it.

Consider also the case discussed in which a cure for Alzheimer's disease is created, but the therapy entails destroying a cloned human embryo every time it is used. If this in fact were to happen, it is conceivable that the supply of "spare" embryos from the cryopreservation tanks of fertility clinics would be quickly exhausted, while the demand for embryos would inevitably increase.[23] In this scenario, large numbers of human reproductive eggs (ova) would be required to generate the cloned embryos for the therapy. This could then lead to a situation in which women could sell their eggs to pharmaceutical companies. This has already begun to occur in regard to the supply of embryos for research purposes.[24] Such commercialization of human ova could involve the exploitation of women who are economically vulnerable. Moreover, if treatments should be discovered for some diseases using stem cells from cloned 4–5 day old embryos, would society be able to resist using the cells, tissues, and even organs from more developed clones, perhaps at the fetal stage of development, to cure other devastating diseases? Admittedly, "slippery slope" arguments (i.e., if one type of behavior is allowed, then others will be more likely to occur) rely less on logic and more on emotions evoked by hypothetical possibilities, but the use of human embryos in the service of other people's interests or, worse, in the service of political and economic interests would seem to have serious potential consequences for the moral attitudes of society toward human life.

While these are concerns of what may come to pass, there are more current concerns for anyone who rejects the moral permissibility of ESC research and human cloning. For example, faith-based organizations, such as Catholic hospitals, must already address concerns regarding ESC research. Clearly, Catholic hospitals should not permit ESC research in their facilities, given the Catholic Church's teaching on the sanctity of human life. But there are other questions. To what extent should an individual who objects to the killing of innocent human life cooperate with organizations that might be funding ESC research or engaging in it directly? Many such organizations exist primarily to eradicate certain forms of cancer or childhood diseases—causes that ethical people should and do promote. Should individuals who reject the moral permissibility of ESC research donate money to such organizations if they fund or engage in ESC research? In terms of our normative basis, we would put the question this way: are relationships that encourage and facilitate the destruction of human life, even in the service of other human life, right relationships?

What if therapeutic treatments like those in these cases become the standard of care? Would it be morally justifiable to use treatments that make use of stem cell lines created from embryos but don't entail the destruction of more embryos (essentially the position of President Bush)? Within our normative framework, it is clear that a preferred alternative that upholds the dignity and sanctity of human life and fosters right relationships at a societal level would be to seek alternatives that don't entail destruction of early human life.

According to our normative basis, ASC research and the therapies derived from it, such as the one discussed in *Case 11B*, are a morally acceptable alternative to ESC research and human cloning. However, ASCs should not be blindly encouraged and recklessly funded. Fostering right relationships at the societal level requires paying attention to all dimensions of the common good. Understood in this light, ASC research does raise ethical questions, though these questions are more akin to those attached to any medical research rather than to ESC research. All medical research raises questions regarding how much of society's resources, how much of the common good, should be dedicated to the search for new therapies. In other words, how much suffering could we relieve by dedicating some of the funds that advocates want to see put toward stem cell research, if those funds were to be used to provide basic preventative care to a portion of the 40,000,000 Americans who lack health insurance?

Though relevant to all medical research, this question becomes even more pressing given the huge amounts of money and all the attention that stem cell research draws.[25] In keeping with the normative basis we have outlined, along with the principle of solidarity, we must ask whether our first concern should be how we will reply to those who in the future might be helped by a therapy that doesn't yet exist, or should it be the meeting of real needs of millions of people who suffer and die today from fully preventable and treatable diseases. We must also ask whether we would be fostering right relationships by creating unfettered access to any form of stem cell research and dedicating large amounts of societal resources to fund it, or by dedicating those funds to those whom we know can be served by such resources.

## Conclusion

From our perspective the moral questions surrounding ESC research and human cloning are rooted not only in a concern for embryonic human life, but in considerations of what kind of society we would become by providing unfettered access, encouragement, and funding for scientific and medical research that entails the destruction of early human life. From this perspective, the debate about the personhood of pre-implantation embryos as the basis for the moral status of ESC research can be considered misplaced. Regardless of whether one is willing to give personal moral status to individual embryos, treating even early embryonic human life as merely an instrument for the benefit of others ultimately leads to its commercialization, to a further eroding respect for life, and to the narrow edge of a slippery slope. Once we go down this slippery slope, will we as a society be able to recognize any limits to the goals of medicine, or will we let the pursuit of new medical technology and cures undermine the value of the very lives it is intended to help?

In the end, we must ask what kind of a society we want to become in and through our collective actions. Are we content to let millions of our fellow community members suffer needlessly from illnesses that are fully preventable, while we search for cures for others? Or do we want to become a society that fosters and exhibits genuine human love for all our neighbors so that we and they can achieve human well-being and human flourishing? Even if we agree to the latter we still must find a way to balance the need to respect all human life, including those yet to be born, with the need to improve the lives of those now in community with us. Though it does not provide any easy answers to this question, our normative basis appropriately reframes the ethical questions regarding ESC research and human cloning in light of promoting right relationships and the social virtues that lead to individual and communal human flourishing.

## Additional Case Studies

**Case 10D:** Having had a sibling with juvenile diabetes, you have been a long time supporter of the Regional Juvenile Diabetes Fund. Even as a young adult, you always donated what you could to the charity in hopes of them one day finding a cure. Now that you have amassed a modest personal fortune through your long career as an innovative CEO for one of the country's largest health systems, you have been giving substantial donations on an annual basis. You have recently learned, however, that the Regional Juvenile

Diabetes Fund funds embryonic stem cell research. You discuss this with a friend and colleague who also considers herself to be pro-life. She says that she donates anyway because the research is going to continue whether she donates or not, and the embryos they are using for the research are destined to be destroyed regardless.

**Discussion Questions.** Would you continue to donate to the Regional Juvenile Diabetes Fund? Why or why not? Would you donate if you could specify that your donation not be used for embryonic stem cell research? Are you persuaded by the argument that embryonic stem cell research is not ethically problematic because the embryos are just going to be destroyed anyway?

**Case 10E:** Your state has recently added a constitutional amendment to the ballot for the upcoming election. If it passes, this amendment would give scientists a constitutional right to engage in human embryonic stem cell research in your state. While the proposed amendment also claims to ban "human cloning," it specifically defines human cloning as implanting an embryo resulting from somatic cell nuclear transfer in the uterus of a woman with the intent of bringing about a live birth. In effect, the amendment would also make it a constitutional right to conduct somatic cell nuclear transfer for the purpose of creating stem cells for research. There are further provisions in the proposed amendment that would allow women to be "fairly reimbursed" for any time and burdens involved in the process of donating their eggs to science.

**Discussion Questions.** Would you support this proposed legislative amendment in its current form? Would you support such a bill with some revisions? Why? What revisions would you like to see?

## Suggested Readings

Branick, Vincent, and Therese M. Lysaught. "Stem Cell Research: Licit or Complicit? Is a Medical Breakthrough Based on Embryonic and Fetal Tissue Compatible with Catholic Teaching?" *Health Progress* 80, no. 5 (Sep.–Oct. 1999): 37–42.

Brock, Dan W. "Is a Consensus Possible on Stem Cell Research? Moral and Political Obstacles." *Journal of Medical Ethics* 32 (2006): 36–42.

Fabbro, Ronald. "Stem Cell Research, Cloning and Catholic Moral Theology." *Linacre Quarterly* 72 (2005): 294–306.

Hall, Stephen S. "Stem Cells: A Status Report." *Hastings Center Report* 36, no. 1 (2006): 16–22.

Kavanaugh, John F. "Cloning, by Whatever Name, Smells Bad." *America* 194, no. 21 (June 19, 2006): 6.

## Multimedia Aids for Teachers

*Miracle Cell.* Films for the Humanities and Sciences. 2004. This 60-minute video depicts several patients who undergo therapies derived from adult stem cells. It is available in DVD or VHS. For information see http://www.films.com/id/6674/Miracle_Cell.htm.

*Stem Cell Research: Frontier of Hope and Concern.* DIA Productions. For information see http://fac.ethicsprograms.com/. This 30-minute video can be purchased separately or in a group with other videos on select issues in health care ethics.

National Institutes of Health. "Stem Cell Information: The Official National Institutes of Health Resource for Stem Cell Research." http://stemcells.nih.gov/. This Web site contains a variety of resources regarding the science and politics of embryonic and adult stem cell research.

## Endnotes

1 Milton Wainwright, Miracle Cure: *The Story of Penicillin and the Golden Age of Antibiotics* (Oxford: Basil Blackwell, 1990).

2 See James A. Thomson, Joseph Itskovitz-Eldor, Sander S. Shapiro, et al., "Embryonic Stem Cell Lines Derived from Human Blastocysts," *Science* 282 (1998): 1145–47; Michael J. Schamblott, Joyce Axelman, Shunping Wang, et al., "Derivation of Pluripotent Stem Cells from Cultured Human Primordial Germ Cells," *Proceedings of the National Academy of Sciences* 95 (1998): 13726–31.

3 Adapted from G. Magill, "Science, Ethics, and Policy: Relating Human Genomics to Embryonic Stem-Cell Research and Therapeutic Cloning," in *Genetics and Ethics: An Interdisciplinary Study,* ed. Gerard Magill (St. Louis: St. Louis University Press, 2004), 253–83, at 254–55.

[4] Alessandro Auiti, Shimon Slavin, Memet Aker, et al., "Correction of ADA-SCID by Stem Cell Gene Therapy Combined with Nonmyeloablative Conditioning," *Science* 296 (2002): 2410–13.

[5] Regarding the science of stem cells, see National Institutes of Health, "Stem Cells: Scientific Progress and Future Research Directions," (2001), http://stemcells.nih.gov/info/scireport/ (accessed August 10, 2006).

[6] Anonymous, "400,000 Embryos and Counting," *New York Times* (May 15, 2003); R. Weiss, "400,000 Human Embryos Frozen in U.S. Number at Fertility Clinics Is Far Greater than Previous Estimates, Survey Finds," *Washington Post* (May 8, 2003). Regarding the scientific utility of these embryos and its limitations, see "The Myth of 400,000 Embryos," http://www.stemcellresearch.org/polisci/lesson04.pdf (accessed February 22, 2007).

[7] See: http://stemcells.nih.gov/info/basics/basics4.asp (accessed February 22, 2007).

[8] For a list of the different therapeutic uses of ASCs, see: http://www.stemcellresearch.org/facts/treatments.htm (accessed February 22, 2007).

[9] Martin F. Pera and Alan O. Trounson, "Human Embryonic Stem Cells: Prospects for Development," *Development* 131 (2004): 5515–25.

[10] See, for example, Malcolm Alison, Richard Poulsom, Rosemary Jeffery, et al., "Cell Differentiation: Hepatocytes from Non-Hepatic Adult Stem Cells," *Nature* 418 (2002): 41–49.

[11] Wilmut Ian, A. E. Schnieke, J. McWhir, et al., "Viable Offspring Derived from Fetal and Adult Mammalian Cells," *Nature* 385 (1997): 810–13.

[12] According to researchers at the Roslin Institute where Dolly was cloned, however, the cloning of one human being for reproductive purposes could require, given existing technology, the use of 1000 oocytes (eggs) and 20 to 50 surrogate mothers. See, Arlene Judith Klotzko, "Voices from Roslin: The Creators of Dolly Discuss Science, Ethics and Social Responsibility," *Cambridge Quarterly of Healthcare Ethics* 7 (1998): 121–40.

[13] For a chart of state laws regarding therapeutic and reproductive cloning, see the National Conference of State Legislators Web site at http://www.ncsl.org/programs/health/Genetics/rt-shcl.htm (accessed August 8, 2006).

[14] *The President's Council on Bioethics, Human Cloning and Human Dignity: An Ethical Inquiry,* Washington, DC: Government Printing Office, 2002, p. 205

[15] Transcripts from the *Jim Lehrer News Hour* on PBS, July 10, 2001, http://www.pbs.org/newshour/bb/health/july-dec01/stem_cells_7-10.html (accessed August 8, 2006).

[16] Anonymous, "Stem Cell Politics," *Religion and Ethics News Weekly*, July 6, 2001, http://www.pbs.org/wnet/religionandethics/week445/news.html (accessed August 10, 2006).

[17] David Korn, "The NIH Guidelines on Stem Cell Research," *Science* 289 (2000): 1877.

[18] Charles Bagington, "Stem Cell Bill Gets Bush's First Veto," *Washington Post*, July 21, 2006, A4.

[19] See, Michael R. Panicola, "Three Views on the Preimplantation Embryo," *National Catholic Bioethics Quarterly* 2 (Spring 2002): 69–97, at 77–82.

[20] Benedict M. Ashley and Kevin D. O'Rourke, *Health Care Ethics: A Theological Analysi,* 4th ed. (Washington, DC: Georgetown University Press, 1997), 234.

[21] G. McGee and A. Caplan, "The Ethics and Politics of Small Sacrifices in Stem Cell Research," *Kennedy of Ethics Institute Journal* 9 (1999): 151–58.

[22] G. Meilander, "The Point of a Ban: or, How to Think about Stem Cell Research," *The Hastings Center Report* 31 (2001): 9–16.

[23] Regarding the following argument see John Paul Slosar, "Genomics and Neurology: An Ethical View," *Health Progress* 81, no. 1 (Jan.-Feb. 2006): 68–72.

[24] Ethics Committee of the American Society for Reproductive Medicine, "Financial Incentives in Recruitment of Oocyte Donors," *Fertility and Sterility* 82 (2004 Suppl.): S240–44.

[25] Regarding adult stem cell research and the common good see, Lisa Sowle Cahill, "Stem Cells: A Bioethical Balancing Act," *America* 184, no. 10 (2001): 14–19.

# CHAPTER 11

# Genomics and Genetic Testing

In 1988 Congress appropriated funds for the Department of Energy and the National Institutes of Health to begin planning the Human Genome Project (HGP), which was to begin in earnest in 1990 to detail the complete set of genetic instructions of the human being. Estimated cost was $3,000,000,000 with a timetable of 15 years; the actual cost was $2,700,000,000 over 12.5 years.[1] The public imagination was captured immediately. The project was dubbed "the search for the holy grail of biology," "a quest for humanity's blueprint," and the uncovering of the "Book of Life."[2] Despite the hype surrounding this event, scientists were united in their goal toward a common good: to understand the genetic contribution to human disease and the eventual eradication of those genetic anomalies. This represented potentially the first attempt in the history of medicine truly to cure people by changing the genetic codes that underlay their diseases.[3]

Amid this fervor for scientific truth about our genetic basis were fears of what might be discovered, the ends to which such discoveries might lead, and the magnitude of the project itself.[4] The HGP was the largest genomics project attempted to date. Critical questions were raised as to whether we could develop the technology required to perform the task, whether the cost of the technology was justified, and what other research would need to be sacrificed as a result of taking on this huge endeavor. Further questions faced society in light of this venture: Would this project settle the nature/nurture debate (i.e., are we predominantly the product of our genes or our environment)? Is one's right to privacy violated if one's genetic code is made public? What about discrimination against those who may have an "inferior" genetic makeup or may be more prone to particular diseases? Questions such as these fed Frankensteinian notions of what might come of the knowledge gleaned from the HGP.[5] In response to these and other questions, the HGP devoted 5% of its overall budget for the purpose of studying the ethical, legal, and social implications of the research, known as ELSI. This amounted to roughly $150,000,000. Unprecedented at the time, ELSI projects and grants helped to shape public policy to deal with ethical and legal issues raised by the research, sometimes in advance of the science.[6]

The scientific publication of the completion of the HGP in April 2003, nearly 50 years to the month after the publication of James Watson and Francis Crick's report of the double helix structure of DNA, marked far more than just the completion of the mapping and sequencing of the human genome. The implication was that medicine would now be able to understand the genetic basis of illness and disease and that the information would revolutionize clinical care. Former president Bill Clinton was so swept up with the accomplishment that at a public speaking engagement announcing the completion of the HGP, he remarked,

> Today we are learning the language in which God created life. We are gaining ever more awe for the complexity, the beauty, and the wonder of God's most divine and sacred gift. With this profound new knowledge, humankind is on the verge of gaining immense new power to heal.

While the full promise of the HGP has yet to be realized, the information has furthered our knowledge about genetics in general and genetic disease in particular. We now know that humans have approximately 25,000 genes—as opposed to 100,000, as was once thought—which means that we have only twice as many as a roundworm, three times as many as a fruit fly, and six times as many as baker's yeast. We also know that 99.9% of all genes in the human genome are the same regardless of ethnicity, sex, and other variables. Information obtained from the HGP has allowed us to identify hundreds of genes located on specific chromosomes responsible for numerous diseases. Below is a list of some of the more noteworthy discoveries.

- *Colon cancer.* A marker was found on chromosome 2 that acts to correct minor errors in cellular DNA. If the gene mutates, however, it apparently triggers a cascade of mutations that result in the familial form of colon cancer. The gene is present in 1 out of 200 people; of those with the gene, 65% are likely to develop cancer. The familial form is responsible for roughly 15% of all colon tumors.

- *Amyotrophic lateral sclerosis.* The familial form of ALS results from a mutation on chromosome 21. This chromosome in its un-mutated form plays a role in eliminating free radicals—if not controlled, free radicals are thought to lead to muscle degeneration. The familial form accounts for 10% of all cases.

- *Type II (adult onset) diabetes.* A more complex process, this disease is felt to have a genetic basis in chromosome 7, which codes for an enzyme critical for the pancreas to produce insulin.

- *Late onset Alzheimer's disease.* The gene ApoE on chromosome 19 codes for a protein that transports cholesterol. A person who has both alleles for the protein E4 has eight times the risk of developing late onset Alzheimer's; with one allele, a person has two to three times the risk.

- *X-linked SCID.* Severe combined immunodeficiency disease is caused by a mutation in a gene passed from mothers to sons on the X chromosome. The normal gene functions to create a protein that is essential to keep T-cells of the immune system functioning. Newborns with a mutated gene have few or no T-cells. Even a mild infection is life-threatening for these newborns.

The list continues to expand as science learns more about disease-causing mutations.[7]

The discovery of a disease-causing mutation often leads to the development of a test for that mutation. Although this research continues at an astounding pace, the concept of a genetic disease is not as straightforward as it may seem. First, it is not the case that a person who carries a certain allele linked to a disease-causing mutation will necessarily develop the disease. This reflects the degree of penetrance of the specific allele. About 75% of women with certain mutations in the BRCA1 gene, for example, develop breast or ovarian cancer. The penetrance of those mutations therefore is 75%.[8] Or it may be that a person is merely rendered more susceptible to a particular disease by the presence of one or more gene mutations and/or a combination of alleles, not necessarily abnormal, associated with the disease (i.e., genetic predisposition).[9]

A number of questions must be raised with regard to the values and dangers of genetic testing because in many cases we do not know how genes function in the body and cause disease, or how genes interact with other important factors such as the environment and behavioral or lifestyle choices, or how proteins function in a given cell, or how proteins interact with other proteins. Yet, advances in genomic medicine continue to (1) individualize preventative care based on the predicted risk of a disease as assessed from one's own genome, (2) develop gene-based therapies to repair individual genomes by replacing defective genes with healthy ones, (3) provide drugs that are more compatible with a person's genome as well as develop new drugs targeted to counteract specific disease-causing mutations, and (4) build organs in cell cultures to replace "worn-out" or "diseased" ones.[10]

## Setting the Context: Genes and Genomics

In order to understand the basis of genetic testing or testing for a genetic disorder, we begin by focusing on the relationship between genetics and disease as currently understood. Our bodies consist of about 100,000,000,000 cells, all of which, except mature red blood cells, contain a complete copy of our genetic code. This genetic code is packaged in chromosomes in the nucleus (or "control center") of every cell. The chromosomes are made up of strands of the chemical deoxyribonucleic acid or DNA. Genes are specific clusters of DNA that are located on the chromosomes. A small number of genes are also contained in tiny packages in the cell called mitochondria (the "power house" of the cell). The entire DNA in the cell makes up the human genome.[11]

There are 46 chromosomes in our body (or *somatic*) cells—23 from mom and 23 from dad. At the completion of fertilization, the egg and sperm come together to form the single-cell zygote, which has 46 chromosomes, made up of 23 pairs, and contains all the genetic material needed for further development. Scientists have numbered the chromosomes from the largest (c. #1) to the smallest (c. #22); these are called the *autosomes*. There are also two chromosomes that have been given the letters X and Y; these are the sex chromosomes. In their somatic cells, a female has 44 autosomes and 2 X sex chromosomes, while a male has 44 autosomes, 1 X sex chromosome, and one Y sex chromosomes. In their germ cells, females have 22 autosomes and an X chromosome and males have 22 autosomes and an X or Y chromosome. Chromosomes consist of strands of DNA that twist and coil up like a ball of string. Each bead of DNA is a gene which has a specific location on the chromosome. They come in pairs, with the exception of the genes on the sex chromosomes. Thousands of genes make up each chromosome (though this varies among sex chromosomes).

Each gene is a different packet of information that has a particular job in terms of directing how our bodies develop and work as well as how we look. The information in the genes is in the form of a chemical (DNA) code, often referred to as the genetic code. Genes issue instructions to the cells by these chemically coded "messages." This is why the DNA that makes up the genes is often called "coding DNA," whereas the DNA string between the beads of genes is called "non-coding DNA" as it does not contain messages that the cells use. Interestingly, genes comprise only 2% of the human genome; the remainder consists of non-coding DNA.

There are four basic "building blocks" (nucleotide bases) that make up DNA: Adenine (A), Guanine (G), Thymine (T), and Cytosine (C). DNA is made up of very long chains of these bases. The bases pair up to form the rungs of a ladder twisted into the now famous double helix structure. The pairing of the bases follows strict rules: A with T, and G with C. The DNA message is in fact made up of three-letter words composed of combinations of these letters A, G, T, and C. A gene can therefore be thought of as a coded message that the body understands. There may be hundreds or even thousands of letters in each gene message; a significant aspect of the HGP is that it has figured out the sequence of these letters.

The DNA message in the genes tells the cell to produce particular proteins, which are large, complex molecules made up of smaller subunits called amino acids. The sequence of three-letter words in the gene enables the cells to assemble the amino acids in the correct order to make up the protein. Although genes get a lot of attention, the proteins perform most life functions and even make up the majority of cellular structures. When a cell needs to make a particular protein, the DNA making up the gene unwinds and the message is "transcribed" into another chemical called messenger RNA or mRNA. The mRNA takes the coded genetic information to the units in the cell where it can be "translated" into a chain of amino acids. Some of the proteins form building blocks for structures within the cells, such as the protein called keratin, from which hair is made. Others, called enzymes, help carry out chemical reactions, such as digesting food. Still others form communication networks between cells. Each gene message can be "read" by the cell in a number of different ways so that each gene can provide a message to make 2 or 3 different proteins, which is the reason why we have more proteins than genes in our bodies.

The body has many different types of cells (e.g., skin, muscle, liver, and brain), all of which contain the same genes. However, not all genes are active in every cell because only certain genes are required for the cell to function correctly. Therefore, different genes are active in different cell types, tissues, and organs, producing the necessary specific proteins for proper cellular function. Sometimes genes can be altered or have mutations causing a change in the message sent from the gene to the cell and thus affecting protein production. Most of the time genetic mutations do not cause any problems or manifest as a genetic disorder. In fact, everyone is born with several gene mutations and sometimes these can even be beneficial because they allow us to adapt to our environment (e.g., faulty hemoglobin gene and malaria).[12] However, genetic mutations can be harmful in at least three different ways: (1) mutations can lead to a genetic disorder; (2) mutations can make us a carrier of a disorder, which we can pass on to our offspring; or (3) mutations can predispose us, thereby increasing our risk of being affected by a specific genetic disorder.

Geneticists group genetic disorders into three general categories: single gene disorders (disorders caused by a mutation in a single gene), multifactorial disorders (disorders caused by a combination of small variations in genes, often in concert with environmental factors such as diet, chemical exposure, and lifestyle choices), and chromosome disorders (disorders caused by structural changes in the chromosomes or the gain or loss of whole chromosomes during either the formation of the egg or sperm or during the process of fertilization).

Scientists believe that mutations in single genes cause about 4000 different severe genetic disorders that affect millions of people worldwide. Many single gene disorders follow Mendelian inheritance patterns, though not all (e.g., "mitochondrial inheritance" and "genetic imprinting"). The inheritance pattern depends on whether the mutant gene is on one of the autosomes or on the X chromosome; it also depends on whether the mutation is recessive or dominant. Thus inherited mutations that lead to single gene disorders are categorized as: autosomal recessive (inheritance of a recessive mutant gene that is carried on an autosome); autosomal dominant (inheritance of a dominant mutant gene that is carried on an autosome); and X-linked (inheritance of either a recessive or dominant mutant gene that is carried on the X chromosome).

As seems to be the norm in other fields of medicine, new discoveries are coupled with new understandings. Beyond the above-mentioned inheritance patterns are the matters of mitochondrial inheritance, imprinting (a biochemical phenomenon that determines which pair of alleles will be active in that individual), and anticipation (the phenomenon of certain genetic disorders being present earlier in successive generations with more severe manifestations). It is beyond the scope of this chapter to delve into all the inheritance patterns as they relate to disease-causing mutations. For further information we direct to you to the National Institutes of Health Web site related to the Human Genome Project at http://www.genome.gov. In order to appreciate the way in which medical genetics can serve a variety of ends, we now turn toward a more cautionary tale of eugenics. Here we begin to see how varying world-views can attempt to justify the use of genetic/scientific research to serve a variety of ends. This backdrop will help to demonstrate the strength of our normative base, which does not separate ends from means (see chapter 4).

## A Cautionary Tale: Promising Science Gone Bad

It is important to note that genetics did not start with the HGP. Questions concerning how traits are inherited or handed down from one generation to the next go back to the beginnings of human history. It wasn't until 1865 that an Augustinian monk named Gregor Mendel, working with pea plants, found that individual traits are determined by "discrete factors," later known as genes, which are inherited from parents. By analyzing purebred and hybrid pea plants, Mendel also found that each trait (e.g., seed color) has two alternative forms (e.g., yellow or green) and that each alternative form of a trait is expressed by alternative forms of a gene. Although Mendel's work was done on pea plants, the knowledge gained was shortly thereafter applied to humans. The study of family pedigrees affected by disorders provided many of the first examples of mendelian inheritance in humans.

## The Slippery Slope to Eugenics

Mendel's ideas not only led to new knowledge about inherited diseases but also spawned the eugenics movement. Francis Galton (1865), a major proponent of eugenics, hypothesized that the human race could be bettered if we multiplied desirable traits and minimized undesirable ones. Positive eugenics (the promoting of desirable traits through reproductive choices) gave way gradually in the early 1900s to negative eugenics (the "breeding out" of undesirable traits by preventing reproduction, either voluntarily or otherwise).[13]

The idea of negative eugenics was accepted in the United States and other "developed" countries and was endorsed by prominent scientists who thought it could eliminate the "feebleminded" (a blanket term used in the early 1900s to describe the mentally ill, the mentally retarded, the slow learners, the ignorant, and the degenerate of all sorts).[14] The idea was to provide no support to the feebleminded and not to allow them "to propagate their unfit kind" by forcing sterilization; there were also attempts to limit the immigration of "inferior races."[15] Several states adopted laws authorizing compulsory sterilization of the feebleminded but were checked by constitutional challenges, except for a Virginia statute upheld by the U.S. Supreme Court in the notorious case of *Buck v. Bell* (1927).

The case of *Buck v. Bell* involved Carrie Buck, an 18-year-old mentally retarded woman who resided at the Virginia State Colony for Epileptics and Feebleminded. In 1924, just months after Virginia adopted a statute allowing for the compulsory sterilization of the feebleminded for negative eugenics purposes, the superintendent of the institution sought to have Carrie sterilized because she represented a "genetic threat to society." Carrie was the offspring of a mentally retarded woman. After being raped by her adopted mother's nephew, Carrie had given birth to a baby deemed "feebleminded," which most likely prompted Carrie's institutionalization. After two lower courts upheld the request for the sterilization, the case eventually made its way to the U.S. Supreme Court, which, in an 8-1 decision, ruled that it was in the state's interests to have Carrie sterilized. Writing the majority opinion, Justice Oliver Wendell Holmes, Jr., stated,

> We have seen more than once that the public welfare may call upon the best citizens for their lives. It would be strange if it could not call upon those who already sap the strength of the State for these lesser sacrifices ... in order to prevent our being swamped with incompetence. . . . Three generations of imbeciles is enough.

The ruling reinforced Virginia's compulsory sterilization statute and encouraged other states to write similar statutes. Fortunately, explicit negative eugenics began to fall out of favor in the wake of the horrible consequences of the Nazi quest for racial purity, which led to the deaths of hundreds of thousands of "inferiors." It was further subverted as new knowledge about human nature and disease was gained, leaving scientists to conclude that the eugenics description of human life was too simplistic and ultimately unconvincing. Simple dominant/recessive schemes did not fully explain complex behaviors and mental illness, which we now know involve many genes, nor did they account for environmental effects on human development. Still, it would be a bit too optimistic to presume that the eugenics mindset does not persist to this day in the form of the new quest for the "perfect child" with the "right traits," the "right gender," and so on. Our current techniques may be a bit more sophisticated than compulsory sterilizations and our language may be more politically correct, but reproductive technologies, prenatal and pre-implantation diagnosis, selective abortion, and the like can and have been used for eugenic purposes.

As bias and bigotry were replaced by hard science, new breakthroughs in genetics resulted. It is evident from these great advances that genomics does indeed hold great promise. However, with great promise can come great peril. Genomic medicine could further the divide between the "haves" and the "have nots" within an already unjust health care system. In other words, if diagnoses can lead to prevention through presymptomatic predisposition profiling, for example, only those who can afford such profiling (either personally or through their health care coverage) would be able to access therapies or cures. Knowledge about genomics could lead to genetic reductionism (the idea that the complexity of the human person can be explained solely via genetics). The limits of privacy and confidentiality could be tested as caregivers are confronted with genetic information that has wider implications. Genetic information could be mishandled and used to discriminate for work or insurance purposes.[16] The peril that genomics may pose does not necessarily mean we should turn away from its promise, however. Rather, it means that we have to proceed carefully and govern ethically our newfound power over the human genome. We must not let technological progress outpace ethical reflection. History has shown us what will come of us if we let this happen.[17]

An avenue that exemplifies both the promise and peril of the information gained through the HGP and earlier work in genetics is genetic testing (GT), which is by far the most significant and immediate spin-off of the advances made in genomics. For this reason and because of space limitations, we will focus on genetic testing and associated ethical issues.

## Discussion: Ethical Issues and Analysis

GT is the examination of a person's chromosomes, the protein product of a gene, or DNA. GT is used to predict risks of disease, screen newborns for disease, identify carriers of genetic disease, establish prenatal or clinical diagnoses or prognoses, and direct clinical care. GT can be done using many different biological samples, including blood, amniotic fluid (from which fetal cells are obtained), or individual embryonic cells.

In the past, GT was used to detect or confirm rare genetic disorders that have a specific inheritance pattern. More recently, however, tests have been developed to detect genetic mutations with links to multifactorial disorders (such as breast, ovarian, and colon cancer and cardiovascular disease), the effects of which generally do not appear until later in life. GT has generally been reserved for individuals who have a family history of the disease; in the future, though, GT will probably be offered to individuals without a family history. At present, there are 614 laboratories testing for 1355 diseases.[18]

The following are some specific types of genetic tests:

- Carrier testing and screening

- Prenatal diagnosis

- Pre-implantation diagnosis

- Newborn screening

- Diagnostic testing

- Pre-symptomatic testing

- Predictive testing

## Carrier Testing and Screening

Carrier testing (CT) is done to assess whether an individual carries one copy of an altered gene for an autosomal or X-linked recessive disorder. CT is usually performed on people who have a family history of an inherited condition to determine if they are carriers of the recessive mutated gene involved. CT may be useful in planning pregnancies so individuals can avoid passing on the mutated gene to their offspring.

Carrier screening (CS) refers to genetic testing applied to a whole population or to a defined group who have a greater than average chance of carrying a particular mutated gene due, for example, to their ancestry or ethnic background. Examples of genetic diseases that are linked to ethnic background for which CS may be used include cystic fibrosis (in Caucasians), sickle cell disease (in individuals of African and Mediterranean descent), thalassemia (in Asians and individuals of Mediterranean descent), and Tay-Sachs and canavan disease in Ashkenazi Jews.

**Ethical Issues.** The acquisition of knowledge is not in itself a justification for CT or CS. Yet such technological advances can be extremely beneficial to individuals with a genetic predisposition to a particular disease. For example, those with the gene for xeroderma pigmentosum are extremely sensitive to ultraviolet radiation, and exposure to such radiation is likely to lead to a form of melanoma that is usually incurable. However, avoiding such exposure usually allows one to avoid developing melanoma; knowledge leads to benefit.

Take however, the case of Duchenne muscular dystrophy (DMD) an X-linked recessive disease. Because females have two X chromosomes, a female can be a carrier of a DMD gene mutation but will usually not develop the condition because she has a normal copy of the gene on her second X chromosome. Knowledge of being a carrier for this condition will in no way lead to treatment or cure. In other words, no way of preventing the disease is known, and early diagnosis and intervention makes no difference in the outcome of the disease progression. Some may wish to know whether they are a carrier of the deleterious gene in order to make informed decisions about marriage, childbearing, and lifestyle. Others might prefer blissful ignorance. This raises an ethical question: in cases where treatment or cure cannot change the outcome of the disease progression, should genetic testing be done as a matter of responsibility to future offspring and society? That is, does an individual with a terminal genetic diagnosis have an obligation to undergo testing so as not to reproduce? If so, the deleterious gene would not harm future offspring and the lineage with the genetic anomaly would cease.[19]

The normative basis offered in this work suggests that the question of what constitutes right relationships between parent and child (or potential child) is relevant in a discussion about CT. Specific to the case of DMD and future children, it is important to recognize that a male child would be at significantly greater risk for having DMD than a female child. Thus the question to reproduce or the obligation not to reproduce begs further ethical questions: should one screen embryos positive for the DMD gene mutation and select only those embryos negative for the mutation, or select only females (who may be carriers but would likely not be otherwise affected)? The question of whether one has an obligation not to reproduce also begs the question of obligations to future generations. Certainly our commitment to human flourishing would suggest that where known gene-based disorders would be clearly transmitted to a future generation, one has an obligation to avoid reproduction to the extent that such a disease would arguably impair that person's ability to flourish. However, such an assertion cannot suggest that the person currently living with DMD somehow lacks human dignity or the ability to flourish as a human person. We will address this line of argumentation in the section on prenatal diagnosis.

What if a gene-based disease is identified as specific to an ethnic background, as in the case of sickle cell disease, an inherited autosomal recessive genetic disorder found mainly in people of West African descent and people of Mediterranean origin? The disease affects the ability of hemoglobin in the blood to carry oxygen. In a sickle cell crisis, hemoglobin is distorted and trapped in small blood vessels, which results in severe pain, blood clots, and even stroke or heart attack. In 1972, the U.S. government decided on a national screening program. Unfortunately, there was no accompanying education regarding the disorder. Because in many states African-American schoolchildren, athletes, and military cadets were targeted, leaders of these communities argued that the mandatory screenings were racially motivated and discriminatory. As a result of these state-sponsored screenings, many individuals, including carriers who were quite healthy, faced discrimination in employment and insurance.[20]

Further ethical questions concern informed consent, that is, whether people are forced to undergo such testing or screening or are fully informed of the implications of such testing or screening. Another concern is whether people are given proper education, support, and counseling related to both the test results and possible applications of such knowledge. Other questions concern whether individuals should disclose genetic knowledge to their offspring, and who should decide when and how much the offspring should know. Finally, what might be the impact of this genetic information on the individual's family?

**Prenatal Diagnosis.** Prenatal diagnosis (PD) refers broadly to a number of different techniques and procedures that can be performed during pregnancy to provide information about the health of the fetus. Initial screening tests may indicate whether the fetus has an average, greater than average, or below average risk of being affected by a particular genetic condition or birth defect. When the results of screening show increased risk, pregnant women may be offered other diagnostic tests to confirm whether the fetus is, in fact, affected. PD may also be offered directly to women whose pregnancies are considered high risk because of age, family history, or other factors.[21]

Several different prenatal diagnostic tests can be offered at various stages in pregnancy:

- *Ultrasound:* a noninvasive procedure that can be done at any time in a pregnancy. It uses high frequency sound waves to produce an image of the fetus inside the uterus. Often an ultrasound is used to determine the age of a fetus based on fetal measurements, to monitor fetal growth, to determine why bleeding is occurring, to check the baby's position in the uterus, to detect multiple births, and to evaluate the general development of the fetus. Most recently, however, first trimester ultrasound has also become a practice for detecting Down's syndrome. A significant ethical concern is raised by the use of ultrasound as a screening tool: what if the mother wishes to terminate her pregnancy because the fetus is positive for Down's?[22]

- *Nuchal fold translucency:* an ultrasound performed by a specially trained physician-sonographer at 10 1/2–13 1/2 weeks that measures the thickness of the skin in the back of the baby's neck. If the skin folds are thickened, there is an increased risk of trisomy 21 or 18 and further testing and counseling are recommended.

- *Chorionic villi sampling (CVS):* a test performed at 11–12 weeks to detect specific genetic abnormalities by obtaining cells from the developing placenta (villi) and examining the chromosomes or DNA in the lab. CVS is performed by inserting either a catheter through the vagina and cervix, or a needle through the abdomen into the villi. The risk of miscarriage is about 1%, but the procedure can be done earlier than amniocentesis.

- *Maternal serum marker screening (MMS):* a simple blood test that is offered to pregnant women at 15–18 weeks to screen for neural tube defects (such as spina bifida and anencephaly) and two chromosome disorders (i.e., trisomy 21 and 18). The MMS for the trisomies have a detection rate of 85% and 60% respectively. MMS measures the concentration of proteins (alpha-fetoprotein, unconjugated estriol, human chorionic gonadotropin, and inhibin A) that are made by the fetus during pregnancy and which circulate in the blood of a pregnant woman.

- *Amniocentesis:* a diagnostic test performed at 15–20 weeks in which a fine needle is inserted through the abdomen to allow for the withdrawal of a small amount of amniotic fluid from the sac that holds the developing fetus. The fetal cells found in the amniotic fluid are grown in a cell culture and studied to detect chromosome abnormalities. Specific enzyme or DNA analyses, which may be indicated based on family or medical history, can also be performed on the fetal cells derived from amniotic fluid. The risk of miscarriage is less than 1%.[23]

**Case 11A:** In 1983 a group of Orthodox Jews in New York and Israel initiated a screening program to eliminate diseases transmitted as recessive genes within their community. The group called itself Dor Yeshorim, "the generation of the righteous." A couple familiar with this program is working with Dr. Cowan and decide that they are going to take their chances despite both of them testing as carriers in 1983. Unfortunately, amniocentesis reveals that the fetus is positive for Tay-Sachs.

The couple knew the odds were stacked against them in terms of their fetus testing positive for Tay-Sachs, but they felt that they had a right to try to have genetic offspring. Now they are wondering whether the unfavorable odds might suggest they had an obligation not to attempt to reproduce. They are struggling with feelings that they have knowingly put their child in harm's way. They are knowledgeable about Tay-Sachs, but it is still difficult for them to conceptualize that it is *their* child who has the disease. Finally, they are struggling with their emotional pain, knowing they will be raising a child who will live less than a year and die as a result of this condition.

**Ethical Issues.** A central tenet of genetic testing is the claim that there is no connection between the offering of prenatal diagnosis, the documentation of fetal abnormalities, and the decision of whether to terminate the pregnancy. The assertion is often made that prenatal diagnosis is for the purpose of providing information to couples about what they can expect. Is this a naïve or overly limited perspective? Is there a responsibility that one has to early human life irrespective of the child's genetic make-up? Once the information is disclosed to a parent about the genetic make-up of his or her child, can one truly obtain non-coercive, unbiased counseling related to matters like selective termination and alternatives?[24] It is argued that knowledge gained from prenatal diagnoses and screening can significantly prepare parents for what they are to expect. Additionally, in cases where outcomes can be affected, prenatal screening may allow for significant changes in obstetrical care (i.e., children with ventral wall defects or neural tube defects can be delivered in an environment that can immediately address these issues as well as adapt modes of delivery to significantly reduce co-morbidities). But can these distinctions be drawn so clearly for parents, who may be in the midst of decisions related to the results of a genetic test or screen?

Given that answers to many of these questions are rooted in a specific definition of what constitutes human life, imperfection, normalcy, and health, it is important that ethical reflection deal with the matter of what constitutes a genetic disorder.[25] In other words, if one's genetic make-up is increasingly going to be the basis for evaluations of normalcy, then should parents have their fetuses tested for obesity, shortness, asthma, migraine headaches, alcoholism, depression, aggressiveness, Alzheimer's disease, and sexual orientation? In an attempt to define these terms, questions will arise. Where there is a test for determining a predisposition toward homosexuality, what if someone wished to use it as a prelude to selective abortion? Should geneticists withhold certain information if they feel it will be used for selective abortion because, for instance, the baby is considered to be the "wrong sex"? Ought society or the medical profession set limits on individual autonomy in the genomics age? Is non-directive counseling for parents at odds with public health considerations? In other words, what if, from a societal perspective, genetic testing is confirming that the gene pool continues to be weakened? Do we have social eugenic responsibilities to correct this negative effect?[26]

Genetic information is deeply personal and yet has profound social implications. If individuals in their reproductive years have deleterious genes that may lead to genetic disorders, the possibility of passing those genes along or the potential harm caused to future generations sets up a unique set of circumstances in a genomics age. Rosamond Rhodes has put forth an interesting argument suggesting that "there is no right to genetic ignorance."[27] She argues there is a duty to inform our family of our genomic heritage based on traditional kinship bonds and a duty of fidelity. Genetic knowledge may be viewed like any other set of knowledge that allows us to make life decisions. Failing to act in accord with genetic knowledge constitutes failure to accept our human condition and to treat ourselves with the inherent respect deserving of human beings.

Our couple in the case study above is certainly struggling with what Rhodes has put forth—suggesting that they may have had an obligation not to reproduce. Our normative basis would suggest that although there is no right to reproduce, offspring is certainly a significant component of human flourishing as it relates to married couples. Yet in this set of circumstances, the couple is presented with unique knowledge prior to a decision to attempt to procreate. This knowledge seems to create responsibility based on the human dignity of the future person.[28] This is a difficult discussion to process, however. What are our obligations to future individuals? We commonly refer to such obligations in such contexts as the reduction in nuclear arms, the removal and treatment of nuclear waste, education regarding the prevention and spread of disease, and concerns about the national debt. However, given that future individuals do not yet exist (and may never exist), the notion of obligation becomes problematic at best.[29] Nonetheless, human dignity suggests that the fetus the couple is going to bring into the world does possess inherent dignity and worth as a human being and must be treated as such despite its limited lifespan and potential for great suffering. The obligations of the couple are now those related to becoming parents as with any other offspring. The question of flourishing as a married couple and the matter of offspring can be addressed through other means, perhaps, like adoption.[30] Although recognized as not completely a fulfillment of the desire to achieve genetic offspring, parenthood through other means may provide an avenue for human flourishing.

**Pre-implantation Diagnosis.** Pre-implantation genetic diagnosis involves removing and testing a polar body (a small cell that is the by-product of meiosis) from an egg cell or, more commonly, a single cell from an early embryo prior to implantation for identification of genetic mutations associated with disorders.

- *Testing polar body:* in vitro fertilization (IVF) techniques are used to obtain eggs from the mother and the genetic makeup of the egg is inferred from the genetic makeup of the polar body cells; eggs determined to be free of the particular disease under scrutiny are then fertilized in the lab with the father's or donor's sperm, and the embryo is implanted.

- *Testing embryonic cell:* one or two cells are removed from the developing embryo 2–4 days after fertilization and the DNA from these cells is examined; results can be obtained within 12–24 hours and the embryos without the genetic abnormality or with the desired genetic traits are then transferred into the uterine cavity.

Almost all genetically inherited conditions that can be diagnosed in the prenatal period can also be detected in the pre-implantation period.

**Case 11B:** Bruce and Laura are little people. They feel that they would not know how to raise a child that is not a little person. They have made numerous changes to their living environment to accommodate their size and wonder what it would be like if their son or daughter soon surpassed their height. Further Laura comments, "We want a child like us. We understand our culture and wish to emphasize that this life is just as dignified as others." Bruce and Laura decide they want to speak with a geneticist to screen embryos prior to implantation for those that are positive for the genetic mutation that produces dwarfism. Bruce and Laura are confident that in speaking with a genetic counselor they will get unbiased information as to the likelihood of pre-implantation genetic diagnosis (PGD) being able to achieve their goals. Yet when they meet with the genetic counselor Bruce and Laura are dismayed that the genetic counselor starts her conversation by asking whether Bruce and Laura have considered whether such a selection might be in the best interests of their child.

Bruce is outraged. He comments, "I thought genetic counselors were supposed to be value neutral. We came to you precisely to avoid this type of discussion." Bruce goes on to ask, "Do you begin your discussion with prospective parents in a similar manner when they are blind or deaf and make similar requests? What is so different in our situation?"

**Ethical Issues.** The advantage of PGD allows a person to detect genetic defects that cause inherited disease in human embryos before they are implanted. PGD offers both selection of healthy embryos leading to presumptively healthy pregnancies and the ability to discard unhealthy embryos at a stage earlier than conventional methods. However, because of PGD's link to IVF, ethical issues that burden the mother include all those related to both technologies (see chapter 9). Other issues are associated with the moral status of the human embryo. While this issue was discussed more substantively in previous chapters, specific concerns related to the moral status of the human embryo and PGD require discussion here.

Although the embryo is apparently unharmed by the process of "cellular biopsy" at the eight-cell stage of embryonic development, the research is somewhat ambiguous. Hence polar body PGD or preconception PGD may be ethically more acceptable to those opposed to the manipulation of the human embryo. These forms of PGD have their limits in terms of reliability, and in the case of preconception PGD has so far failed to establish a pregnancy.

To date, steps have been taken through legislation or public policy to set parameters around the use of PGD. For example, in the United Kingdom alteration of an embryo's genes, even for gene therapy or for cloning of embryos, is illegal. All IVF clinics must be licensed by a government-appointed authority; this authority can withhold a license if the proposed use of PGD is not ethically acceptable or otherwise justified. This may include the use of PGD for sex selection exclusively.

Several ethical questions call for reflection. If harmful effects could occur to the embryo, can the benefits of genetic knowledge ever outweigh the harm? What is our responsibility to early human life even if it does exhibit deleterious genes? What are the obligations of medical practitioners who offer IVF in conjunction with PGD to the prospective parents, and what are their obligations to any embryos created? What of questions of access and distributive justice? Do all prospective parents have access to the technology? Is knowledge of the technology made available to all people regardless of socioeconomic status, race, ethnicity, education, and other factors that have traditionally limited access?[31]

Returning to the case of Bruce and Laura, further questions abound. May a prospective parent utilize PGD to screen embryos for conditions like dwarfism, deafness, or blindness? Is it appropriate to consider, as Bruce implicitly asserts, all such conditions as equal? Our normative basis would definitely affirm that all such people are equally valued as human beings and therefore present inherent dignity and worth because they are all created in the image of God. Yet the issue is not whether such people maintain such dignity and worth, but can prospective parents utilize technology intentionally to attempt to bring only individuals positive for these conditions into existence? A simplistic view of autonomy might suggest that prospective parents with the means to do so should be allowed the opportunity to screen their embryos for a variety of conditions and thereby utilize technology to achieve the ends they desire. However, recall that we are framing these ethics issues in the context of human flourishing and right relationships. In that context one must ask whether the parents are selfishly constraining the parameters of their offspring's capabilities in an effort to feel more comfortable about their ability to raise their offspring. Should the parents utilize technology as a means to legitimize a culture or should it be more a matter of how actively they pursue such a cause to the exclusion of purposefully screening their embryos for particular characteristics.

In order to make the latter claim, however, our conception of human anthropology and human flourishing must be robust enough to suggest that blindness and deafness and dwarfism are conditions that prospective parents ought to, at the very least, purposefully chose for their offspring. Laura Purdy attempts to deal with this difficult issue insofar as she constructs what she calls criteria for a "minimally satisfying life."[32] Admittedly, the term "minimally satisfying" is a shifting concept based on the relative concept of normal health in a given culture. It is difficult to know what to make of this claim, or even what demands it places on us presently.[33] Yet, as argued earlier, to ignore such a claim would result in creating unnecessary constraints on human flourishing and in certain cases suffering and purposeful disadvantage for some people.[34] Hence, despite its relativity, the claim is somewhat satisfactory, for it implies that "parents ought to try to provide for their children health normal for that culture, even though it may be inadequate if measured by some outside standard."[35]

**Newborn Screening.**   Newborn screening (NS) is performed in newborns as part of state public health programs so that certain genetic disorders can be detected soon after birth and early intervention or therapy can begin. Through NS programs, more than 4,000,000 newborns in the United States are tested each year for diseases such as phenylketonuria (PKU), hypothyroidism, sickle cell disease, and cystic fibrosis. All states, the District of Columbia, Puerto Rico, and the U.S. Virgin Islands now have their own mandatory NS programs. Because the federal government has set no national standard, however, screening requirements vary from state to state and the comprehensiveness of these programs varies. States routinely screen for anywhere from 2–30 disorders, with the average state program testing from 4–10 disorders.[36]

NS is done within the first two or three days of life by pricking the baby's heel and drawing a small sample of blood that is then applied to a card (called a Guthrie card after the scientist who developed a blood test for screening newborns for PKU). In general, consent to screening is not required; however, parents can refuse screening if they notify the health care provider in advance. Most states have identified a state or regional laboratory to which hospitals send the samples for analysis. Although NS is designed to detect infants with metabolic illnesses, certain tests can identify the infant as a carrier who may be clinically asymptomatic. Such information is important for the family in terms of planning future pregnancies and could be important to the infant when he or she reaches reproductive age.

**Ethical Issues.** More than four million newborns are screened in the United States each year. The intention of newborn screening as a public policy is prevention of serious illness where parents may not even be aware of genetic risk. The ethical issues in the area of newborn screening, therefore, are many. Matters of informed consent, access, confidentiality and privacy, adequacy of social support services, and resource allocation highlight the complexity and multidimensional array of ethical issues involved in newborn screening. Difficulties associated with obtaining adequate informed consent in this area are compounded by the difficulties facing any issue within the context of labor and delivery and its associated anxieties and pressures. Furthermore, the disorders for which a child is screened may depend upon the place the child happens to be born. Once this knowledge is gained, ethical reflection shifts to adequacy, availability, and access to social support services to help families with children in whom disorders are discovered. This raises corollary ethics questions concerning resource allocation: (1) what tests should society consider in light of its ethical aims, and (2) what criteria do we use to select the disorders for which we test, given issues of access and availability of resources in the local community?[37]

Privacy and confidentiality in the area of newborn screening takes on special significance because third parties have some legitimate interests regarding reimbursement or insurance. It may have implications for further access to health care services. Given that the genetic information gleaned from newborn screening will follow the person throughout his or her entire life, agencies and health care institutions must ardently guard the privacy of this information.

**Diagnostic Testing/Predictive Testing.** Two forms of genetic testing are used to identify or predict diagnoses. Diagnostic testing is used to identify or confirm the diagnosis of a disease or condition in an affected individual. It may also be useful to help predict the course of a disease and determine the choice of treatment. Predictive testing is used to determine the probability that a healthy individual with or without a family history of a certain disorder might develop that disorder (e.g., mutations to BRCA1 and/or BRCA2 genes are associated with an increased risk of breast and ovarian cancer). Predictive testing that leads to the detection of a mutated gene provides the person with an increased risk estimate rather than certainty that he or she will develop a particular disorder later in life.

Pre-symptomatic testing is used to determine if a person has a particular genetic mutation that will lead to a certain disorder later in life, though the person is not yet experiencing any symptoms. Pre-symptomatic testing is available for several neurodegenerative diseases such as Huntington's disease and some forms of bowel cancer. A key difference between pre-symptomatic testing and predictive testing is that the likelihood of developing the disorder is very high as opposed to having an increased risk of developing the disorder.

**Case 11C:** Cory has recently read about breast cancer and the possibility of genetic testing. A friend who was diagnosed with breast cancer tells her that early detection is important. She continues to do self-examinations, but wants a more definitive test to let her know whether she is going to have breast cancer. Cory decides to approach her OBGYN about getting the genetic test. Her physician asks, "Has any close relative, like your mother, sister, or grandmother, ever died of breast cancer?" Cory replies that no one had, but she wants to take all measures possible to avoid this horrible disease. Cory's physician understands and agrees to offer her a referral for testing for BRCA1 and BRCA2.

After their office visit, Cory's physician briefly contemplates whether she is simply offering Cory the test because it exists and her patient has requested it. Given that Cory's family history does not really suggest such a test is warranted, her physician wonders on what basis she is providing this test. Then Cory's physician realizes that she never really discussed with Cory the difference between risk and diagnosis related to the tests for BRCA1 and BRCA2, but she knows that such a discussion will occur at the referral site before the testing is undertaken. She wonders whether, as a matter of informed consent, she should have explored these issues further. More practically, she wonders whether she should go back and address these issues, although she has already agreed to refer Cory for the genetic test.

**Ethical Issues.** In addition to many of the previously discussed ethical issues related to differing forms of genetic testing, there are ethical issues unique to these three types of genetic tests. In the area of diagnostic testing, ethical issues raise concerns whether there is a duty on the part of the patient who may be diagnosed with a genetic disease to disclose information to family members. Other concerns relate to the usefulness of the information. That is, are there curative or preventative measures available, psychological relief, and the like? Who should decide for minors, and on what grounds?

In the area of predictive testing there are concerns about false positives and false negatives of the tests. In other words, a patient may incorrectly test positive for the disease, experience the psychological burden associated with such knowledge, and perhaps disclose the genetic disorder to other family members, but not actually have the genetic disorder.

Genetic discrimination or stigmatization because of the diagnosis is also possible. Finally, issues of social justice must be raised as well, namely, is there fairness in testing and equitable distribution of the benefits and burdens?[38]

Returning to our case of predictive testing for BRCA1 and BRCA2, it seems that Cory is not truly aware of how genetic testing works or what might be appropriate indications. Cory's fears, brought on by listening to her friend's experience, are legitimate. But do such fears warrant a genetic test although there are no indications for such a test based on her family history? Cory's understanding of whether or not she should obtain a predictive genetic test for BRCA1 or BRCA2 is lacking. It seems to her that simply because she wants the test and has the means to pay, it should be made available.[39]

Herein lies the significant ethical issue: for women with family histories of early onset breast or ovarian cancer the BRCA1 and BRCA2 gene are apparently responsible for 80% of the breast cancer that occurs.[40] Yet only 7% of women from families with breast cancer have a BRCA1 mutation.[41] Without a family history, however, a number of factors complicate the specificity of the test: (1) BRCA1 and BRCA2 are such large genes that a great number of mutations are possible, many of which may not indicate a susceptibility to breast cancer; and (2) the mutations that often occur throughout the genes occur without reoccurrence.[42] Essentially this means that Cory's request for testing without a family history is simply uninformed. Cost effectiveness and reliability questions relate to the responsibilities of Cory's physician. An additional concern, already raised, is the matter of a false positive.

An approach that may be more in line with our normative basis (specifically the principles of stewardship and equitable distribution) would be for women at high risk for hereditary breast cancer (those with a family history of ovarian or breast cancer) to undergo the testing if adequate funding is available and consent is given.[43] In such cases the information obtained would actually benefit the women and allow them to take preventive steps to avoid getting cancer. Since genetic testing is never without risk, counseling must always be coupled with such testing in order for it to be respectful of the human dignity of the patient. That is, there may be risks associated with the psychological uncertainty, interpretation of results, and concerns about the implications of the results, including impact on future health coverage, privacy of information obtained, and duty to tell family members.

Finally, because Cory is engaged in a health care system that allows some to purchase services others cannot access, the role of the medical professional in terms of guidance and recommendation is essential. Cory's physician is right to question why she should provide Cory access to this test. Testing anyone who wishes to have knowledge about their genetic make-up simply for "peace of mind" without such a test being clinically indicated in light of family history or other relevant information is not medically sound, socially sustainable, or ethically defensible.[44] On the other hand, if the OBGYN did not feel that she had the expertise to sort through the complexities of cancer genetic testing, was a referral appropriate, given that a referral does not necessarily mean the testing will occur? In other words, the referral may provide the information necessary for Cory to make a prudent decision in light of her real (versus perceived) risk. Our normative basis would suggest that the physician's professional obligations to informed consent should compel her to revisit the issue with Cory before moving forward with the test, since the evidence suggests that Cory is not an appropriate candidate for a BRCA1 and BRCA2 predictive genetic test.

## Conclusion

While many issues are likely to surface in the legal and public policy discourse about genetic testing and screening, the focus will likely be on privacy and confidentiality of genetic data. Many are concerned that genetic information may be used in a manner that might deny, limit, or cancel an employee's health insurance or allow employers to discriminate in the workplace based on certain genetic "deficiencies." Ethics must be at the forefront of this debate, asking questions concerning access, distributive justice, and considering whether people are likely to be ostracized or stigmatized by such information. Are people being adequately informed regarding the uniqueness of the genomics context of testing and screening? What are one's duties to family and others with regard to disclosure of a genetic diagnosis? What is the obligation of practitioners when a genetic diagnosis would most certainly affect future offspring but the person tested does not wish to disclose the information to a spouse? Maintaining a focus in these areas should keep the ethical debate properly focused on genetic testing and screening without becoming myopic regarding issues of autonomy and the right to know.

## Additional Case Studies

**Case 11D:** In May of 2002 the Burlington Northern Santa Fe Railroad (BNSF) Company agreed to pay $2,200,000 to settle charges of illegally testing workers for genetic defects. BNSF had performed genetic tests on over 30 employees who sought worker's compensation and medical attention for carpal-tunnel syndrome. The employees claim that they did not give consent for nor have knowledge of the genetic tests at the time blood samples were taken. It was also their contention that BNSF conducted the tests in order to avoid costs of medical care associated with the syndrome.

The BNSF employees filed a complaint with the Equal Employment Opportunities Commission, who in turn filed suit against BNSF on the rounds that the railroad violated the American's with Disabilities Act (ADA). The EEOC asked the court for an order directing BNSF to (1) halt its policy requiring genetic testing for track worker employees who file worker's compensation claims related to carpal tunnel syndrome, and (2) halt disciplinary action or termination of employees who refused to submit a blood sample for genetic tests.

BNSF settled out of court and agreed to stop testing employees. It also agreed to destroy all blood samples from workers who were already tested and delete the genetic results from their employment record. BNSF also agreed to promote efforts to create federal legislation prohibiting genetic testing related to employment.

Discussion Questions. Should BNSF have settled out of court, or did they have an ethical basis upon which to justify testing? There are often restrictions on certain types of jobs that require minimal levels of strength, endurance, or ability; why should BNSF's claim be any different? Is there something different about attempting to seek a perceived genetic basis for carpal tunnel syndrome in order not to be required to provide worker's compensation for a work-related injury?

Case 11E: In January 2007, The American College of Obstetricians and Gynecologists (ACOG) released new recommendations for Down's syndrome screening. The recommendations suggest that all pregnant women, regardless of their age, should be offered screening for Down's syndrome. Previously, only women age 35 and older were offered genetic testing and diagnostic testing for Down's syndrome. According to the guidelines, the goal is to provide screening tests with high detection rates and low false positive rates that "provide patients with diagnostic testing options if the screening test indicates that the patient is at an increased risk for having a child with Down syndrome." Given that there are a variety of approaches to this level of early screening strategies, the recommendations are intended to offer guidelines to meet the best interests of the patient.

You are the director of benefits for a non-profit, faith-based organization whose health plan is self-funded. You also have a daughter that has Down's syndrome. You wonder why your organization would fund screening tests for Down's syndrome earlier in a woman's pregnancy. You suspect that the reason the ACOG recommendations have changed is to allow women to be able to terminate pregnancies positive for Down's syndrome early in the pregnancy, although you hope that this is not true. Through inquiry on the recommendation you find that some suggest that earlier screening allow parents to prepare early for a child diagnosed with Down's syndrome. You approach your vice president of human resources to inquire whether the benefits plan should cover this set of screening tests.

## Suggested Readings

Collins, F. C. "Shattuck Lecture—Medical and Societal Consequences of the Human Genome Project." *New England Journal of Medicine* 341 (1999): 28–37.

Ensenauer, R. E., V. V. Michels, and S. S. Reinke. "Genetic Testing: Practical, Ethical, and Counseling Considerations." *Mayo Clinic Proceedings* 80 (2005): 63–73.

Clayton, E. W. "Genomic Medicine: Ethical, Legal, and Social Implications of Genomic Medicine." *New England Journal of Medicine* 349 (2003): 562–69.

McCormick, Richard A. "Moral Theology and the Genome Project." In *Controlling our Destinies*, edited by Philip R. Sloan, 417–28 (Notre Dame, IN: University of Notre Dame Press, 2000).

Keenan, James F. "What Is Morally New in Genetic Manipulation?" *Human Gene Therapy* 1 (1990): 289–98.

## Multimedia Aids for Teachers

*Gattaca*. Directed by Andrew Niccol. Starring Ethan Hawke. Rated PG-13. 1997. This movie depicts a future world where genetic technology has run amuck.

*Rabbit Proof Fence*. Directed by Phillip Noyce. Starring Everlyn Sampi. Rated PG. 2002. This movie depicts the tragedy that befalls an aboriginal family caught in the web of a eugenics-minded Australia in the 1930s.

*A Question of Genes: Inherited Risks*. PBS. 1997. This 2-hour television special follows the personal journey of individuals and families who confront questions about genetic testing. For more information on purchasing the VHS, see http://www.backbonemedia.org/genes/educator/44_video.html.

## Endnotes

[1] Francis Collins, "Shattuck Lecture—Medical and Societal Consequences of the Human Genome Project," *New England Journal of Medicine* 341, no. 1 (July 1, 1999): 28–37.

[2] Lily E. Kay, "A Book of Life? How a Genetic Code Became a Language," in *Controlling Our Destinies*, ed. Philip Sloan (Notre Dame, IN: University of Notre Dame Press, 2000). 99–124.

[3] Collins, "Shattuck Lecture," 30.

[4] Timothy Lenoir and Marguerite Hays, "The Manhattan Project for BioMedicine," in *Controlling Our Destinies*, ed. Philip Sloan (Notre Dame, IN: University of Notre Dame Press, 2000), 29–62.

[5] Willard Gaylin, "The Frankenstein Factor," *New England Journal of Medicine* 297 (September 22, 1977): 665–67.

[6] J. Jin, "An Evaluation of the Ethical, Legal and Social Implications program of the U.S. Human Genome Project," *Princeton Journal of Bioethics* 3, no. 1 (2000): 35–50; and E. M. Meslin, T. J. Thomson, and J. T. Boyer, "The Ethical, Legal, and Social Implications Research Program at the National Human Genome Research Institute," *Kennedy Institute of Ethics Journal* 7, no. 3 (September 1997): 291–98.

[7] For a substantive listing of single-gene disorders see "Online Mendelian Inheritance in Man at Johns Hopkins University," http://www.ncbi.nlm.nih.gov/entrez/query.fcgi?db=OMIM.

[8] J. G. Shaw, "Cancer and Genetic Medicine: A Medical View," *Health Progress* 86, no. 5 (2005): 31–35; and C. Bayley, "Cancer and Genetic Medicine: An Ethical View," *Health Progress*, 86, no. 5 (2005): 35–37.

[9] See "Genetics Home Reference," http://ghr.nlm.nig.gov

[10] F. S. Collins and A. E. Guttmacher, "Genetics Moves into the Medical Mainstream," *JAMA* 286, no. 18 (2001): 2322–24; and P. R. Billings, R. J. Carlson, J. Carlson, et al., "Ready for Genomic Medicine? Perspectives of Health Care Decision Makers," *Archives of Internal Medicine* 165, no. 16 (2005): 1917–19.

[11] Graphics of different DNA structures can be found in the illustrated glossary provided at the site for GeneTests, www.genetests.org, which is funded by the National Institutes of Health.

[12] For an understanding of the relationship between faulty hemoglobin gene and malaria see the article "Malaria and the Red Cell" at the Information Center for Sickle Cell and Thalassemic Disorders Web site: http://sickle.bwh.harvard.edu/malaria_sickle.html.

[13] It is important to note a possible link between the widespread promotion of birth control and racism. Historically, this link was most evident in the appearance of new government-funded clinics in the 1970s seemingly targeting African-Americans. At that time many religious leaders within the African-American community accused family planning clinics of "genocidal" intentions. See Linda Gordon, *Women's Body, Women's Right: Birth Control in America*. (New York: Penguin Books, 1976); Ellen Chesler, *Woman of Valor: Margaret Sanger and the Birth Control Movement in America* (New York: Simon & Schuster, 1992).

[14] Jael Silliman, Marlene Gerber Fried, Loretta Ross, and Elena R. Gutierrez, *Undivided Rights: Women of Color Organize for Reproductive Justice* (Cambridge, MA: South End Press, 2004).

[15] Douglas S. Diekema, "Involuntary Sterilization of Persons with Mental Retardation: An Ethical Analysis," *Mental Retardation and Developmental Disabilities Research Reviews* 9 (2003): 21–26.

[16] For information on genetic non-discrimination legislation introduced, see the National Human Genome Research Institute: http://www.genome.gov/media.

[17] A number of other sources may be important to the reader: Martin S. Pernick, "Define the Defective: Eugenics, Esthetics, and Mass Culture in Early Twentieth-Century America," in *Controlling Our Destinies*, ed. Philip Sloan (Notre Dame, IN: University of Notre Dame Press, 2000), 187–208; Arthur L. Caplan, "What's Morally Wrong with Eugenics?" in *Controlling Our Destinies*, ed. Philip Sloan (Notre Dame, IN: University of Notre Dame Press, 2000), 209–222; Philip Kitcher, "Utopian Eugenics and Social Inequality," in *Controlling Our Destinies*, ed. Philip Sloan (Notre Dame, IN: University of Notre Dame Press, 2000), 229–62.

[18] This information is provided at the site for GeneTests, www.genetests.org, which is funded by the National Institutes of Health.

[19] B. Modell and A. Darr, "Science and Society: Genetic Counseling and Customary Consanguineous Marriage," *Nature Reviews Genetics* 3, no. 3 (March 2002): 225–29; R. M. Nelson, J. R. Botkjin, E. D. Levetown, et al., "Ethical Issues with Genetic Testing in Pediatrics," *Pediatrics* 107, no. 6 (June 2001): 1451–55.

[20] J. E. Bowman, "To Screen or Not to Screen: When Should Screening Be Offered?" *Community Genetics* 1, no. 3 (1998): 145–47; M. S. Yesley, "Genetic Privacy, Discrimination, and Social Policy: Challenges and Dilemmas," *Microbial and Comparative Genomics* 2, no. 1 (1997): 19–35.

[21] C. Slack, K. Lurix, S. Lewis, and L. Lichten, "Prenatal Genetics: The Evolution and Future Directions of Screening and Diagnosis," *Journal of Perinatal and Neonatal Nursing* 20, no. 1 (Jan.–Mar. 2006): 93–97.

[22] B. Bromley, E. Lieberman, T. D. Shipp, and B. R. Benacerraf, "The Genetic Sonogram: A Methods of Risk Assessment for Down Syndrome in the Second Trimester," *Journal of Ultrasound Medicine* 21 (2002): 1087–96.

[23] D. A. Driscoll, "Second Trimester Maternal Serum Screening for Fetal Open Neural Tube Defects and Aneuploidy," *Genetic Medicine* 6 (2004): 540–41; I. R. Merkatz, H. M. Nitowsky, J. N. Macri, and W. E. Johnson, "An Association between Low Maternal Serum Alpha-Fetoprotein and Fetal Chromosomal Abnormalities," *American Journal of Obstetrics and Gynecology* 1 (1984): 926–29.

[24] M. B. Mahowald, M. S. Verp, and R. R. Anderson, "Genetic Counseling: Clinical and Ethical Challenges," *Annual Review of Genetics* 32 (1998): 547–59.

[25] W. French Anderson, "Human Gene Therapy: Why Draw a Line?" in *Bioethics*, ed. Thomas A. Shannon, 4th ed. (Mahwah, NJ: Paulist Press, 1993), 140–51. He states, "Because our knowledge of the human body and mind is so limited, and because we do not know what harm we might inadvertently cause by gene transfer technology, the use of genetic engineering to insert a gene into a human being should first be used only in the treatment of serious disease. . . . The initial 'line' should be those diseases that produce significant suffering and premature death." See also Carol A. Tauer, "Preventing the Transmission of Genetic Diseases," *Chicago Studies* 33, no. 3 (November 1994): 213–39. She writes, "The fact that reasonable people may disagree about the seriousness of particular conditions does not mean that no distinctions can be made."

[26] U. Kortner, "The Challenge of Genetic Engineering to Medical Anthropology and Ethics," *Human Reproduction and Genetic Ethics: An International Journal* 7, no. 1 (2001): 21–24.

[27] R. Rhodes, "Genetic Links, Family Ties, and Social Bonds: Rights and Responsibilities in the Face of Genetic Knowledge," in *Healthcare Ethics in a Diverse Society*, ed. M. C. Brannigan and J. A. Boss (Mountain View, CA: Mayfield, 2001), 291–303.

[28] L. M. Purdy, "Children of Choice: Whose Children? At What Cost?" *Washington and Lee Law Review* 52 (1995): 197–224; L. M. Purdy, "Genetic Diseases: Can Having Children Be Immoral?" in *Genetics Now: Ethical Issues in Genetic Research*, ed. John J. Buckley (Washington, DC: University Press of America, 1978), 25–39.

[29] Carol A. Tauer, "Preventing the Transmission of Genetic Diseases," *Chicago Studies* 33, no. 3 (November 1994): 213–39; Jan Christian Heller, *Human Genome Research and the Challenge of Contingent Future Persons* (Omaha, NE: Creighton University Press, 1996).

[30] There are other options, such as adoption (in which the parent forgoes genetic offspring in order to prevent the potential spread of disastrous genetic disease), egg or sperm donation (in which the parent with the deleterious genetic makeup would forego contribution to the genome of the offspring to prevent possible genetic disease), and voluntary sterilization (in which the diseased contributor makes the "genetic sacrifice" to forgo possible reproduction so damaged genes cannot be passed to future generations). Joseph Fletcher made this argument when he considered the possibility of such an act virtuous in the context of a technologically advanced society: J. Fletcher, *The Ethics of Genetic Control* (New York: Prometheus Books, 1988).

[31] G. Pennings and G. de Wert, "Evolving Ethics in Medically Assisted Reproduction," *Human Reproduction Update* 9, no. 4 (2003): 397–404; G. Pennings, R. Schots, and I. Liebaers, "Ethical Considerations on Preimplantation Genetic Diagnosis for HLA Typing to Match a Future Child as a Donor of Haematopoietic Stem Cells to a Sibling," *Human Reproduction* 17, no. 3 (March 2002): 534–38; R. J. Boyle and J. Savulescu, "Ethics of Using Pre-Implantation Genetic Diagnosis to Select a Stem Cell Donor for an Existing Person," *BMJ* 323 (2001): 1240–43.

[32] Laura M. Purdy, "Genetics and Reproductive Risk: Can Having Children Be Immoral?" in *Biomedical Ethics*, ed. Thomas A. Mappes and David DeGrazia (New York: McGraw-Hill, 2001), 520–27.

[33] While some claim that there exists a duty to avoid human suffering for future generations through interventions in the human genome, others feel that such a view is anti-feminist and places a huge burden on women to give birth to perfect babies. See Abby Lippman, "Prenatal Genetic Testing and Geneticization: Mother Matters for All," *Fetal Diagnosis and Therapy* 8 Supplement (April 1993): 175–88; Abby Lippman, "Mother Matters: A Fresh Look at Prenatal Genetic Testing," *Issues in Reproductive and Genetic Engineering: Journal of International Feminist Analysis* 5 (1992): 141–54; Abby Lippman, "Prenatal Genetic Testing and Screening: Constructing Needs and Reinforcing Inequities," *American Journal of Law and Medicine* 17 (1991): 15–50. Others have argued that a duty to avoid human suffering for future generations may imply genetic interventions in utero without consideration of the impact of that intervention on the mother, see: Purdy, "Children of Choice," 197–224; L. M. Purdy, "Genetic Diseases: Can Having Children Be Immoral?" in *Genetics Now: Ethical Issues in Genetic Research*, ed. John J. Buckley (Washington, DC: University Press of America, 1978), 25–39; L. M. Purdy, "Are Pregnant Women Fetal Containers?" *Bioethics* 4 (1990): 273–91. Still other feminist writers focus on the differing roles related to reproduction and caregiving between the sexes insofar as that those roles are impacted differently by current advances in genetics: see Mary B. Mahowald, "A Feminist Standpoint for Genetics," *The Journal of Clinical Ethics* 7 (1996): 333–40; R. Rapp, "Gender, Body, Biomedicine: How Some Feminist Concerns Dragged Reproduction to the Center of Social Theory," *Medical Anthropology Quarterly* 15 (December 2001): 466–77; Maura A. Ryan, "Cloning, Genetic Engineering, and the Limits

of Procreative Liberty," *Valparaiso University Law Review* 32 (Spring, 1998): 753–71; Patricia Spallone and Deborah Lynn Steinberg, eds., *Made to Order: The Myth of Reproductive and Genetic Progress* (New York: Pergamon, 1987); Maura A. Ryan, "The Argument for Unlimited Procreative Liberty: A Feminist Critique," *Hastings Center Report* (July/August 1990): 6–12; S. Squier, "Fetal Subjects and Maternal Objects: Reproductive Technology and the New Fetal/Maternal Relation," *Journal of Medicine and Philosophy* 21 (Oct. 1996): 515–35. Although this discussion is outside the scope of the dissertation, the dissertation is aware of the debate.

[34] Harris, *Clones, Genes, and Immortality: Ethics and the Genetic Revolution*, 211–14; See also: Andrew Czeizel, *The Right to Be Born Healthy* (New York: Alan R. Liss, 1988), 65–81.

[35] Purdy, "Genetics and Reproductive Risk," 524.

[36] T. S. Raghuveer, V. Garg, and W. D. Graf, "Inborn Errors of Metabolism in Infancy and Early Childhood: An Update," *American Family Physician* 73, no. 11 (January 2006): 1981–90; American Academy of Pediatrics, S. R. Rose. Section on Endocrinology and Committee on Genetics. "Update of Newborn Screening and Therapy for Congenital Hypothyroidism," *Pediatrics* 117 (2006): 2290–2303; R. I. Raphael, "Pathophysiology and Treatment of Sickle Cell Disease," *Clinical Advances in Hematology and Oncology* 3, no. 6 (June 2005): 492–505; D. Paul, "Contesting Consent: The Challenge to Compulsory Neonatal Screening for PKU," *Perspectives in Biology and Medicine* 42 (1999): 207–19.

[37] T. Lewens, "What is Genethics?" *Journal of Medical Ethics* 30, no. 3 (June 2004): 326–28; B. Wicken, "Ethical Issues in Newborn Screening and the Impact of New Technologies," *European Journal of Pediatrics* 162 Supplement (December 2003): S62–S66; M. J. McQueen, "Some Ethics and Design Challenges of Screening Programs and Screening Tests," *Clinica Chimica Acta* 315, no. 1–2 (Jan. 2002): 41–48.

[38] M. Harris, I. Winship, and M. Spriggs, "Controversies and Ethical Issues in Cancer-Genetics Clinics," *Lancet Oncology* 6, no. 5 (May 2005): 301-10; J. P. Mackenbach, "Genetics and Health Inequalities: Hypotheses and Controversies," *Journal of Epidemiology and Community Health* 59, no. 4 (April 2005): 268–73.

[39] L. Beckman, "Are Genetic Self-Tests Dangerous? Assessing the Commercialization of Genetic Testing in Terms of Personal Autonomy," *Theoretical Medicine and Bioethics* 25, no. 5–6 (2004): 387–98; S. Sherwin, "BRCA Testing: Ethics Lessons for the New Genetics," *Clinical and Investigative Medicine* 27, no. 1 (2004): 19–22; S. C. Hull and K. Prasad, "Reading Between the Lines: Direct-to-Consumer Advertising of Genetic Testing in the USA," *Reproductive Health Matters* 9, no. 18 (Nov. 2001): 44–48; and B. A. Koenig, et al., "Genetic Testing for BRCA1 and BRCA2: Recommendations of the Stanford Program in Genomics, Ethics, and Society. Breast Cancer Working Group." *Journal of Women's Health* 7, no. 5 (1998): 531–45.

[40] K. F. Hoskins et al., "Assessment and Counseling for Women with a Family History of Breast Cancer: A Guide for Clinicians," *Journal of the American Medical Association* 273 (1995): 577–85.

[41] F. J. Couch et al., "BRCA1 Mutations in Women Attending Clinics that Evaluate the Risk of BC," *New England Journal of Medicine* 336, no. 20 (1997): 1416–21.

[42] Olufunmilayo I. Olopade, "The Human Genome Project and Breast Cancer," *Women's Health Issues* 7, no. 4 (1997): 211.

[43] Mary Briody Mahowald, *Genes, Women, and Equality* (New York: Oxford University Press, 2000): 199.

[44] Mahowald, *Genes, Women, and Equality*, 200.

# CHAPTER 12

# Medical Research on Humans

## Balancing Scientific Inquiry and Human Dignity

The book, *Institutional Review Board: Management and Function,* includes a foreword by Paul Gelsinger, whose nineteen-year-old son, Jesse, died as a result of a gene therapy protocol. The case's relevance here rests in Jesse's father's final plea to the institutional review committee (IRC, sometimes termed the institutional review board, or IRB):

> I supported these doctors for months, believing that their intent was nearly as pure as Jesse's. They had promised to tell me everything. Even after the media started exposing the flaws in their work, I continued to support them. I discovered that federal oversight was woefully inadequate, that many researchers were not reporting adverse reactions, and that the FDA was being influenced into inaction by industry.

Please remember Jesse's intent when you review studies or when you make policy. You are professionals and you know the issues. I ask—and life itself demands—that you take the time and energy to review each protocol as if you were going to enroll your own child. Please use Jesse's experience to give you the strength to say no or the courage to ask more questions.

If researchers, industry, and those in government apply Jesse's intent—not for recognition, not for money, but only to help—then they will get all they want and more. They'll get it right.[1]

Revealed in this quote is the powerful tension that can arise when the desire to pursue scientific inquiry is pitted against the protection of individual human beings. This tension is inescapable when experimentation and research are carried out on humans. Yet ethics demands that we never allow the desire to pursue scientific inquiry to trump the interests and inherent value of the unique and irreplaceable human beings who are enrolled in such research. Historical challenges to this norm, and seminal works that have resulted from such challenges, will be considered in this chapter.

Mr. Gelsinger's letter rightly alludes to the significance of the work and mission of an IRC to protect the rights and welfare of human research participants. This is another critical area in medical research and one that we will take up specifically by elaborating the ethical principles that ought to guide such bodies. Finally, we will expand on some of the fundamental topics related to human research, namely (1) the distinction between research and therapy; (2) the ethics of randomized clinical trials, especially the use of placebos in research; (3) impartiality and consent in selecting research subjects; and (4) special concerns related to research involving vulnerable populations.

Our goal for this chapter is to raise your level of awareness about the ethical issues that are central to research on human beings and to help you to address these issues in light of our normative basis. We especially want you to understand "Jesse's intent" better, because that gets to the true meaning and ethics of research on humans. Let us consider the following case to illustrate these concepts:

Case 12A: On October 14, 1984, a baby was born in a community hospital in southern California with a heart malformation known as hypoplastic left-heart syndrome (HLHS). This essentially means that the child was born with an underdeveloped mitral valve or aorta on the left side of the heart. Therefore, only the right side of the heart functions properly. The occurrence of this disease affects roughly 300–2000 children a year. At the time of this case most babies suffering from HLHS died within a few weeks of birth; today, however, survival rates are significantly better as surgical techniques have improved.

Baby Fae, as she was known to the public, was taken to Loma Linda University Hospital Center. There Baby Fae was given a heart transplant with a baboon heart. This first ever baboon-to-infant transplant was performed by Dr. Leonard Baily. Baby Fae died twenty days later.

## Setting the Context: Basic Concepts and Definitions in Research on Human Beings

Throughout history research on human beings has been central to the practice of medicine. Advances in medicine cannot occur without the involvement of human beings. This presents a difficulty when one attempts to distinguish between clinical practice and medical research. Take, for example, the case of Baby Fae: is this experimental research or clinical practice? The distinction is essential in determining how processes are reviewed and the degree to which people are therapeutically engaged. In a seminal work on the ethics of research on human beings Jay Katz observed, "Drawing the line between research and accepted practice ... (is) the most difficult and complex problem."[2]

Thomas Chalmers adds, "It is extremely hard to distinguish between clinical research and the practice of good medicine. Because episodes of illness and individual people are so variable, every physician is carrying out a small research project when (s)he diagnoses and treats a patient."[3] Yet, we must work with a standard definition of research on human beings, so we will define it as research involving human beings in carefully designed protocols in a manner that will allow the knowledge gained to be analyzed with the intention of contributing to the greater good of science and humanity.

One can see from this definition that a number of issues come to the fore. In contrast to the practice of good medicine, which intends to offer a therapeutic effect to the patient, research on human beings is truly research. That is, its benefit to the subject is not known. This raises a number of important questions that we will address in this chapter: How do we ensure that people receive a reasonable level of information to permit them to consider adequately whether to enroll in a protocol that may have little or no direct benefit to them? How does one weigh contributing to the good of humanity against potential risk to individuals? How does a review body ensure that the principal investigators will not inappropriately influence people to enroll? Ought not research participants, in certain circumstances, be compensated for their participation? If so, what is to prevent such compensation from having a coercive influence on decisions to enroll?

## Individual versus Social Good

These questions lead us back to the central tension facing all research on human beings: the polarity between the common good and the individual. Animals often fulfill the role of experimental subject in research, but in order to determine the effects of an unknown on humans, ultimately humans are needed for research. We are convinced that the following norm must be upheld in all considerations of research on human subjects: the desire to pursue scientific inquiry must never be allowed to trump the interests and inherent value of the unique and irreplaceable human beings who enroll in such research. Our normative basis calls us to respect the inherent dignity of all human beings because that is essential for right relationships and ultimately human flourishing. Here we are just being more specific to the issue at hand by saying that in research humans must never be treated as a means to an end and that research must never subject humans to unethical protocols. But what does it mean for a protocol to be unethical?

Many have turned to the process of informed consent to resolve the question of what is an ethical protocol, but this resolution is not entirely satisfactory. Might there be research that ought never to be done, even if some people give their informed consent to it? Furthermore, if only autonomous adults can give truly informed consent, is research with all others inherently unethical? And is it truly possible for any research subject to give informed consent, given the competing interests in human research and the inherent knowledge differential between researcher and subject?

Turning to a model where the common good may take precedence, however, begs questions regarding the inherent dignity of the individual human and that individual's interest in protecting his or her own person from violation. History offers examples of the dangers of weighing the interests of the many above the interests of the few (i.e., research subjects). And yet this same argument—that the interests of the many outweigh the interests of the few—is widely supported as a general philosophical principle, even though no one person would desire, presumably, to be the one whose sacrificed interest can be justified for the greater good.

Unfortunately, individuals' dignity, rights, and interests have often been violated in pursuit of generalized scientific knowledge. The Nuremberg Military Tribunals referred to atrocities that must never be forgotten carried out on innocent human beings in Nazi concentration camps:

> In every single instance appearing in the record, subjects were used who did not consent to the experiments; indeed, as to some of the experiments, it is not even contended by the defendants that the subjects occupied the status of volunteers. In many cases experiments were performed by unqualified persons; were conducted at random for no adequate scientific reason, and under revolting physical conditions. All of the experiments

were conducted with unnecessary suffering and injury and but very little, if any, precautions were taken to protect or safeguard the human subjects from the possibilities of injury, disability, or death. In every one of the experiments the subjects experienced extreme pain or torture, and in most of them they suffered permanent injury, mutilation, or death, either as a direct result of the experiments or because of lack of adequate follow-up care.

Manifestly human experiments under such conditions are contrary to the principles of the law of nations as they result from the usages established among civilized peoples, from the laws of humanity, and from the dictates of public conscience.[4]

Though the Nazi atrocities awakened the world to the potential for abuses in research, abuses still occurred, even in the United States, where individual autonomy and liberty otherwise prevailed above the interests of the state. The withholding of newly discovered penicillin for African Americans in the U.S. Department of Public Health's Tuskegee syphilis study was cited in chapter 1, but there are many other examples. In the Willowbrook Hepatitis Experiments, children who were profoundly cognitively delayed were used as experimental subjects. Some were deliberately infected with the strain of the hepatitis virus prevalent at Willowbrook, with serious ethical concerns about the method of obtaining informed consent from some parents. Live cancer cells were injected into patients at the Jewish Chronic Disease Hospital without their knowledge. Cold-war radiation experiments were conducted on a variety of people (some pregnant women and prisoners), who received high doses of radiation and injections of plutonium. At a residential school in Fernald, MA, from 1946–1956, nineteen children with cognitive disabilities were fed radioactive iron and calcium in their breakfast oatmeal—the consent form mailed to parents made no mention of radiation.[5]

In response to explicit violations of human dignity in the United States related to research on human beings, a number of guidelines were established that incorporate and even expand on the principles put forth in the Nuremberg

Code. These formal statements include (1) The Belmont Report from the Department of Health, Education, and Welfare, Office of the Secretary concerning Ethical Principles and Guidelines for the Protection of Human Subjects of Research, issued in 1979; and (2) the Declaration of Helsinki from the World Medical Association, issued in 1964, most recently revised in 2000.[6] These documents, along with other seminal works, have offered a set of principles that govern the ethics of research on human beings. Given the significance and groundbreaking nature of such works, the ethical principles for the evaluation of human subjects research are highlighted here: the principle of human dignity (core to all research involving human subjects), the principle of free and informed consent (a corollary to human dignity but grounded uniquely in the development of a well-formed conscience and human freedom), and the principle of totality and integrity—relevant to therapeutic experiments.[7] These principles should be familiar from our normative basis.

While these principles provide a general framework for ethical reflection, they need to be further specified as norms that ground such reflection. To this end, Benedict Ashley and Kevin O'Rourke propose six norms consistent with our normative basis and supported by the Belmont Report, The Declaration of Helsinki, and The Nuremberg Code. To this list we wish to add three more essential norms: items 7–9, below.

1. The knowledge sought through research must be important and obtainable by no other means, and the research must be carried on by qualified people.
2. Appropriate experimentation on animals and cadavers must precede human experimentation.
3. The risk of suffering or injury must be proportionate to the good to be gained.
4. Research candidates should be selected so that risks and benefits will be distributed equitably among all members of society.
5. To protect the integrity of the person, free and informed (voluntary) consent must be obtained.

6. At any time during the course of research, the subject (or the guardian who has given proxy consent) must be free to terminate the subject's participation in the experiment.
7. Research that is flawed methodologically may never be performed even were people willing to provide free and informed consent.
8. Where a standard of care therapy exists, a placebo control arm may not be utilized in a research protocol.[8]
9. As soon as a protocol's research shows conclusive evidence of a study drug or device's therapeutic effect, the research must be suspended and the investigated drug or device should be offered as therapy.

Principles 1–3 and 7 are necessary in view of the principle of human dignity. Thus from the perspective of our normative basis, human research cannot proceed unless these four norms are met. Norm 3 is perhaps the most operative where the other three norms have been met, namely, the benefit-burden analysis. This is difficult to calculate, but our unwavering commitment to the inherent dignity of all humans requires that principal investigators must attempt to represent to the potential subject, as accurately as possible, the level and nature of the risk from any potential research protocol. The more true this process, the better further norms will be met in terms of free and informed consent and the ability of the research subject to terminate his or her involvement at any time during the protocol.

Returning to the central issue raised earlier in this chapter, the individual versus social good, the norms listed above provide an absolute norm related to the risk a person can incur in light of the social good achieved through research. The desire to pursue scientific inquiry must never be allowed to trump the interests and inherent value of the unique and irreplaceable human beings who are enrolled in such research. Experiments may be quite beneficial in terms of scientific progress or information gained, but when they proceed at the expense of human beings such experiments are a violation of human dignity and therefore unethical. Stated more succinctly, the individual cannot be sacrificed for "the interests of the state or for scientific progress."[9]

So far we have elaborated on the fundamental principles and norms necessary to frame and guide research on human subjects. Now we must turn to a discussion of the committee functions required to carry out the evaluation of human research protocols in light of these guiding principles and norms. We understand that many of you may not serve on an IRC or may not even be aware of the process of reviewing human subjects' research. Given that much of the ethical analysis on human research is performed by these groups throughout the country, we feel it is important not only to make you aware of the IRC, but to ask you to engage some of the issues IRCs work through when evaluating human research protocols.

## Discussion: Ethical Issues and Analysis

### Institutional Review Committee (IRC)

The Department of Health and Human Services, Code of Federal Regulations regarding the Protection of Human Subjects has outlined a number of criteria that focus on the requirements for review of research on human beings. Before human participation in any research can occur, IRCs must review and approve all clinical research protocols. The federal regulations mandate this IRC review and approval. Review and approval of research protocols entails (1) that the protocol itself is consistent with sound research design and does not expose the participant to excess risk, thereby minimizing risk to potential participants; (2) risks to potential research participants are reasonable in relation to the benefits; and (3) informed consent will be obtained and documented from all potential enrollees before involvement in the research protocol.[10] Additionally, in actual practice IRCs review the protocol, the informed consent documentation, and supporting information. In certain cases this also includes amendments and continuing protocol review reports.

The work of the IRC as it relates to the Code of Federal Regulations is merely the floor in terms of ethics review. Although the federal regulations are deeply rooted in the ethical principles set forth in the Belmont Report, the Declaration of Helsinki, and the Nuremberg Code, they are designed to be the starting point for IRC review. In other words, IRCs are free, and encouraged, to move beyond these ethical principles to incorporate the values and principles unique to an institutional or a particular normative framework, or a particular cultural milieu of a community. Additionally, institutional values, mission statements, and simple administrative capacity also determine whether research is suitable for a particular institution. For example, a cancer research protocol designed by a cooperative research group through the National Institutes of Health might wish to enroll participants at a community hospital. Let's presume the IRC has reviewed and approved the protocol. Despite the approval of the IRC, hospital administration may decline to enroll subjects at its facility for reasons related to the mission of the community hospital, or simply the inability to staff an oncology unit, in this example, in order to facilitate the necessary requirements of the protocol. It is important to note that an institution may not implement a research protocol after that institution's IRC has found the protocol unacceptable for research on human beings.

Internal or external audits of the IRC files, minutes, and documents can verify whether the IRC is meeting the requirements set forth in the federal regulations. A far greater challenge is determining whether the IRC is meeting the requirements intended in the over-arching documents: the Belmont Report, the Declaration on Helsinki, and the Nuremberg Code. Here a greater deal of trust must be placed in the competency and level of commitment of the IRC to carry out a prudent review of human research protocols. The difficulty of attaining this threshold of review can be understood when one examines the complexity of the research environment today.

## The Research Environment

The research environment has attained a level of complexity that was not present in 1974 when IRCs came into existence. First, new technology across all disciplines of medicine have added a level of intricacy to new research protocols of which only a few specialists in the field may have complete understanding. The ability of an IRC to understand the details of the research protocols regarding their impact on the human subject may be severely constrained, therefore, even when able to seek outside counsel from experts in the field. Second, institutions have become the new recruiting grounds from for-profit companies seeking to test new medical devices and drugs. The increasing pressure over the past thirty years from health care institutions seeking to have a robust research program (and thereby establish a new lucrative revenue stream) has added a new level of institutional pressure. Third, there seems to be an increasing blur between research and therapy. That is, the medical device industry as well as the pharmaceutical industry seems to be targeting medical professionals directly with the goal of enrolling patients in human research. Thirty years ago institutions were very aware of the research being carried out by a few medical practitioners. Today, with the size of medical staffs, the desire to have a nationally recognized research program, pressure for tenure within academic medical centers, and increasing flow of research dollars coming into an institution, institutions are far less aware of the research that is occurring within their walls and therefore potentially ignorant of the interface between the institution's patients and medical research. Here, the IRC may not even be involved in review of research protocols due to ignorance or claims made by the manufacturer that the protocols have already been reviewed by the manufacturer's own IRC. As noted earlier, this is not an acceptable level of review, as the federal regulations mandate an institution's IRC review and approval of human research protocols.

As the level of research continues to increase in complexity and the level and nature of the potential for conflicts of interest also increase, the IRC must maintain itself as a well-educated and authoritative body within the institution. IRCs must continue to work to protect human subjects in research and continue to have the courage and wherewithal to be able to challenge, raise questions, and in certain cases reject research proposals that do not meet the expectations of both the federal regulations and the ethics principles that govern review of research protocols.

Let us now return to the case of Baby Fae presented at the outset of this chapter. Although Baby Fae was not the first to receive such a transplant, questions arose immediately about the legitimacy of the experimental procedure on a number of levels. Should a human donor have been ruled out prior to using the heart of an animal? This question is grounded in an understanding of the justification for research that relates to our primary norm. Recall we stated that IRCs are never to allow the desire to pursue scientific inquiry to trump the interests and inherent value of the unique and irreplaceable human beings who are enrolled in such research. This norm requires that (1) the knowledge sought through research must be important and obtainable by no other means, and the research must be carried out by qualified people; and (2) appropriate experimentation on animals and cadavers must precede human experimentation. Using the Loma Linda case as our context, our principles would suggest that although a baboon-to-infant heart transplant may have offered great potential for Baby Fae, its experimental nature requires us to ensure that the baboon heart is truly the method of last resort for Baby Fae. Also, it suggests that the transplant surgeon(s) and his or her team must carefully discern the extent to which the desire to be the first to achieve this medical feat played a role in their decision to move forward with such a procedure. Finally, because Baby Fae could not express interests for herself, the difficulty of surrogate decision making comes into play. We discussed this at some length in chapter 6 in regard to the care of critically ill newborns. The same ethical issues are relevant to this case: who decides, and by what criteria? The relational best-interests standard we offered in that chapter applies here as well: would such a procedure allow Baby Fae to achieve a level of human flourishing that is proportionate to her inherent human dignity in light of the risks of such a procedure?

Further complicating the ethical analysis of this case is the existence of the Norwood procedure, available in Boston and Philadelphia, which could have been used on Baby Fae, although the procedure would necessarily have been invasive and repetitive (continued surgical interventions are required as the child grows and develops).[11] Was the potential for research or experimentation placed before the well-being of the patient? Was there an obligation to utilize the Norwood procedure before attempting to use an animal organ? Recall our norms for evaluating research protocols, especially number 3 (the risk of suffering or injury must be proportionate to the good to be gained). Certainly curing Baby Fae's heart anomaly (by means of an animal organ transplant) would be preferable to continued invasive procedures throughout her lifetime (Norwood procedure). Yet the notion of proportionality suggests that although most children with this heart condition die within a few weeks, great caution should have been used lest Baby Fae become an object of experimentation.

One manner of preventing such exploitation is the principle of informed consent. Again, examining this principle within our normative basis raises further questions. Namely, even if informed consent were obtained from the parents, can the parents ethically offer their child for such experimental procedures if a known alternative exists? In other words, might the parents have been so persuaded by the potential cure the procedure offered that true informed consent was really not obtainable given the emotional factors at play: the high rate of morbidity and mortality related to the illness, the desire to have the child live at all costs, and the inability to process proportionality between risk and benefit ("children should never die this young"). That is not to say that emotional factors should be irrelevant to such intense decisions, but that parents and health care providers must recognize the limitations such emotions may place on principles traditionally used to assess and protect patients against unwarranted procedures or experimental therapies.

## Human Research: The Protocol

Recall the definition of research on human beings used in this chapter: research involves humans in carefully designed protocols in a manner that will allow for the knowledge gained to be analyzed with the intention of contributing to the greater good of science and humanity. Since it is also required that an IRC review all human research protocols within the IRC's institution, it is important that we briefly review the areas of accountability for protocol review. These areas include the rationale, objectives, procedures, outcomes of interests, experimental design, protection for human subjects to minimize risk, methods of analysis of data, endpoints of protocol, and the method for review and monitoring of adverse events. Additionally, the IRC is charged with assessing the qualifications of the principal investigator in light of the research proposed. In what follows we will cover the substantive areas of IRC review for research on human beings, intermingled with case studies to illustrate each concept.

**Number of Participants in Protocol.** Without getting into a great deal of statistical methodology, participant number is critical to research on human beings. Research proposals must have a specific number of participants in order to "power" the study so that it will be generalizable. In other words, a certain number of participants are necessary both to legitimize the research and to make it relevant for further study or justifiable as therapy. Not to do so would unnecessarily expose a small number of participants to research risk without the potential for gaining any scientifically substantiated knowledge from the research itself. Conversely, protocols must not enroll too many subjects because such levels of participation would expose too many people to unnecessary risk. The principal investigator is responsible for setting this number appropriately with the aid of a biostatistician.

The matter of participant number is also crucial for administrative review by the IRC. Recall that IRCs are charged with review of a protocol's impact on the health care institution, including staffing levels, interference in patient care, and training of personnel for implementation of protocol. If a research protocol requires a significant number of test subjects, the facility may be too small to accommodate the number of participants necessary, or the number of participants required may affect operations within the facility so profoundly as to have a negative impact on patient care. IRCs are required to consider these factors as part of human research protocol review. In certain cases the research may be very appropriate methodologically and statistically but unfeasible within a particular site and therefore unethical insofar as it affects an institution's primary responsibilities to the health and well-being of its patients.

**Experimental Design.** A significant issue in experimental design is the use of a placebo such as a sugar pill in research studies. A placebo-controlled clinical study is only justified when no satisfactory treatment exists for the disease that is being investigated in the research proposal. Norm 8 (in the beginning of this chapter) states that where a standard of care therapy exists, a placebo control arm may not be utilized in a research protocol. If scientific and medical practice indicates that there is a standard-of-care treatment for a disease, people may not be enrolled in a protocol that exposes them to the risk of receiving neither the experimental treatment nor the existing beneficial treatment. The use of a placebo in such cases is unethical and therefore protocols with such an arm should be rejected.

Some protocols randomly place human subjects into either a treatment group or a placebo group with neither the researcher nor the subject knowing whether the subject is receiving the treatment or the placebo  (called a randomized, double-blind, placebo-controlled clinical trial). For various reasons many researchers and manufacturers prefer this experimental design. Such protocols raise a number of ethical issues in addition to that cited in the preceding paragraph. If a manufacturer of a drug or mechanical device is studying their drug or device only against a placebo and a known therapeutic exists, the research is inherently faulty because it will not be known whether the new drug or device is actually safer or more efficacious than that which already exists. A case study may help to illustrate this point.

 **Case 12B:** A physician at your health system submits a protocol to the IRC. In that protocol he has created two arms for research purposes and will utilize a randomized, double-blind,  placebo-controlled trial as the experimental design. The physician argues that the hypothesis they are trying to test is the effectiveness of a new lipid-lowering drug for high cholesterol. The drug has gone through animal and safety Phase I and II trials and is now looking

for efficacy in a Phase III trial. The principal investigator notes that they have designed the placebo to be indistinguishable from the investigational drug. People who will be selected for the study must have a cholesterol level significant enough to require a 10–15% reduction in bad cholesterol. The physician explains that potential subjects will be informed that they will be participating in an experiment to test the efficacy of a new lipid-lowering drug and that the drug will not hurt them. In fact, they may see a lowering of their cholesterol while in the study.

You remark to the principle investigator that you feel the research design may be problematic and that patients will not be informed that they may receive a placebo where there is known therapy for high cholesterol. The physician responds by noting that a placebo-controlled trial is the best way to determine whether the drug is effective and therefore requires this type of trial. He also feels he has adequately informed the research subject because the Phase I and II trials were sufficient for moving to Phase III and the participant will not be harmed. The principal investigator ends by saying, "We usually have no trouble recruiting for studies. Patients want access to the latest and greatest drugs. I feel this is the next step in the progression of lipid-lowering drugs. I would really like to see this study approved."

Would you recommend approval for this study? If so, on what grounds would you recommend it? Recall our proposed norm: where a standard of care therapy exists, a placebo control arm may not be utilized in a research protocol. Given that the safety of the drug has been tested on animals and a small cohort of human beings, the principal investigator (PI) claims that the drug is essentially safe. He also asserts that potential subjects only care about whether they will be harmed or not. The PI feels that it will be ethical to proceed to Phase III testing of the new drug because the safety of the drug has been determined. Ethical concern, however, requires a more robust discussion as to whether there are problems with the design of the study; it may be unethical to enroll people in the trial by virtue of the fact that the study is flawed. Even if the test drug is essentially safe, potential research subjects should not be exposed to a placebo when standard therapies exist for lowering one's cholesterol. This argument, based upon recognition of the human dignity of the potential research participant, finds the Phase III trial unethical in its present design, regardless of the drug's safety.

If you answered "no" to the opening question about whether to recommend approval for the study, an interesting follow-up question might be, how would you challenge the PI's use of placebo in this trial? You might also discuss ways to structure the Phase III so that it meets the ethical principles and norms put forth in this chapter.

Again, the normative basis put forth in this work calls into question competing claims against human dignity, like those of the manufacturer regarding dollars or time lost while the investigational study drug or device is in the clinical research phase. These are valid concerns, and some (consequentialist) ethical theories could be made to override the concern of the human subject. The primary consideration of our normative basis, however, is human flourishing. From this perspective, research trials are unethical when they attach more weight to benefit to the researcher or manufacturer than to concern for human beings.

**Selection of Human Test Subjects.** In recruiting human subjects for research, risk must be distributed equitably across the study population and the matter of inducement must be carefully evaluated by the IRC. Studies typically do not involve monetary compensation to participants, as such compensation may be construed as an incentive to enroll in the research. However, the costs for medical care directly related to the study and the drug or device that is being tested is typically included for potential participants in the research protocol. In studies where participants are compensated for volunteering, the IRC must ascertain that the amount offered is not coercive and that payments are not incrementally spaced so participants would need to complete the entire study to receive compensation. No specific federal guidelines exist for this evaluation. Nevertheless, the possibility that the potential study population might be exploited must be taken into consideration.

Coercive inducement is not necessarily limited to monetary payment. Ethical questions arise when researchers, for reasons of convenience, wish to enroll their staff, colleagues, students, or other personnel. Such participants may fear to refuse to participate lest they incur the displeasure of their employer or colleague, or may feel that participation would enhance their prospects of future employment or promotion. An IRC has an obligation to remove such potential conflicts of interest. The difficulty here is for the IRC to protect potential research subjects from coercion in whatever form without being overly paternalistic. Consequently, nonspecific solicitation of potential enrollees is generally preferable because it rules out a number of potential ethical problems. A case study may help to illustrate this point.

Case 12C: An ad in a local campus newspaper reads, "Subjects (male and female) ages 18–24 are wanted to participate in a scientific study to test the impact of a study drug on daily activities. Participants will receive $1500 upon completion of the study. You must be available for 8 weeks to be eligible for the research study." Given that you are behind on rent and the second semester is approaching, you feel that perhaps a few weeks of winter break could be sacrificed to enter the research study. You figure it will only involve a few additional weeks at the beginning of the semester and you could really use the money, so you decide to enroll in the research.

Upon arriving at the research facility you are asked "to fill out some paperwork essentially saying you are willing to participate in the research." A researcher then places before you a cup containing a number of pills and asks you to take them. He claims, "There is no reason to worry, the pills are not known to have any significant adverse effects." You are asked to keep a daily journal related to specific questions. At the end of the study you will be required to turn in the journal.

This case raises a number of significant ethical issues. Most notable is the vulnerability of the study population. Given that $1500 is paid to participants—who will most likely be college students, given the scope of advertising and the target population desired for the study—some may enroll simply for the money. On the other hand, a job over the winter break at minimum wage would pay roughly the same, working 40-hour weeks. As such, the $1500 payment could be viewed merely as compensation for not being able to take a job; one could even argue that it should be higher to compensate for the potential risks associated with the investigational drug. Here the IRC may also wish to consider whether such payment demonstrates a flawed view of human dignity insofar as it seems to suggest a belief that people will be willing to submit their bodies to research solely for monetary gain.

Ethical arguments not based on our comprehensive normative basis might suggest that so long as informed consent is achieved, people should be free to enter whatever research protocols they want as a matter of human freedom and respect for autonomy. While our normative basis does not deny the importance of these principles, it argues that human flourishing supersedes all other goals—it is the goal to which all others should be directed. Therefore, despite the fact that the $1500 would certainly help you with your financial problems, the relevant question is whether enrollment in the research protocol (regardless of the money involved) offers you the possibility of living a good life, a life in which you flourish as an individual in relation to others. Notice that in this case "others" would be those who might truly be served by the outcome of the research.

Finally, consider the fact that participants will receive their compensation only upon completion of the study. We have already noted that contingencies can be ethically problematic in human testing. In this case, the contingency is that research subjects will not receive compensation until completion of the study. One of the norms for ethical research we offered at the beginning of the chapter insists that at any time during the course of research, the subject (or the guardian who has given proxy consent) must be free to terminate the subject's participation in the experiment. In this case study, will participants truly feel free to drop out at any time given the fact that compensation will be offered only to those who complete the study? Such a design has clear advantages to the PI, as it helps guarantee a solid and stable cohort throughout the duration of the study. It would shorten the time needed for the study because it would decrease the likelihood that new subjects would need to be enrolled, and thus would also limit costs to the drug or device manufacturer. Yet our normative basis calls into question such a practice. Given that the primary consideration of our normative basis is human flourishing, the IRC should minimally require that disbursement of compensation be periodically distributed throughout the subjects' participation in the research. This would ensure that fear of lost compensation will not serve to coerce human subjects to maintain enrollment who might otherwise decide that, for whatever reason, they must withdraw from the study.

Aside from questions concerning the potentially coercive influence of the $1500 stipend, there are also ethical issues related to the process of informed consent. We encourage you to revisit this case after reading the section on clinical research and informed consent.

**Qualifications of the Investigator.** The IRC has the responsibility to ensure that the PI is qualified to carry out the proposed research protocol. Is the PI trained in the areas of clinical expertise required in the protocol? Is the PI's institution well versed in the procedures or medication described in the protocol? Is the PI trained in performing clinical research?

There are obvious areas the IRC should examine with regard to the qualifications of the PI, namely, whether he or she is board-certified in the area of specialty required by the research protocol, but also whether the hospital has granted privileges to the PI with regard to the investigational drug, procedure, or device. The requirement that a clinician is trained in performing clinical research is often more difficult to ascertain. Many institutions require that clinicians who are interested in carrying out human research receive training in ethics and compliance for human research either through federally sponsored training programs or institution-specific training programs. This has gone a long way to familiarizing researchers with ethical and legal issues related to human research. However, such training is not standardized and great variability exists in the level of researchers' competency. Data safety monitoring boards—external boards that are designed to monitor a research protocol for participant safety—may be essential for the protection of human research subjects.

**Worth of the Research.** IRCs are also charged with evaluating the worth of the proposed research protocol. Research protocols can be designed so as to be statistically significant and methodologically sound but still not worth performing because the small amount of knowledge to be gained does not justify the risks.

In order for the IRC to determine whether the research is worthwhile, the objectives of the project must be explicit in the research protocol. The IRC may also need to know the external agency funding the research; the competition for such research is significant and may imply the level of worth. This rationale must be scrutinized lest funding and market share become the primary motives. A third method to determine worth of research may include the commitment of the institution to cancer research, for example, wherein a protocol is related to maintaining the institution's center of excellence standing. Again, the IRC should carefully evaluate the potential conflict of interest between the desire to be a part of such research and the true worth of the project. Finally, an IRC should be receptive to its required community members in this area. That is, the community members on the IRC should help decide whether such research is significant and worth pursuing for those for whom the protocol will be directed. Perhaps a case study will help to flesh out these criteria.

**Case Study 12D:** Leah is a member of an independent IRC that reviews protocols for the military. The particular protocol in question relies upon the data gathered from the Nazi altitude experiments. The protocol is funded by NASA and is designed to determine the necessary oxygen requirements in a rescue mission to return a shuttle flight crew safely to earth in the event of an emergency. A flight simulator will be used to gather the data that will simulate oxygen levels at certain altitudes. Only high-altitude Air Force pilots who are familiar with safety precautions will be allowed to enroll in the study.

Leah is aware that the Nazi altitude experiments took prisoners from concentration camps against their will and flew them to extreme altitudes without the benefit of oxygen to determine what would happen to the human body when exposed to such high altitudes—for example, should a pilot have to bail out at high altitude. She recalls the horrors of such experiments as recounted to her by her grandmother, who was a concentration camp survivor. She argues that the knowledge gained from such atrocities should not be memorialized in this way and recommends that the study be rejected given the fact that it utilizes knowledge gained from exploitive and unethical research.

In this case we face an interesting question regarding the worth of research.[12] In this proposed protocol the data gathered from the Nazi altitude experiments helps to protect research participants from unnecessary harm. If these data are protecting human subjects in the proposed protocol, how can use of this knowledge be ethically problematic? None of the principles and norms put forward in this chapter seem to be directly related to this question either. Recall chapter 3, however, where we mentioned a principle called *solidarity* under the broad category of *justice*. This principle was defined as "the responsibility we have to stand with our fellow human beings in times of need." One might suggest that Leah is acting from a position of solidarity with those who were exploited in Nazi human experimental atrocities. Out of a position of solidarity Leah wishes to reject any research that builds upon data gathered from such an abuse of human beings. Alternatively, Leah is suggesting that out of a responsibility to the *common good* she cannot allow the voices of those who were so exploited to be muted by permitting the use of such data, even if beneficial.[13]

On the other hand, one could argue that Leah fails to take into account the additional dangers that researchers are likely to face if the experiments do not draw on the knowledge gained from the Nazi experiments. The principle of solidarity in this case might require that the potential research subjects not be exposed to unnecessary harm. In this way, one could suggest that although the data were obtained in a completely unethical manner, the use of the data might actually provide an important good. In other words, in certain circumstances good may come out of something horribly evil.

Given the relevant considerations raised by the principle of solidarity in both instances, a proper reading of our normative basis would suggest that the latter use of solidarity is not faithful to its context, namely human dignity. Recall that the principle of solidarity is to be understood in the context of human flourishing and right relationships with God and neighbor. In this way, solidarity with those who were at the most extreme end of vulnerability and completely exploited to obtain these data tends to rule out the use of the data completely, regardless of the circumstances. In other words, as Henry K. Beecher noted, it would seem that "this loss . . . would be less important than the far reaching moral loss to medicine if the data were to be published." The principles of human dignity and solidarity demand that we memorialize those people not through utilization of the data garnered via experiments that denied their dignity, but rather by halting research that attempts to utilize such data. In this way we have not "conferred a scientific martyrdom on the victims," but rather recognized that such violence against human beings should never be permissible regardless of what good may someday come of it.[14]

This section sought to highlight some of the relevant factors IRCs are to consider when evaluating the ethical legitimacy of a proposed human subject research protocol. It should be evident that the responsibilities of an IRC member include the protection of human beings from potentially harmful research, and extend far beyond simply examining the process of informed consent. Nevertheless, informed consent remains a significant component of the work of the IRC.

**Clinical Research and Informed Consent.** After an IRC has considered all of the above elements and found that the human research protocol is ethical and meets compliance standards, it still must consider the issue of informed consent. The Department of Health and Human Services, Code of Federal Regulations (often referred to simply as 45 CFR 46) requires the following eight elements:[15] (1) a statement that the study involves research along with an explanation of the purposes and procedures, duration of participation, and identification of experimental elements; (2) a description of risks; (3) a statement of benefits to the individual or to others that may reasonably be expected to benefit from the research; (4) alternatives to participation; (5) provisions for confidentiality; (6) medical treatments and compensations available in the event of research-related injury; (7) identification of individuals or groups that may be contacted for answers to questions about the research, for information about a research-related injury, and for information about the rights of research subjects; and (8) assurance that participation is voluntary and that participants may discontinue participation at any time without penalty or loss of benefits. All IRCs must meet these regulatory standards for informed consent. IRCs must also see that informed consent language is appropriate to a broad audience and understandable to the potential participant.

The consent document is the most important piece of the protocol review process for the IRC. As such, many IRCs require that investigators adapt their documents to templates created by the IRC. In this way IRCs can ensure that essential elements have been properly addressed by the principal investigator. Additionally, the use of such templates helps the IRC to establish a set of guidelines that each PI is required to meet. This can minimize pressure on an institution from an influential investigator or company looking to offer particular research at its institution. A problem with templates, however, is that these documents are not standardized and may vary greatly among institutions. Lack of standardization becomes especially problematic in the case of cooperative multi-site studies. Utilizing such templates requires a great deal of "template language" that is nonnegotiable if the researcher or manufacturer wishes to perform research at that particular institution. This can lead to lengthy consent documents with exhaustive lists of risks and benefits that become incalculable to the potential participant.

The IRC, therefore, must provide to potential research subjects the information they need in order to make a truly informed choice as to whether to participate in the proposed research protocol. Minimally the consent documents should be written at a sixth- to eighth-grade reading level, contain no technical language, and rank risks and benefits in accordance with likelihood of occurrence. It must be noted, however, that simply having an adequate form does not make informed consent. The informed consent process should be a dynamic process between researcher and potential subject wherein the form acts as a starting point for further discussion to evaluate whether the research is appropriate for the individual considering participation. Here it is important to note that it is within the scope of the IRC to review the entire informed consent process, not just the consent documents. IRCs may wish to consider random review of the informed consent process where there may be areas of concern.

This leads to a final point about presentation of informed consent to potential participants. Certain research protocols, by virtue of their design, require approaching a potential research participant in the midst of medical treatment. In such cases, it is not appropriate to allow for only a limited parameter for participants to consider involvement, especially when concurrent with another medical procedure. Furthermore, the vulnerability of the patient population must be taken into consideration insofar as participants in emotional or acute pain may not be appropriate for participation in research. In such circumstances, assuming the research is considered ethically appropriate, therapy and research must be clearly distinguished so as not to allow for therapeutic misconceptions in the research. That is, there must be no misperception on the part of the patients (research subjects) that their involvement will benefit them personally in the form of a cure or relief of symptoms.[16]

## Conclusion

Human research continues to increase in complexity. This has been the case since 1974 when IRCs began as formalized bodies to review such research. IRCs must continue to place the protection of human beings at the forefront of their responsibilities when reviewing proposed human research protocols. To that end, IRCs must continually strive to ensure that the informed consent process is accurate, truthful, and understandable to the potential participant.

IRCs must also have a profound sense of humility that allows them to ask questions and seek answers where necessary. They must also have the courage to table, suspend, or reject studies that do not meet the requirements set forth by legal and ethical norms for human research. All IRCs must know the federal regulations (45 CFR 46) for human research and require them of the protocols they review. However, translating the ethical principles and norms put forth in this chapter and those outlined in the Belmont Report, the Nuremberg Code, and the Declaration of Helsinki is not easily accomplished. IRCs will need to debate these principles and determine each principle's relevance for the protocol before them. Appropriate training and education must be required for all IRC members, especially the IRC chairperson. The IRC will do well to remember that their primary goal is the protection of human beings in research protocols. The IRC will do even better if it has a clear sense of the norm we have posited in conjunction with the goal of human flourishing, namely, never to allow the desire to pursue scientific inquiry to trump the interests and inherent value of the unique and irreplaceable human beings who are enrolled in such research. In this way, as Paul Gelsinger notes, "researchers, industry, and those in government will get it right—not for recognition, not for money, but only to help."

# Additional Case Studies

**Case 12E:** In the early 1980s it was discovered from a suit filed in Illinois that patients of a state-operated mental health facility underwent "therapeutic surgery" in the 1950s and 1960s, possibly without consent. The surgery, intended to relieve or ameliorate symptoms of schizophrenia, involved removing the subjects' adrenal glands. A theory put forward at the time surmised that removal of the adrenal gland might correct a hormone imbalance that some psychiatrists believed to be a cause of schizophrenia.

The investigation that ensued as a result of the suit found that the surgery did not lead to improvement in any of the patients. It was unclear, however, whether the patients had given informed consent. All of those who had their adrenal glands removed required injections of cortisone for the rest of their lives to compensate for the loss of function of their adrenal glands.

**Case 12F:** In the early 1990s research on Parkinson's disease focused on ways to ward off the diminishment or disappearance of specific brain tissue. It was thought that, in certain cases, Parkinson's assault on the central nervous system could be ameliorated or significantly lessened if there were ways to stimulate redevelopment of specific brain tissue. One method to do so would be to deliver fetal tissue to desired locations within the brain through holes drilled in the skull.

To determine whether this therapy might work, a control of some sort would need to be devised. Given that in the early 1990s no good treatments were available for severe Parkinson's, it seemed that the best study model would be to have a group of people with Parkinson's serve as a control. The control group would not receive the delivery of fetal tissue. However, in order to eliminate study bias by the research subjects, all of the people enrolled in the study would need to have the holes drilled in their skulls. This would mean that some of the study participants would, by virtue of their enrollment in the study, be required to have holes drilled in their skull without any intention of delivering fetal tissue.

## Suggested Readings

Vanderpool, Harold Y. "An Ethics Primer for Institutional Review Boards." In *Institutional Review Board: Management and Function*, edited by Elizabeth A. Bankert and Robert J. Amdur, 3–8. Boston, MA: Jones and Bartlett, 2006.

The World Medical Association Declaration of Helsinki. Web site: http://www.wma.net/e/policy/17-c_e.html

## Multimedia Aids for Teachers

Deadly Medicine. Creating the Master Race. United States Holocaust Memorial Museum. http://www.ushmm.org/museum/exhibit/online/deadly medicine/.

*Miss Evers' Boys*. Directed by Joseph Sargent. Starring Alfre Woodard. Rated PG. 1997. This movie documents the true story of the U.S. Government's Tuskegee Study of untreated blacks with syphilis. It provides a powerful example of how research subjects can be abused. It is available on DVD or VHS through retailers.

Steven Spielberg Film and Video Archive. A collection of video footage documenting the Holocaust and World War II. United States Holocaust Memorial Museum. http://www.ushmm.org/research/collections/filmvideo.

## Endnotes

[1] Paul Gelsinger, "Jesse's Intent," in *Institutional Review Board*, ed. Elizabeth A. Bankert and Robert J. Amdur (Sudbury, MA: Jones and Bartlett Publishers, 2006), xi–xix.

[2] Katz, *Experimentation with Human Beings*. (New York: Russell Sage Foundation, 1972).

[3] T. C. Chalmers, "The Clinical Trial," *Milbank Memorial Fund Quarterly* 59 (1981): 324–39.

[4] Trials of War Criminals before the Nuremberg Military Tribunals under Control Council Law, No. 10 Vol. 2, Nuremberg, October 1946-April 1949. Washington DC: U.S. G.P.O., 1949–1953, 181–82.

[5] Baruch A. Brody, *The Ethics of Biomedical Research* (New York: Oxford University Press, 1998), 31–36.

[6] World Medical Association Declaration of Helsinki: Recommendations Guiding Medical Doctors in Biomedical Research Involving Human Subjects. Adopted by the 18th World Medical Assembly, Helsinki, Finland, 1964, and as revised by the 52nd WMA General Assembly,

Edinburgh, Scotland, October 2000, with Note of Clarification on Paragraph 30 added by the WMA General Assembly, Tokyo, Japan, 2004.

[7] Kevin O'Rourke and Benedict Ashley, *Health Care Ethics: A Theological Analysis* (Washington, DC: Georgetown University Press, 1997), 346.

[8] This is notably a more rigid position than that of the Declaration of Helsinki. In the clarifications of paragraph 29 (added in 2002 at the WMA General Assembly in Washington), it adds, "The WMA hereby reaffirms its position that extreme care must be taken in making use of placebo-controlled trial and that in general this methodology should only be used in the absence of existing proven therapy. However, a placebo-controlled trial may be ethically acceptable, even if proven therapy is available, under the following circumstances: (a) where for compelling and scientifically sound methodological reasons its use is necessary to determine the efficacy or safety of a prophylactic, diagnostic or therapeutic method; or (b) where a prophylactic, diagnostic or therapeutic method is being investigated for a minor condition and the patients who receive placebo will not be subject to any additional risk of serious or irreversible harm." We believe, however, that in general this principle does hold and that for the purposes of this work the general principle serves the reader well.

[9] Pius XII, "Allocution to the First International Congress of Histopathology (1952)," in *The Human Body: Papal Teachings*, selected and arranged by the Monks of Solesmes (Boston: Daughters of St. Paul, 1960), n. 349; John Paul II, "Medicines at the Service of Man," (Oct. 24, 1986).

[10] Department of Health and Human Services, Protection of Human Subjects, Title 45, Code of Federal Regulations, Part 46.111.

[11] O. Jonasson and M. A. Hardy, "The Case of Baby Fae (letter)," *Journal of the American Medical Association* 254 (1985): 3358–59.

[12] David Bogod, "The Nazi Hypothermia Experiments: Forbidden Data?" *Anaesthesia* 59, no. 12 (December 2004), 1155–56.

[13] For a similar argument see: H. K. Beecher, "Ethics and Clinical Research," *New England Journal of Medicine* 274 (1966): 1354–60.

[14] Baruch C. Cohen, "The Ethics of Using Medical Data from Nazi Experiments," *Jewish Virtual Library*, http://www.jewishvirtuallibrary.org/jsource/Judaism/naziexp.html#1 (accessed July 31, 2006).

[15] Department of Health and Human Services, Protection of Human Subjects, Title 45, Code of Federal Regulations, Part 46.116.

[16] G. Sreenivasan, "Informed Consent and the Therapeutic Misconception: Clarifying the Challenge," *Journal of Clinical Ethics* 16, no. 4 (2005): 369–71.

# INDEX

**A**

Abortion, 4, 14, 20, 35, 86, 97, 209
 Direct, 89
 Indirect, 88, 99
 Induced, 86
 Legal context of, 86, 90, 91
 Selective, 164
Absolute rules, 56
Access to health care, 262
Acting virtuously, 27
Action-guides, 40, 56
Actions, 4, 6, 28, 27
Adult stem cells (ASCs), 217
Aggressive treatment, 12
Allocation of scarce resources, 19
Anencephaly, 102
Antibiotics, 85
Aquinas, Thomas (saint), 4, 172
Aristotle, 4, 25
Artificial insemination (AI), 192
Artificial nutrition and hydration, 135, 142
ASC. *See* adult stem cells

Ashley, Benedict, 279
Autonomy, 8, 57

**B**

Baby Fae, 275, 284
Bacon, Francis, 167
Becoming virtuous, 51, 52
Beecher, Henry K., 295
Being/Doing, 4, 10, 23, 24, 25
Beliefs, 2, 29, 45, 69, 158, 218
Belmont Report, 279, 282
Beneficence, 8, 19, 57
Benefits and burdens, 139, 142
Best interests, 11
Best interests standard, 122
Birth control. *See* Contraception
Blastocysts, 216
Bodily integrity/ totality, 58
Breathing machine (mechanical ventilation), 12, 59
Brodeur, Dennis, 124
Brown, Louise, 193

Bush, George W., 223

**C**

Caesarian section (c-section), 87
Callahan, Daniel, 163, 165
Capacity, 6
Capital punishment, 34
Cardiopulmonary resuscitation (CPR), 135
 Survival rates for, 147
Caregivers, 11, 159, 176
Catholic tradition, 137, 139, 199
CDF. *See* Congregation for the Doctrine of the Faith
Chalmers, Thomas, 276
Character, 3, 4
Charity, 19
Charlesworth, Max, 162
Child-bearing, 195, 250
Chorioamnionitis, 85, 98
Christian religious traditions, 208
Chromosomes, 242